Family Life and Social Control

A Sociological Perspective

John J. Rodger

Consultant Editor: Jo Campling

MACMILLAN

First published 1996 by
MACMILLAN PRESS LTD
Houndmills, Basingstoke, Hampshire RG21 6XS
and London
Companies and representatives
throughout the world

ISBN 0–333–60463–6 hardcover
ISBN 0–333–60464–4 paperback

A catalogue record for this book is available
from the British Library.

10 9   8   7   6   5   4   3   2   1
05 04 03 02 01 00 99 98 97 96

Printed in Malaysia

To John and Agnes Rodger

Contents

List of figures and tables

Figure

Tables

Acknowledgements

Some of the ideas contained in the book were incubated in earlier publications. The concepts discussed in Chapter 2 were originally developed in articles published in *Sociology*, vol. 22, no. 4, 1988, and the *British Journal of Social Work*, vol. 21, no. 1, 1991, and an earlier version of Chapter 4 appeared as 'Family structures and the moral politics of caring', *Sociological Review*, vol. 39, no. 4, 1991. I am grateful to Sage Publications for permission to reproduce Figure 4.1 from D. Olson and H. McCubbin, *Families: What Makes them Work*.

Encouragement to pursue the original idea behind this book came from Jo Campling and I am very grateful to her for the supervisory role she has fulfilled. My colleague Tony Clarke read and commented in detail on the first draft of the book. His critical comments were perceptive and helpful. Whilst he may not recognise fundamental changes in the final version in line with his advice, his observations were valued. Pam Rodger read the final draft and offered detailed comments on it of a substantive and stylistic nature. Her opinions are particularly appreciated.

JOHN J. RODGER

Introduction

The central theme of this book is 'family life' as an object of social policy interest and welfare intervention, rather than 'the family' as a social institution. There has been a considerable amount of debate in both sociology and social policy analysis about what constitutes 'the family' in modern society (see Bernardes, 1985; Cheal, 1991; Gittins, 1993). That debate has tended to revolve around the issues of the structure and meaning of the family: whether an essentially white, middle-class, patriarchal and nuclear concept of the family should define what the family is, or whether lone-parent families, or indeed homosexual couples, have a validity as alternative forms of family deserving of equal recognition both socially and legally. The critical focus of our attention is not the semantic debate about 'what is family?' but rather the analysis of family life as a focus for policy debate and, in particular, intervention by practitioners from the fields of health and welfare.

Bernardes (1985, 1986) has argued that the social meanings attached to family-type relationships should be the starting point for sociological analysis. He insists that we should not presume that a social entity called 'the family' exists unproblematically. Indeed the social institution which we accept in a taken-for-granted way is constructed and reconstructed as people negotiate their way through the life cycle. Gubrium and Holstein (1990) share this constructionist approach to family studies and they discuss the role of language and familial discourses used by professional practitioners and lay people to assemble the social meanings of family. This type of work has been valuable for redirecting our attention towards the essentially contestable nature of the notion of family. People seem to display a concern for the moral, political and social nature of *family relationships* in a way which they do not for other types of social relations, and this concern has manifested itself in a number of projects and political debates in the 1990s. For example, the United Nations Year of the Family in 1994 was one such international project specifically directed at encouraging both governments and individuals

1

to re-evaluate the place of family relationships and obligations in society in a rapidly changing world; divorce, illegitimacy, reordered families and, of course, child abuse and neglect have been particularly prominent themes. Indeed Hewlett (1993), writing under the banner of the United Nations Children's Fund, has drawn attention to the scope of the problem of child neglect in rich nations and reinforced a growing feeling among policy makers and social commentators within the rich OECD (Organization for Economic Cooperation and Development) countries that problems relating to family structure must be confronted rather than be treated with the complacency which has characterised the past two decades. In Britain a battle has been joined between those on the right who are struggling to set a policy and political agenda on family issues around the motif of 'back to basics' and those on the left who wish to ground a concept of 'ethical socialism' in notions of community service, personal responsibility and family obligation. This debate is centred on which of the political positions can present a clear perspective on what the *Observer* journalist Melanie Phillips has called 'civic morality': the balancing of the growth in individual rights with a stronger sense of personal, familial and community responsibility.

It is the existence of a socio-political agenda surrounding the idea of family, therefore, which has given rise to an increasing interest in the social changes affecting family life. That interest has generated a wide-ranging debate in social policy and politics about whether the family is merely changing or whether it is 'deteriorating'. Politicians, the mass media and the public at large are now engaged in what often appears to be a rather superficial debate about social policy and family life, focusing obsessively on issues such as welfare dependency, single parenthood and categories such as 'underclass', but the very populist nature of the debate appears to be exerting increasing pressure on policy makers and opinion formers to respond to the issues raised by public anxiety about family life. At the heart of the debate has been the issue of how, or whether, family life should be made subject to social control. In response to this debate and the political stimulus of New Right Ideology which has dominated official policy thinking on both sides of the Atlantic in the past decade, a host of professional practitioners from the fields of health and welfare have focused their attention on family life as something to be monitored and changed, with increased intensity.

They have developed an expanding number of theoretical explanations for something called 'family pathologies'.

There are a number of issues which have stimulated interest in the social control of family life at both an academic and a political level. First, there has been an enduring debate in social policy and social theory about the relationship between clinical models of social behaviour, often associated with the control of deviance viewed as the product of individual pathology, and those paradigms which place their stress on the wider social influences on behaviour such as family, occupation and community. The classic example of this debate can be found in the sociology of mental illness, especially in the critique of medical models of mental illness, offered by anti-psychiatry theorists like Thomas Scheff, Howard Becker and Thomas Szasz (see Grusky and Pollner, 1981). Whilst the labels used to define and describe mental patients were very often interpreted by some health and welfare workers as signifying an objective medical condition, those academics working within the anti-psychiatry perspective adopted a sceptical view of clinical practice, seeing labels in the area of mental health as reflecting the social mores and values of the community and having more to do with the social control of deviance than the practice of medicine. Writers in the anti-psychiatry tradition, therefore, emphasised the provisional nature of the labels which were applied to deviant behaviour. There have always been differences in inclination within the caring professions about the most appropriate model to use in the diagnoses and 'treatment' of social problems. The anti-psychiatry debate merely encouraged the wider exploration of these issues with the growth in welfare systems and the increasing frequency with which the state in the name of welfare intervened in family life. The application of a label of sickness or pathology to an individual or a family represented for many the ultimate instrument of social control, and the tension between caring and controlling, albeit in the name of clinical therapy, has been a source of professional acrimony in the development of social work. For example, in the early history of both British and American social work with families it was the language of medicine which was predominant. As Rojek, Peacock and Collins (1988) put it 'at the heart of this thinking was the idea of the defective or diseased organism to which some sort of therapeutic intervention could be applied' (p. 20). The development of social work since the 1960s has continued to be influenced by psychiatry and psychoanalytic theory with their close association with clinical forms of intervention. However, contemporary family therapy and social work with families are now influenced less by the ideas of Freud and have moved to embrace *systems theory* which is more compatible with social psychology and sociological thinking. The application of therapeutic intervention into family life remains, however, very much focused on the 'treatment' of conditions labelled 'family pathologies' and 'family dysfunctions'. The clinical orientation of practice based on systems theory is, therefore, never far from the surface in a great deal of contemporary family therapy and social work, even though there are those working in the field of welfare who subscribe to a sociological perspective on family problems.

The fundamental difference between clinical and sociological perspectives on family problems in this context is that in the former there is a presumption that deviance in family life is in need of *correction*, whereas much of family sociology is content with the *appreciation* of the plurality and colour in human social behaviour. I will develop this distinction further in Chapter 2 and refer to it as the analysis in the book progresses.

Sociologists, of course, are rarely employed in settings where social deviance within a family situation has caused problems for the community and the well-being of children. The application of social control in the context of welfare policy is something for sociologists to study, rather than contemplate its most effective use. Their task is different from that of the therapist or social worker; they must describe and critically analyse the possible difficulties which might arise from the application of professional judgements rather than provide practice solutions for the problems encountered when dealing with deviance. This book, of course, is written from the perspective of the sociologist, not the professional practitioner working in the field of family problems, although it is written with an *appreciation* of the complexities of the problems surrounding welfare work and an acceptance that much of what passes as informed criticism of health and welfare workers is ill-judged and often plain wrong.

The second issue which has given rise to public debate and concern about family life has been the rapidity of change in social behaviour, especially from the 1960s onwards. Concerns about divorce, illegitimacy, lone parenthood, and their connection to juvenile delinquency, appeared to have subsided as social problems for a while during the 1960s and 1970s as they made the transition from issues which society got agitated about to matters that were 'just part of life'; the assumption in many quarters was probably that divorce and illegitimacy were part of the diversity of human life. They were seen as an outgrowth of the process of self-exploration and the growing acceptance of the right to make choices about emotional and sexual existence, and not necessarily associated with criminality. We were encouraged by the theoretical relativism of 'the new criminology' in the 1960s, of which labelling theory was the most prominent example, to view delinquency and criminality as products of the way we *defined* people rather than the way they lived and experienced growing up (see Becker, 1963). In the 1980s and 1990s these issues have again attained the status of major social problems, seen by many to threaten the social and 'moral' fabric of community and family life. Those who were pioneers of radical criminology in the 1960s and 1970s are now more inclined towards what has been called 'new realism' which recognises the existence of high levels of criminality and family disruption in the inner cities and peripheral housing estates (see Matthews and Young, 1992; Young and Matthews, 1992). The association of deteriorating social and economic conditions with changing patterns of family behaviour is, therefore, generating a policy and research agenda which has family life at the centre of enquiry.

The third issue which has emerged in the 1980s is connected to the notion of 'moral hazard', particularly the view that the growth of the welfare state has undermined the purpose and role of families in modern societies, whilst ostensibly seeking to help them. The presentation of changes in family life and family structure, particularly the rise in the numbers of living patterns alternative to the nuclear family model, as not only a 'moral' question confronting modern societies, but fundamentally a problem of the distribution of responsibilities between the state and the private sphere of family relationships, is at the heart of this issue. The welfare state whose beneficence everyone took for granted in the 1960s and 1970s is now subject to severe criticism for being costly, and also destructive of the institution of marriage and a sense of family duty within our culture. These issues have manifested themselves in a number of public debates about family obligations in the context of divorce, community care, child abuse and neglect and the emergence of an 'underclass' family type. Chapters 3 to 7 will examine each of these issues because they have become the focus of policy debate and have generated professional activity among family welfare workers, therapists and others charged with the responsibility of monitoring family life and social behaviour in contemporary society.

The aim of this book is to provide a critical discussion of the dominant theoretical ideas which inform thinking in welfare work with families and an examination of some of the most pressing social policy issues which have stimulated intervention into family life. An outline of the central themes of each chapter can be identified.

Chapter 1 reviews three theoretical perspectives which have been influential in recent years in the areas of family studies and social policy. *Systems theory* is selected for discussion because it has been the most influential theoretical paradigm in social work and family therapy; *post-structuralism* has established itself rapidly in the social sciences in the past decade, transforming the way questions about power and social control are posed in sociology and social policy analysis, and, of course, it has become increasingly powerful as a critical perspective on professional practice; *feminism*, despite taking a variety of conceptual forms, competes with post-structuralism to provide sociological analyses of family life with a radically critical perspective capable of changing the way people think about 'family' and gender relationships. A central theme running through Chapter 1 is the issue of social control and how it should be conceptualised in the context of studying welfare intervention into family life. The chapter closes by considering the concept explicitly and concluding that social control is rarely allowed to be exercised in one direction: those subject to social control in the context of social work often attempt to counter, resist and defend themselves against the exercise of statutory powers. The ways in which power and social control are exercised must, therefore, be differentiated because they will vary from one social context to another.

Chapter 2 develops the theme of social control in the context of practitioner–client relationships. The specific intention of the chapter is to develop the outlines of a theory of family intervention. It is argued that we require a vocabulary to describe and analyse the relationships which characterise the interaction between the private aspects of family life and the practices of both the social sphere of welfare work and the public sphere of policy formation processes. Whilst the principal effort in the chapter is concerned to demonstrate the usefulness of applying Basil Bernstein's sociological analysis of language and communication to the description and analysis of social work, the secondary intention is to generate concepts which can be used as a form of shorthand throughout the book for conceptualising discourses on family life as revealed by a variety of social and political interests. In particular, the chapter identifies what are described as *correctional* and *appreciative* codes which act as a shorthand to describe different orientations to meaning reflected in the relationship between different kinds of knowledge and information and different power relationships in society and practitioner–client interaction.

The utility of the theoretical framework sketched in Chapter 2 can be seen in Chapter 3, which deals with marriage issues and conciliation. The argument that is developed is that there has been an historical shift away from a view of marriage as a social institution to be defended by punitive matrimonial law towards a more open and negotiable view of marriage in which individuals pursue personal happiness and fulfilment: the movement is described as a shift from a *correctional* view of marriage, which is bound up with the idea that it is an institution of society which should be influenced by a range of religious, material and legal considerations, to an *appreciative* view which treats marriage as a 'pure relationship' which is valued solely in terms of the satisfactions intrinsically derived from the relationship. This movement has, of course, created an opportunity for new knowledges and new forms of intervention in family life to evolve. The professional 'experts' who have emerged in recent years, and who focus their gaze on the problems of marital disharmony and breakdown, are depicted in Chapter 3 as the 'technicians of human relations', following the term used by Christopher Lasch (1977). The chapter traces the unfolding of different approaches to marriage conciliation and locates an explanation for the rise in both divorce and marriage intervention in the social characteristics of society as it moves into an era of late modernity.

The analysis contained in Chapter 4 seeks to explore the theme of family obligation in the wider social policy context of community care. One increasingly debated public issue in the past ten years has been about where the responsibility should fall between the state and the family for the provision of care for the frail elderly and the mentally and physically handicapped. The analysis developed in Chapter 4 is grounded in concepts of family structure and family system, with its explicit objective being that of pointing up the way that family structures vary in their forms and in their capacity to provide care. Increasingly, as the notion of a 'mixed economy of welfare' becomes generally accepted by both the public and policy makers, the role of social work intervention in family life will be to construct care packages for people using family rather than state resources, albeit augmented by voluntary and commercial help. The emphasis on family care, whilst ignoring the family's capacity to provide care, will lead to a range of social problems of which elder abuse is a recently acknowledged and disturbing example. The chapter concludes, therefore, by connecting this emerging social issue to the theme of the 'moral politics of caring' lying at the heart of my analysis.

Chapter 5 and chapter 6 are closely related. The social policy context of family life is discussed in Chapter 5: in particular the increasing emphasis in public debate upon reducing the state's obligations in the sphere of welfare alluded to in Chapter 4 is further developed in relation to the contemporary hostility towards unconventional family forms, especially single-parent households. By placing Britain's approach to family policy in the context of Europe, it is argued that British social policy lacks an explicit commitment to the idea of family life, and that *moral regulation* is the term which most accurately reflects official policy towards family life in contemporary Britain. This policy stance has been evidenced in recent Government strategies to develop the themes of 'back to basics' and 'pro-family· values' as the foundation of Conservative social policies. The result of this policy debate has been to encourage the idea that an 'underclass' family type is emerging in contemporary Britain. This issue is explored in Chapter 6. The analysis suggests that we can identify at least three prominent models of the 'underclass' family stemming from the variety of theoretical and political studies which have focused on disadvantaged and poor families: the *structured underclass family*, the *fatherless underclass family* and the *criminal underclass family* reflect the competing explanatory emphases found in a range of contemporary investigations into the connection between poverty, disadvantage and family life. The chapter concludes by briefly discussing the phenomenon of the 'family centre' which has grown up in inner city areas and peripheral housing estates to manage and monitor 'underclass families', who may be regarded as 'dangerous' in a variety of ways which the following chapter discusses.

Chapter 7 develops the theme of the 'dangerous family' and unconventional family life with reference to the issue of child protection and abuse. The purpose of this chapter is to round out the analysis offered on social control and family life by highlighting the public reflection on child protection failure which has punctuated social policy debate in the personal social services since the 1970s. The emphasis in this chapter is on the concept of *the public sphere* which emerges as a particularly potent area for studying the mechanisms for monitoring *the social sphere* of welfare work and making it more accountable. This distinction between *the social sphere* and *the public sphere* discussed in Chapters 1 and 2 is, therefore, seen clearly through the phenomenon of the public inquiry sitting to consider matters of child protection failure.

Chapter 8 provides concluding observations. A distinction is drawn between what I call 'real movements' and 'ideological movements': the former attempt to conceptualise the change in social attitudes and behaviour over time, the latter delineate the shift in what Stanley Cohen (1985) has called *social control talk* which may or may not have a real connection to what people are doing or how they may behave. My view is that 'real movements' cannot be fundamentally changed by rhetoric or ideological currents aimed at changing people's behaviour without attention also being given to the conditions of existence within which many families live in an increasingly polarised society. Recent evidence from the Joseph Rowntree Foundation study on Income and Wealth (Barclay, 1995; Hills, 1995) indicates that since 1977 the proportion of the population with less than half the average weekly household income of £254 in 1995 has more than trebled, and is estimated to be about 62 per cent of the population. Families with children have increasingly been caught in social policy movements which have undermined the task of caring for children. The relationship between family life and social control in recent years appears to be distinguished by censorious rhetoric and moral panic rather than social support for what remains the most crucial responsibility people can take on, that of supporting family dependents in an economically uncertain world.

1

Social theory and family life

Of the main developments which have taken place in social theory, three perspectives stand out as being of particular importance for our understanding of the debate about family life, namely, *systems theory, post-structuralism* and *feminism*. First, *systems theory* continues to be the most influential theoretical perspective for those health and welfare professionals working in the area of family problems. Systems theory has in particular become the pre-eminent perspective for those involved in clinical intervention into family problems, both in social work and in family therapy settings. Second, there has grown up in recent years what has become known as *post-structuralism*. This perspective has been especially influential with those who seek to evaluate critically the forms of social intervention into family life found in professional practice. A central theme of this work has been a concern with what Foucault called the development of 'panopticism' in the 'carceral society' (Foucault, 1973, 1977): that is to say, post-structuralism has articulated a critical anxiety about the expanding number of locations where discipline, regulation and the monitoring of social behaviour take place. In the twentieth century, the growth of the welfare state, and the wide range of professionals charged with the responsibility of attending to social and health problems in society, has given rise to a greater sense that social and 'moral' behaviour is subject to 'surveillance'. Those professional practitioners working in the fields of health and welfare who concentrate their attention on family life have, therefore, become of particular interest to those social analysts influenced by the post-structuralist theory fashioned by Foucault and followers such as Donzelot (1980). Third, the emergence of *feminism* as an intellectual force in the social sciences has transformed the way questions are posed about family life. Central to the feminist perspective is the critique of the patriarchal structure of family life and, in particular, the failure of both systems theory and post-structuralism to integrate adequately the insights of feminist scholarship; for example, the failure of systems theory to acknowledge family life as characterised by inequalities of power and violence, and the suspicion that post-structuralism has no normative position from which to criticise and so challenge existing social relationships, especially patriarchal ones.

The need for a critical theory which can integrate feminism and post-structuralism has been evident for some time (see McNay, 1992). A number of feminist analyses of women and welfare have been using the language of post-structuralism (Smart, 1993, 1989; Worrall, 1990). There is also emerging a feminist critique of the premises of systems theory in the context of family therapy (see Perelberg and Miller, 1990). An alternative set of intervention methods are being developed by feminist therapists to counter the mutuality of influence often assumed in systems approaches to family therapy. Recently there have been a number of attempts to integrate feminism and post-structuralism with critical theory (see Agger, 1991; Fraser, 1989). The success of that project for developing new insights into family life is, perhaps, something to await for future evaluation rather than contemplate here.

Systems theory

American social science has embraced the clinical potential of systems thinking to a much greater extent than is evident in European work. A core feature of that research and theorising has been the idea that a distinctive sub-discipline called 'familology' can be developed (see Burr *et al.*, 1988). This perspective is multidisciplinary in character, incorporating psychiatry, psychology, sociology, family therapy and, interestingly, medicine (see Schmidt, 1983, and Candib and Glenn, 1983). It tends to straddle the clinical/academic boundaries, with a great deal of theoretical work being developed in relation to therapeutic work with families deemed to have some kind of 'pathology', invariably a member with a psychiatric disorder or what is considered to be a behavioural problem in need of correction. In the United Kingdom, social work intervention into families in response to the growing concern about child abuse and domestic violence has stimulated systems thinking, perhaps hastening the decline of psychodynamic approaches which focus on individual 'pathologies'. Family therapy is becoming increasingly important as a mode of intervention into child abuse cases (see Dale *et al.*, 1986).

The project of developing a distinctive domain of study based on the family rests on the assumption that there is a conceptual and institutional space called 'the family realm'. It directs analysis towards the private sphere of family living rather than engaging with the public sphere of policy making and, most significantly, it concentrates upon refining a systems perspective on family members' interactions with each other rather than accounting for the behaviour or idiosyncrasies of an individual family member. Problems in the family are therefore understood within the framework of a circular rather than linear concept of causation: no single individual is deemed to cause disorder because the family constitutes a bounded system of social interaction. It is the total configuration of family relationships which becomes the focus of analysis and clinical remedy.

R. Hill (1971) was one of the earliest systems theorists in sociology to set out the parameters of systems concepts in the context of studying the family. He stressed the interdependence of family positions and roles; the relatively closed boundary-maintaining processes of families; their equilibrium-seeking and adaptive characteristics; and the 'task performing functions' of families for external agencies. The unavoidable implication of this way of viewing family life is that a 'conventional' conception of the family lies at the heart of the theory. Stability and equilibrium are presumed to be disturbed by actions or behaviour which destroy the interdependence of roles and functions within the family, such as a father who deserts his wife and child; a woman who refuses to play the motherhood role; or a child who refuses to display expected patterns of filial duty.

Zimmerman (1988) makes the observation that the primary functions which families are expected to perform are to a large extent ideological, reflecting social and cultural relativism. For example, the main functions of the family typically cited in the functionalist and systems literature include the following: the physical maintenance and care of members; facilitating the addition of new members through procreation or adoption; the supervision and socialisation of children for adult roles and including the social control and disciplining of the family's deviant members; the production and consumption of goods and services to maintain the family unit; and, finally, the maintenance of family morale and motivation to ensure that members can function within the family and other social groups. However, she rightly points out that the ways in which these tasks are understood and performed will vary according to social class, ethnic and religious background, age and gender. The perception of deviance in the family social system may, therefore, incorporate ethnocentric and gendered understandings of what constitutes 'stable family functioning'. The emergence of family systems theory as a problematic perspective will be explored at various points below, but a few indications of its controversial nature can be discussed at this stage. Two areas currently being developed are the application of systems theory to identify and treat medical conditions from a family perspective and the rapidly expanding use of systems theory in family therapy work (Franklin, 1983; Cheal, 1991, 60–4).

The concept of 'family medicine' as something which literally involves the whole family in processes of diagnosis and treatment is evolving rapidly, particularly in the United States, but there is evidence that a number of general practitioners throughout Europe are also exploring the relationship between family therapy based on systems theory and the treatment of illness (Huygen, 1978). The stimulus for this development is the increasingly well researched and documented connection between clearly defined medical conditions or problems and their associated family effect. For example, it is well understood that chronic illness, or severe depression, in one family member will have consequences for other family members, both psychologically and somatically. Further, the flow of influence from family members to a particularly ill member can have significant consequences for the prognosis of an illness. A troublesome pregnancy can be helped by support from the family, as can certain cancers. Family attitudes to an illness and treatment programme can be crucial for supporting a patient's adherence to a medical regime or encouraging abandonment of a course of treatment (Schmidt, 1983). Beyond the more clearly defined medically treatable conditions are a range of what can best be described as problematic behaviours which are increasingly involving a partnership between general practitioners and family therapists. Recurrent childhood poisoning or anorexia nervosa are examples where the purely medical and the behavioural boundaries become blurred. The application of family systems thinking to the 'treatment' of these problems is being developed. Where once the analysis, diagnosis and treatment of the problem would have been exhausted by reference to the 'deviant' individual, now the family is viewed as part of a wider medical programme of therapy and intervention. The extent to which this type of practice will become widespread remains difficult to predict (see Candib and Glenn, 1983). Resources of both time and money will obviously inhibit its widespread application in general practice, but its development in local specialist units is something to expect in the coming years. We are perhaps witnessing a reverse of the phenomenon of the *medicalisation of social problems* which has been discussed in sociology for a number of years, and are now to experience the 'sociologisation of medical problems' on an increasing scale. The historically weak professional position of social workers in relation to medical practitioners and the comparatively less exalted status of psychiatry in Europe when compared with the United States probably means that progress on this side of the Atlantic will be much slower than has been evident there. However, the full implications of this type of movement will require close monitoring and critical analysis.

The value of family systems theory and family therapy will vary. In terms of sociological thinking, the concepts of family systems theory can be useful for ordering complex variations in social interaction; systems theory can assist in building models to aid systematic analysis (see Chapter 4). With respect to alleviating the distress of social and behavioural difficulties experienced by some families, the application of systems thinking in the context of therapy again assists in the organisation of complex data, helping to focus attention on particular problems generated by the pattern of social relationships; the meaning lies in the configuration of relationships, within their *gestalt* rather than through one set of meanings articulated or expressed by an individual. However, Gubrium (1992), in his ethnographic study of two different types of family therapy projects, reveals something of the ambivalence surrounding this area of family theory.

Gubrium, like a number of other sociologists and psychologists working in the area of family therapy, has found it useful to conceptualise families in terms of what Durkheim would have understood as a *collective representation*: families develop a sense of their unity through a wide range of mundane, everyday acts, routines and symbols which have the consequence of constructing an abstract sense of family which is above and distinct from the individual family members (see Chapter 4 and the work of Reiss, 1981, and Dallos, 1991). This notion is increasingly accepted by those working in the area of family therapy, and it is towards an understanding of the functioning and breakdown of the 'family paradigm' that much therapeutic intervention is aimed (Reiss, 1981). The combination of studying family discourses (the language and meanings attached to relationships and events: the ways in which family members talk about their family life) and the analysis of the everyday interactions and family rituals provides insight into family constructs. Crises or major troubles confronting a family make visible what was previously taken for granted: the family paradigm shaping and ordering family patterns of behaviour and interaction can suddenly be disrupted. Family therapy which bases its understanding of family functioning on the family's *collective representation* will therefore focus on the troubled household and the configuration of family relationships rather than singularly on an event or an individual's personal crisis. With respect to this type of perspective, Gubrium makes a number of useful observations through his study of two family-therapy projects. First, there is a tendency perhaps to overstress the degree of consensualism in the concept of 'family paradigm'; it would be essential, for example, for the therapist to be sensitive to the multiple narratives which shape a family's sense of itself as an entity. A mother's and a father's images of family may well be different. Family discourses include a number of competing voices which may be more or less absorbed or negated in the processes of family interaction. Second, the question of who within a family should be accorded the privilege of 'speaking for' the family becomes a highly problematic issue. Indeed, the very idea that someone within a family can fully understand and articulate the feelings of all family members in 'normal' circumstances is doubtful; at a time of crisis or severe family breakdown, it seems unlikely. It is at this point of crisis that the family therapist would offer direction and, crucially, *interpretation* of family life.

Gubrium develops two related themes in his analysis of the two therapeutic settings. First, he argues that family troubles take on meaning through the interpretation of the family disorder in the therapeutic setting. Secondly, he suggests that the abstract entity of the family as an embodiment of many acts and symbols approximates to what Levi Strauss called *bricolage*: the 'bits and pieces' of everyday family life relating to conversation, posturing and routine interaction together make a meaningful whole. These 'bits and pieces' are deconstructed and assigned meaning by the particular organisational principles underlying the structure of the therapeutic setting. Whilst it may be objected that signs, symbols and interpretations of behaviour can mean what people want them to mean, Gubrium maintains that the organisational setting of the therapeutic project embeds particular meanings in line with its initial analysis of the problem, its methods of intervention and its objectives. Conceptions of family disorder are shaped by the organisational understanding of what constitutes order; the therapeutic practice provides a 'framework' for the interpretation of household events. The two projects studied by Gubrium differed in terms of their understanding of family and the therapeutic process. On the one hand, the therapists at Westside held to a view of the family as a *system of knowledge* which underpinned its dynamics, whilst the therapeutic project was understood to be a 'moral system of principles, preferences and polemics'; the therapeutic encounter was therefore viewed as an engagement between two epistemological systems. Fairview, on the other hand, took a different approach by targeting the family authority structure. Particular attention was paid to language and conversation. The assumption was that family order/disorder would be displayed through observation of the *hierarchies of communication*: who said what to whom and when. The construction of an understanding of domestic disorder, in the cases studied by Gubrium, is worked out through the range of seminars, discussions, videotaped sessions and other activities constituting the therapeutic encounter. The reconstruction of meaning and the making visible of that which remains hidden or unclear or abstract to family members by specialists external to the family make family systems theory and family therapy fraught with difficulties. The issues of professional knowledge and power which lie at the core of the clinical application of family systems theory are addressed most clearly in post-structuralism.

Post-structuralism

Turner (1987) helps us to link the problems identified with family therapy in Gubrium's analysis with the theoretical insights of poststructuralism. He reminds us of the philosophical underpinnings of post-structuralism in the work of Nietzsche (1974). It was Nietzsche who argued that modern medical practice constituted a new form of control. Medical science represented for Nietzsche a form of language which interpreted reality, and interpreted conceptions of 'pathology' and illness. Medical science and, importantly, the application of medical models to the analysis and 'treatment' of social behaviour, constitute a *system of interpretation*. Developing this insight, Turner uses Parsons' (1951) concept of the 'sick role' to point up that 'illness behaviour is structured and patterned according to specific expectations in the interaction between doctor and patient, but also that disease and sickness are products of general values relating to that which is esteemed significant within a given society' (Turner, 1987: 216). The 'sick role' is therefore *interpreted* by both patient and medical practitioner in accordance with the prevailing cultural expectations about how the role should be performed. Our understanding of 'pathology', whether physiological or that relating to family functioning, is constructed through language; our understanding of it is shaped by the authority of those offering diagnoses, classification and definition of the problematic core of a social action or a piece of social behaviour.

The most interesting insight of post-structuralism with respect to the issues being addressed here is that the concept of what constitutes 'pathology' or disease is the product of medical discourses. In the context of family therapy, the professional discourses of psychiatrists, social workers and family therapists shape and pick out of social reality that which is problematic in accordance with the dominant paradigm informing the value orientation in the therapeutic setting. This is precisely what Gubrium (1992) describes in his analysis of the two therapeutic settings, Westside and Fairview. Foucault argued that we see what our language permits us to see (Foucault, 1974). Professional status confers the power to talk authoritatively and with legitimacy about a range of matters from the worlds of medicine and 'social pathology' in the modern welfare societies in the west. Problems and 'pathologies' become *visible* because an increasing variety of knowledges, such as psychiatry, psychoanalysis, sociology and social work, combine with new and emerging forms of professional power, allowing practitioners to define, classify and prescribe remedies for an infinite number of problematic social behaviours and 'pathological' conditions; knowledge and power are, within Foucault's conception of post-structuralism, an indivisible pairing.

[P]ower and knowledge directly imply one another; that there is no power relation without the correlative constitution of a field of knowledge, nor any knowledge that does not presuppose and constitute at the same time power relations. These 'power-knowledge relations are to be analysed, therefore, not free in relation to the power system, but on the contrary, the subject who knows, the objects to be known and the modalities of knowledge must be regarded as so many effects of these fundamental implications of power-knowledge and their historical transformations. (Foucault, 1977, 27–8)

This conception of power transcends the idea of underlying structures determining courses of action (hence the label 'post-structuralism') (see Hirst, 1976). The subject is constituted by language rather than underlying structures in institutions or language itself.

One way in which Foucault's concept of power can be understood and its relevance for the analysis of welfare intervention into family life demonstrated is by focusing on the use of the concepts of *rationalisation* and *normalisation* in his work. With respect to the first concept of *rationalisation*, Turner (1987) sees parallels between Weber's concept of *rationalisation* and Foucault's argument that western societies have become subject to increasing forms of regulation (see Dandekar, 1990). The application of science to everyday life leads to an inevitable uniformity in human affairs, bolstered by a range of professional practitioners, particularly from the fields of health and welfare, who are charged with the responsibility of controlling not only social deviance but also medical deviance within large populations. (For example, recent developments in bio-technology, and in particular the isolation and commercialisation of genetic testing for gene mutations such as fragile X which causes mental abnormalities and learning difficulties, may well lead to mass screening for a range of defective genes carried in the population. In the United States such screening has been carried out in schools in co-operation with bio-technology companies. The possibility of the identification of a genetically inferior 'underclass' is just one issue raised by this development.) The consequence of these developments has been the emergence of a modern form of social regulation based on the surveillance of social behaviour through routine administrative practices and mass medical screening called 'panopticism'. The concept of *normalisation* grows out of this process of the rationalisation of social life; it is a mechanism of social control well adapted to ordering the lives of large populations effectively without recourse to instruments of coercion. As Burns (1992) suggests when drawing a likeness between Foucault, Goffman and Gramsci on this issue, '*normalisation* is a complex form of organisation in which we are all agents of power, all involved in the exercise of power' (p. 164). It is the discipline of the school, the hospital and the factory to which post-structuralism draws our attention – also, Foucault maintained, 'the disciplines of the family, of neighbourhood, and of the encounters of everyday life' (Burns, 1992, 164). It is this sense of power being effective by exercising pressure on people to conform to social norms through *self-control* that we can understand as 'normalisation'. Power, therefore, does not operate solely, or indeed mainly, through the coercive authority of the state in modern industrial societies, as Gramsci understood very well, but rather it operates through a hegemonic and dispersed authority whereby those subject to surveillance co-operate and consent to their own monitoring and regulation: they watch over themselves. An integral part of this process is what Foucault (1977) called *normalising judgement*, which refers to the power yielded to professional practitioners, such as social workers, health visitors and others involved in community medicine, to evaluate each individual in accordance with a measure of what constitutes normality in society. In this way, welfare practitioners are cast as central figures monitoring and effecting change in family life. The medicalisation of social problems is one particularly growing form of social and moral regulation highlighted by post-structuralist analysis.

Dingwall and Eekelaar (1988), drawing on the post-structuralist perspective of Donzelot (1980), describe how the state resolves its dilemma of regulating the family life of the poor whilst avoiding the ideological transgression of direct intervention into the private sphere by sponsoring the development of moral-hygienism through the 'do-gooders' of the Charity Organisation Society, and, later in the twentieth century, through the agents of the welfare state such as social workers and community medicine professionals. In an analysis which is consistent with much contemporary sociological theory in its rejection of a fixed conception of *the family*, Donzelot draws attention to the construction of problems and identities by those who intervene in family life. In a similar vein, Dingwall and Eekelaar describe how the nineteenth century concern for issues of public health and morality led philanthropists to construct a discourse rooted in what can best be described as moral-hygienism, which identified working-class family life as both the problem and the solution to 'public health and moral decay'. The cause of both 'pathological' behaviour and epidemics which threatened public health was located in the inadequate child rearing practices and poorly ordered domestic life of working-class families. The solution to these problems lay in the creation of an identity for working-class women around the role of motherhood.

Symonds (1991) captures the character of what post-structuralists have referred to as 'soft policing' in her investigation into the different social class identities of district nurses and health visitors. She concludes her analysis by pointing up an important conceptual distinction between the role of the two nursing statuses within the social space of the household: the expertise of the district nurse does not threaten the ownership of social space because she provides practical help to her clients; it is illness, not the state of the house or parenting competence, which is the focus of their concern. The expertise of the health visitor does challenge the ownership of social space by virtue of their educational, advisory and monitoring role which claims authority on matters of health and childcare. The intervention into the privacy of the family sphere therefore enables the health practitioner to construct an image of a competent or incompetent, or indeed 'dangerous', mother through the application of professionally grounded language and training. In a similar vein Abbott and Sapsford (1990) apply the insights of post-structuralism to determine whether the description of 'policing the family' is appropriate when applied to health visitors. They acknowledge the absence of statutory powers underpinning the health visitor's role, but point to their possession of extensive routine authority to visit and advise on a range of health and childcare issues. Without coercion, and most often with the consent of mothers, they monitor and construct conceptions of 'good' and 'bad' mothering habits. The blurring of the boundaries between 'caring functions' and 'controlling functions' in professional practice has been a significant insight gained through post-structuralist perspectives on welfare intervention. It is possible to see why the concepts of *rationalisation* (the application of medical science to the regulation of family living), *normalisation* (the inculcation of 'good' domestic habits through schooling and advice) and *panopticism* (the surveillance of family and household) are apt for the description of the professional role of the health visitor.

The contemporary application of post-structuralism to the analy-

sis of social work, and hence to the critique of statutory intervention into family life, can be found in Rojek *et al.* (1988). They
develop what they call 'subjectless social work'. The object of their
criticism is the presumption that social problems have an underlying objectivity, so leading to the construction of a 'developmental
view of humanist social work which portrays 'pathologies' and 'symptoms' as developing in an unbroken chain of cause and effect towards an assigned end or point of origin' (p. 128). The alternative
perspective. suggested by Rojek *et al.* is that post-structuralist influenced social work practice should acknowledge the need for 'lateral
analysis' of the many ways in which everyday social work vocabulary is constructed through professional and client discourses. It rejects
both the idea that there are fixed meanings in language and that
clients have 'essential' needs which are described by social work
vocabularies and professional discourse. The idea of subjectless social
work derives from the idea that social workers construct a subject
(the client) and her 'needs' through the use of social work discourse
rather than respond to an already formed subject with *essential*
human 'needs' which are yet to be fulfilled; it is a rejection of the
notion that social work clients are 'characterised by a universal
subjectivity, one which applies to all individuals and yet no one in
particular' (p. 137).

The troubling aspect of post-structuralism is its apparent rejection of what Habermas has called the political ideals of the enlightenment: Foucault's failure to make clear his normative stance on
issues such as freedom, autonomy of the individual, and emancipatory movements including gender inequalities in society. Feminist scholarship, in particular, has been attracted to the iconoclastic
nature of Foucault's work, but is also somewhat uneasy about its
stance on matters such as power and inequality in family life (see
Fraser, 1989, 65–6). There are also issues which should be examined
with respect to the concept of agency in post-structuralism, but I
will delay discussion of that theme until Chapter 2 when practitioner–
client relationships will be discussed.

Feminism

The issue at the heart of feminist work on family life is the failure
of existing theoretical perspectives to adopt a normative stance on
the inequalities of power and control which shore up the institution

of the family. Against systems theories which stress concepts of circular causality, feminist analysis will focus on the linear direction of power and control in family life from men over women and children leading to family breakdown and distress through child abuse and domestic violence. Against post-structuralism, which appears to hold to a neutral view of power, stressing its dispersal through all social relationships and accentuating its positive and productive capacities, feminist analysis will tend to focus on the hierarchical nature of gender relationships and, as some feminists would have it, the 'class-like relationships' characterising the marriage relationship (see Delphy and Leonard, 1992). As Fraser (1989) has argued, there are 'good' forms of power, but there are also 'bad' forms of power which many theorists believe Foucault failed to incorporate into his theoretical project.

From the perspective of feminist social work, the broader social context of the domestic division of labour provides the backcloth to the tensions which give rise to family problems. Feminist social work practice and family therapy will unavoidably reorientate strategies of family intervention so that they more adequately appraise the needs of women rather than the family system. It is the imposition of patriarchal forms of control over women's lives which becomes problematic. By briefly considering the broader analysis of patriarchal power, an insight into the feminist viewpoint can be illustrated. Delphy and Leonard (1992), for example, argue that men and women should be conceptualised as two socially differentiated categories: two genders, one of which dominates the other. Sexual relationships, and our understanding of emotional fulfilment through the marriage relationship, are socially constructed and not biologically based mechanisms for relating men and women together. They advance this perspective by developing a materialist analysis of marriage in terms of the 'class-like relationships' between men and women. This idea was prepared in an earlier work by Delphy (1977) where she argued that relations between husband and wife are actually exploitative rather than just unequal because they involve the exploitation of women's labour. Within households social categorisations determine work tasks 'flexibly by age but more fixedly by gender'; the obligation for women to undertake household labour is lifelong. Children are exploited not because of their gender but because they are young. Women are exploited because of their gender. The problem for women when compared with workers under the

capitalist mode of production is that they cannot change their husbands as workers can theoretically change their employer; it is this
entrapment in exploitative labour within the marriage or cohabiting
relationship which constitutes the core of the *domestic mode of production*. A further feature of the marriage relationship is that its
exploitative character does not cease with divorce because women
continue to perform domestic labour in the form of childcare for
their ex-husbands. So by examining the conditions of performance,
remuneration and status of household work, Delphy and Leonard
reveal the *relations of production* shaping family and marriage relationships. The important insight of this work is its insistence that
household tasks should not be extracted from their *relations of production*; they argue that 'we are moving towards an understanding
of the gender constitution of classes and the class constitution of
gender' (p. 160).

Patriarchal authority, which anchors the relations of household
production, is stable because it is a form of what Weber understood
as *traditional authority*: like master and servant or officer and soldier,
marriage appears to be a natural coupling. Underlying this popular
conception of the 'natural' division between the sexes is what Delphy
maintains is a common misunderstanding that gender, or socially
constructed differences between men and women, is grafted on to
basic biological distinctions. This notion is rejected by Delphy (1980,
1984); patriarchal forms of domination bring about gender divisions
rather than emerging as epiphenomena of pre-existing differences
between the sexes. The relationship between the sexes is class-like
because, like Marx's notion of the differences between bourgeois
and proletarian, the social roles of men and women presuppose one
another. Oakley (1974) provided an earlier analysis of domestic labour,
stressing it as 'work'. The central features of domestic work and
the housewife role were their association with economic dependency; the common perception of it as not being 'real' work, that is,
productive work for a wage or salary; and its almost exclusive allocation to women. Oakley's analysis was particularly interesting for
the description of the ways in which the association of the housewife role as being essentially 'feminine' pressurised women to identify
with it. Research on dual-earning households by Brannen and Moss
(1991) and by Martin and Roberts (1984) on women and employment indicates that the burden of domestic labour does not lessen
with paid employment but rather accumulates and leads to the problem

of role strain, with all that that implies for women's health.

Family life consists, therefore, of class-like differences which give rise to differences in consumption based on differential status and power. Patriarchy is, therefore, to be understood as a form of hegemonic control of one social group by another. Not all practitioners will subscribe to the materialist version of feminism described in Delphy and Leonard's work. However, their analysis strips away the veneer of 'naturalism' often associated with family life and reveals the underlying power relationships which structure the relationships which often underpin family problems.

The line of continuity running through the analysis of the domestic division of labour and the analysis of its impact on the health and well-being of women and children is *patriarchy*. Feminist perspectives on family life vary with respect to the degree to which they focus on the interior or exterior of family relationships, but they share a common interest in the inequality of power inherent in gender relationships. The systematic control over the routines of family living which lies in the hands of men gives rise to a more widespread system of *patriarchal power*. For instance, the explanation for violence against women and children within the family follows from the analysis of *patriarchy* rather than other bases of control and authority in society. There are a number of competing explanations for male aggression and violence, and many of them could be used to support a general feminist perspective in social work practice. The main critical measures, however, for delineating what is or is not compatible with a feminist perspective must be, first, whether the account relies on an underlying conception of *human nature* and so explains male violence and aggression in terms of some 'natural' animal instinct beyond human control and adjustment; and, second, whether the account effectively treats women as being culpable, contributing to their own victimisation through the way they have related to their male partner (M. Fine, 1981). Feminism which identifies patriarchal power as *the problem* will invariably stress the social construction of violent male attitudes, ultimately concentrating attention on the wider institutional and cultural supports for male aggression rather than on 'abnormal' individuals who are somehow outside of the influence of social processes: it is the social construction of masculinity which becomes problematic. It follows, therefore, that feminist social work or family therapy will treat women's rejection of conventional domestic responsibilities as an attempt at renegotiating inequitable gender relationships rather than as being a manifestation of 'pathology'.

Feminist practice in therapy and social work

The feminist critique of family therapy and social work practice can be divided into two distinct parts: that which attacks the underlying theoretical premises of practice theory, which has meant overwhelmingly offering a critique of systems theory, and that which has attempted to establish guidelines or critical measures for redirecting professional practice.

Goldner (1985) locates the modern development of family therapy in the 1950s, which she characterises as a particularly 'familialistic' era. In fact, it was a time when there was concern to reinforce traditional conceptions of the patriarchal nuclear family, motherhood and domesticity in order to encourage women to vacate the factories and offices for men returning from military service. This was also a time when sociological theory in the form of Parsonian structural functionalism was at the height of its influence, and its specific emphasis on social system equilibrium and stability had the effect of reinforcing what appeared to be visible: the family as a unique domain in which women were charged with the functional task of family maintenance. A common clinical problem which has emerged in family therapy, that of the over-involved mother and the peripheral father is, according to Goldner, not so much a 'pathology' of family living but rather an outgrowth of the exaggerated split between the public and private spheres of work and home which has been a feature of historical change in industrial societies and which was accentuated by systems theory grounded in functionalist dogma. The attachment to systems thinking has led family therapists to pathologise deviations from the ideological model of the middle-class patriarchal nuclear family which lies at the heart of orthodox clinical conceptions of 'healthy family functioning'; maternal centrality and paternal marginality are 'ideological categories and not states of nature' (p. 32). Notions of complementary sex roles and functional domestic divisions have, therefore, obscured inequalities in family power which systems theory has been unable to conceptualise.

One enduring issue in feminist analysis is, of course, the tendency in law and clinical practice to blame the woman victim. The problem of what Goldner (1985) calls 'mother's overexposure' at the centre of family living because of the unequal domestic burden imposed on women also makes them vulnerable to therapeutic manipulation operating a systems logic. Too often family therapy treats the mother as 'the problem' because she is the fulcrum upon which everything balances. Osborne (1983), for example, criticising systems theory in this context, specifically structural family therapy, sees dangers in assuming an equality in the power balance between husband and wife when attempting to disengage the mother from 'over-involvement' with her children in order to create space for the marginal father: the assumption that men as husbands and fathers will be there for the children and wife is to ignore the broad and deep foundations of gender divisions in society and family life. However, the paradox at the centre of this scenario is that the therapist exploits the woman in the family in order to get access to the private sphere and to the husband. The woman's position as the cooperative therapeutic subject is used instrumentally to appease the reluctant and poor therapeutic subject which is the man. But access to the reluctant male is gained at the expense of devaluing the needs of the woman. One particularly neglected aspect of the woman's role in family life, and one which diverges from the rather fundamentalist materialism of someone like Delphy, is that the relations between the sexes are, as Goldner (1985) observes, both complementary and hierarchical at the same time; women within the family are socially powerful but this position is undermined, even 'denigrated', by the wider system of power based on patriarchal assumptions and practices. Family therapy cannot succeed whilst ignoring this paradox and ignoring the woman's needs in preference to some notion of family system and stable family functioning. The case of child abuse raises similar issues. Besides the fact that child abuse as a social problem overwhelmingly, although not exclusively, involves men abusing children, the culpability of women within the configuration of an abusing family is often assumed. The charge that the mother 'failed to protect' the child is often made, and acts to divert attention from the male abuser who is actually culpable. Feminist analyses of child abuse link this phenomenon to other forms of patriarchal abuse: child abuse is always seen as an act of violence and, most importantly, an extreme expression of male power. Feminists working in social work and family therapy are therefore more likely to talk about particular abusers than problem families.

The analysis of this problem requires a broader analysis of the masculine and feminine discourses which inform everyday social life. Indeed the problem is not one which should be exclusively the concern of feminists but really ought to involve the as yet undeveloped analysis of masculinism in modern society (see Hearn, 1987; Hearn and Morgan, 1990).

The question that remains to be debated actively by feminists, however, is that of how feminist practice in social work and family therapy can encompass a stress on family interaction which systems theory has developed. It has been objected that feminism too readily rejects the insights of systems theory and so overlooks the complexities of family dynamics. As a result it slips into what has been called a 'victimisation paradigm' which rests on rather absolute assumptions that social control always operates in a 'top down' direction (see Fetherstone and Fawcett, 1995).

With respect to guidelines for a feminist family therapy, the core theme is undoubtedly that therapy must never 'pathologise' women who reject the conventions of feminine behaviour. This must also involve an approach which can accept women as operating without men; without having to service male needs. Urry (1990) sets out six principles and a number of guidelines for therapists wishing to develop a feminist-sensitive practice, and Schneider (1990) describes their application in the practice situation. First, gender divisions are based on inequalities in the public world which are reflected in the private world. So therapists have to acknowledge this and enquire into the assumptions about men and women within the present and past family, combined with a focus on the power distribution and use of language, particularly such things as possessive pronouns such as *yours* and *mine* when the participants refer to property or children. Second, the therapist needs to identify the different power bases within the family, whether they be domestic, affective, sexual, economic, language or physical, and then work to negate their destructive impact. Third, the therapist can never be gender neutral and this involves self-reflection on the part of the therapist or therapy team about their own position on matters such as feminism and gender relations. Fourth, the therapist's thinking and practice must not be contradictory. The use of methods must be such that there should not be reliance on strategic means which are intrinsically sexist and unfair to women in order to achieve 'a sound goal'. With respect to this particular principle, it would be considered intrinsically wrong to use the woman in strategic therapy in order to gain acquiescence from the man (see Osborne, 1985). Fifth, a conscious effort should be made by the therapist to empower women by validating their experience: sexist assumptions that may be made routinely by both males and females need to be challenged; responsibility for the 'dysfunction' in family life should not be placed on the woman; and the therapist should relate to the woman as a named person and not a social role. And finally, sixth, there is always a need to connect the private relational difficulties encountered in the therapeutic setting to the wider public political culture and the patriarchal institutions which shape people's lives.

The precepts set out here for the guidance of family therapists are equally valid for social workers. Increasingly social workers are working with methods which aim to balance the power differentials between them and their clients. A range of approaches are adopted involving contracts, task centredness and therapeutic intervention in locations such as family centres (see Hare-Mustin, 1978). Each approach could be organised around an anti-discriminatory and/or feminist strategy. I will discuss the issue of practitioner–client relationships in Chapter 2 where the implications of these ideas will be explored more fully.

Social control and social policy in social theory

By way of concluding this chapter, we can review more generally the way in which the concept of *social control* has developed in the social analysis of welfare. There has been a widespread rejection of the view that welfare has been the product of an evolving humanitarianism (see Baker, 1979). In terms of the growth of the welfare state, Thane (1982) emphasises at the beginning of her book on *The Foundations of the Welfare State* that

> to interpret its growth simply as a manifestation of altruism, of a desire to remove poverty and other social evils, renders mysterious the fact that much poverty remains, that those in greatest need have often gained least and that their gains have been hedged around with restrictions designed . . . to keep benefits below normal wages (Thane, 1982, 2).

Similarly, Ignatieff (1983) underlines the agreement to be found amongst a host of scholars studying social welfare and penalty, including Piven and Cloward (1972), Scull (1979), Rothman (1971) and Foucault (1967, 1973, 1977), by emphasising that they have all concluded that there has not been a simple passage from 'cruelty to enlightenment' (see Squires, 1990). Social welfare provision since the nineteenth century has had at the centre the theme of societal discipline, whether one thinks of Donzelot's (1980) argument that the family has been subjected to a 'tutelary complex' at the hands of child welfare agents, or, as Ignatieff has put it in relation to reforms within the prison system:

> This strategy of power could not be understood unless the history of the prison was incorporated into a history of the philosophy of authority and the exercise of class power in general. The prison was thus studied not for itself but for what its rituals of humiliation could reveal about a society's ruling conceptions of power, social obligation and human malleability. (Ignatieff, 1983, 77)

Contained within Ignatieff's remarks is a glimpse of two elements which have emerged in recent scholarship to challenge the overly sanguine view of social policy development: first, that social policy has as its objective the maintenance of class power, and second, that a wider social discipline has been evolving which has only become visible through the scholarly examination of the relationship between the prison and the factory (Melossi and Pavarini, 1981) and the interchange between penal policy and social policy. The Marxist tradition and Foucault's archaeological method have each been instrumental in developing these insights.

On the one hand Marxists have focused on the process of incorporation accomplished by the welfare state, treating social policy as a tool of social crisis management, though it has not always been successful (Offe, 1984; Griffin, Devine and Wallace, 1983). On the other hand, Foucault has encouraged us to view the welfare state, or at least institutional developments within it, as part of a large-scale historical transformation in the techniques of power, in which social control is made effective by the intricate and multifaceted ways in which surveillance in modern society is maintained (Foucault, 1967, 1973, 1977). In the case of Marxism the problem of agency is *located* in the notion of ruling-class power, but in the work of Foucault the conception of power employed is *dispersed*. There is no possessor of power from which the capacity to exercise social control can flow. As suggested above in relation to post-structuralism, power is conceptualised by Foucault in relation to processes of *rationalisation* and *normalisation*; it is the phenomenon of *panopticism* rather than elite power which characterises modernity in his work. It is this latter type of analysis which has enlivened recent debate about social control theories as applied to social welfare practice. There is, as a consequence, a gathering disquiet about the way the theme of social control has been used and, to some extent, ignored by those involved in delivering welfare services (see Pratt, 1985). The seduction of working with conceptions of large-scale historical and theoretical 'master shifts' does, however, leave understanding of their concrete implications undeveloped.

In reviewing the range of social control theories of social policy, Higgins (1980) classifies the radical critique of the welfare state into three categories. First, under the rubric of *Marxism*, John Saville's classic paper on the welfare state (Saville, 1957) was taken as an exemplar of the 'social policy as concession to working class' approach, while O'Connor (1973) and Gough (1975) were cited as examples of Marxist analysis, emphasising the processes of ideological and political integration of class struggle through the legitimatory functions of the welfare state. Secondly, Higgins isolates what she calls *urban crisis theory*, which includes amongst many others Alcaly and Mermelstein's (1977) analysis of New York's fiscal crisis, Castells (1977) on the urban question and Piven and Cloward (1972) on relief policies in the USA. Within this type of work the analysis of class and racial conflict in the urban context again treats social policy initiatives as being aimed towards integrating and pacifying dissident groups through community development and welfare projects. Thirdly, Higgins identifies what she calls *radical social work* analyses which stress the 'social tranquillising effect' of social work (Corrigan and Leonard, 1978). Her conclusion is that, despite the varieties of social control theories, they all assume too much intent and unity among a ruling class. Further, they work with 'reified constructs' at too high a level of generality and on the whole tend to 'rely too heavily on assertion rather than empirical data'. Whilst acknowledging the importance of 'social control theories' for injecting more realism into the evaluation of social policy, and posing important questions about the limits of altruistic and humanitarian motives in welfare provision, Higgins nevertheless argues for a more empirical and differentiated approach to analysing social control arguments. In the context of social work she rightly points out that to assert that social workers are 'agents of social control' avoids examining the different roles and types of work undertaken by social workers. Further, to dismiss them in this way is to abrogate any responsibility for unpacking the concept of 'social control agent' or for providing an answer to the questions 'In what ways are social workers social control agents?' and 'How might they behave and act otherwise?'

Van Krieken (1986, 1991) undertakes a critical scrutiny of the social control theme in social policy analysis with special reference to child welfare. The work of Anthony Platt (1977), Christopher Lasch (1977) and Jacques Donzelot (1980) are singled out for particular mention because they all stress in their own way the imposition of social control on mainly working-class families by professional social welfare interventionists. The work of Lasch and Donzelot in particular provides interesting analyses of the 'colonising' and 'policing' effects on working-class families of the penal/welfare complex emerging in the twentieth century (see Cohen, 1985; Garland, 1985).

Van Krieken, however, points out that too often the social control theories he reviews fail to acknowledge the historical evidence that working-class families displayed resistance to welfare control. And, indeed, he cites examples where working-class families have actively sought to use 'bourgeois' welfare institutions to socialise and constrain their own members (Tholfsen, 1976; and Philips, 1977). He lays particular stress on the social and cultural divisions that have existed within working-class communities. A similar observation is made by Mann (1991) in his analysis of the historical divisions internal to working-class formation, giving rise to social groupings variously labelled the 'aristocracy of labour' and, more recently, 'the underclass' or 'claimant class'. What these historical analyses indicate is the need for a more discriminating and empirical analysis of how social control works, acknowledging the intra- as well as inter-class uses of power. By way of underscoring his argument, Van Krieken quotes approvingly de Swaan's view (1990) that collusion between parents, state officials and third party professionals, such as doctors and social workers, often means that *all* gain by child welfare actions. It might mean that a family crisis is resolved for the parents, delinquency is prevented in the local community and the professional status of social workers and doctors is enhanced. This line of argument perhaps leaves many issues relating to the child's welfare unresolved, but it has the virtue of suggesting a more pragmatic approach to the analysis of social control in welfare contexts, and encourages us to examine the complexities involved in such professional–client relationships.

Whilst our analysis should build into it an account of the words and motives of policy makers and social workers, Van Krieken is surely correct to warn against collecting together 'the most colourful and strident quotations one can find about the evils of the lower classes and how this or that institution or piece of legislation will civilise and regulate them'. He continues by warning us that 'this is presented as conclusive proof that child welfare was clearly part of a process of social control' (Van Krieken, 1986, 407). His argument is well made when he suggests that one either chooses to study such intentions and objectives in their own right or, alternatively, to investigate empirically the effects of child welfare on the families and clients of the social work services. The particular form in which social control is exercised must therefore be demonstrated and not assumed. The questions at issue are how does social control operate in social work practice and, most importantly, how are disciplinarian regimes negotiated and modified by those involved? We should try and understand the nature of intervention into family life by agents of the welfare state in a more differentiated way. This is the issue we will turn to in Chapter 2.

2

Understanding family intervention: theorising professional practice

It is one of the central weaknesses of recent critical work in the sociology of welfare that the practitioner–client relationship has either been ignored or characterised crudely as simply one of power. What is lacking is a framework which can focus analysis on the interaction between social worker or therapist and client(s). There are two interrelated dimensions involved in all social interaction but too often analysis focuses attention on one at the expense of the other. Knowledge, and its possession, yields power and authority. It enables people to have a voice and influence outcomes by virtue of their expertise. Social structures also constrain and organise social interaction in terms of axes of division such as class, age, race and gender. Foucault was absolutely correct to say that power and knowledge are inextricably paired. However, we should not examine discourses independently of the social structures which enable some voices to be more influential than others. And, of course, incivility and deviance often mean that the voices of the authoritative are treated irreverently, or are undermined by strategies adopted by those apparently without power.

Central to the project of developing a critical understanding of family intervention is the identification of a theoretical framework which can provide insight into how the wider ideological and policy debates which rage in our public institutions take form. It is also helpful if that theoretical framework can assist in the analysis of transactions within practitioner–client relationships which lie at the heart of welfare practice and intervention in family life. In this chapter I want to set out a framework of analysis which will assist us in understanding how the principle of social control in professional practice with families is shaped and, importantly, how it varies between different types of practitioner–client relationships. However, beyond the specific analysis of practitioner–client relationships, the conceptual framework described in this chapter will be used throughout the book as a shorthand to describe different orientations to meaning which are shaped by the relationship between distinctive kinds of knowledge and information on the one hand, and the power to assign a positive or negative value to that knowledge and information on the other hand.

Towards a critical theory of family intervention

One of the central concerns of this analysis is the tension between family life as a private experience, and family life and the institution of the family as a focus for public debate and public policy. This divide between the public and the private spheres of society hinders attempts to elevate women's issues to the top of the political agenda and so force social and political change in those policy areas which impact on women and family life. Direct political intervention into the private affairs of family living is generally considered to be unacceptable in liberal-democratic societies. This prohibition was, of course, established much earlier in history when the governance of families was rooted in patriarchal authority (see Donzelot, 1980). Other means of influencing the character of family life which do not entail the destruction of the aura of privatism surrounding the institution of 'the family' have had to evolve.

One of the most interesting insights of Donzelot (1980) in his post-structuralist analysis of the family is his notion of the creation or construction of 'the social sphere' as a direct product of intervention by nineteenth-century philanthropists to regulate socially the family life of the poor; the social sphere became an integral part of the development of the welfare state (see Squires, 1990) and a solution to the problem of how family life could be directed in the interests of public authorities without using coercive law and political intervention. However, the post-structuralist vision of 'governance *through* families' lying at the centre of Donzelot's perspective should be complemented by the notion of 'the public sphere' which has been developed both in classical political theory (see Arendt, 1958) and in the critical theory of Habermas (1989). The concept of the public sphere makes visible the institutional and political space whereby ideas, opinions and social movements form and individuals, professional practitioners and social and political movements confront one another and enter into conflict with opposing belief systems and practices. Most importantly, it directs our attention to the question of how public languages and professional discourses, which are accorded status because they are anchored in educational, legal and public political institutions, encounter the local and often subversive discourse of the social work client in their struggle to shape social interaction and communication; it assists us in focusing on both the ideal and distorting processes which organise social relationships and the social construction of meaning. For example, Smart's analysis of the construction of the concept 'woman' in nineteenth-century legal discourse pays particular attention to both the legislative frameworks generated to bring about 'social engineering' and the moral purity campaigners and voices which occupied the public sphere to shape public conceptions of social problems, family life and women (Smart, 1992). However, too often the lure of post-structuralist vocabulary overlooks the real political dimension of discourse analysis. The *social sphere* may well be the focus of political and policy activity, but the *public sphere* draws our attention to the conflicts over the formulation and presentation of views which are obscured by an overly sterile analysis of professional discourses as if they were unlocated universes of meaning. Whilst acknowledging the authentic reaction of women against attempts by policy makers and the law to regulate public conceptions of womanhood through struggles over abortion, contraception, childcare and sexuality, Smart's analysis only hints at the public political processes at work in the construction of public images of womanhood. There is a danger in seeing social regulation and social control as singularly emanating from the powerful middle-class professional elites in medicine and social science. There are two problems with this. First, it tends to neglect the influence of clients and lay people in shaping and negotiating the outcomes of social and political interaction. Secondly, it fails to provide a conceptual space for the public conflict and debate about what constitutes a valid representation of a problem, an image or an identity. The concept of the *public sphere* is therefore essential for a grounded analysis of language and communication, particularly the heated public debates about family life.

Habermas has given us a rich theoretical framework through which many of these conceptual problems can be confronted. For him, material reproduction and symbolic reproduction are irreducible functions of society. Neither is foundational; the one is not determined by the other as might be implied in classical Marxism, which gives priority to the sphere of material production. The sphere of material reproduction encapsulates the range of activities which take place within the capitalist market economy and the state system of political institutions and public policy formation. The sphere of symbolic reproduction includes those social practices concerned with socialisation and the reproduction of a society's culture and normative system. From this basic theoretical framework we can see that the area of family life is conceptualised as being anchored in the symbolic sphere and *predominantly* concerned with issues of solidarity, socialisation and cultural transmission. In a useful appreciation of Habermas from a feminist perspective, Fraser draws our attention to the distinction between what Habermas calls system-integrated action contexts characterised by 'self-interest, utility-maximizing calculations typically entertained in the idioms . . . of money and power' (Fraser, 1989: 117) and 'socially integrated action contexts'.

> Socially integrated action contexts are those in which different agents coordinate their actions with one another by reference to some form of explicit or implicit intersubjective consensus about norms, values and ends, consensus predicated on linguistic speech and interpretation. (Fraser, 1989, 116–17)

Fraser continues by focusing on Habermas's further distinction between *normatively secured social integration*, which is characterised by taken-for-grantedness, convention and pre-reflective consensus, and *communicatively achieved forms of social integration*, characterised by explicit norms, reflectively achieved consensus and, above all else, unrestrained discussion, freedom, equality and fairness. Building on this distinction Fraser argues that family life is normatively rather than communicatively secured: we tend to accept unquestioningly the nature of family relationships, even when they are not perfect, because there are routine, everyday normative expectations attaching to them.

Whilst Habermas has not explored the gender issue thoroughly, there is much in his framework that is of value. A core feature of his method is to contrast the actual distortions in communication and institutional practices with a clear conception of the ideal (Habermas, 1970). So in order to point up the real distortions in communication he establishes the ideal or counterfactual model of the 'idealised speech situation' (an abstract simulation of communicative interaction where power and hierarchy are suspended and the power of reason is presumed to allow only the force of the better argument to prevail) where undistorted communication can at least be conceptualised and distortions measured. Similarly, by positing a distinction between normatively and communicatively secured contexts of social integration, he provides us with a useful ideal model guiding practice in terms of both political action and social policy intervention.

The objective of a critical strategy in therapy or social work with respect to family life would be the replacement of a context for family relationships which was normatively secured either by taken-for-grantedness, or sheer power, by one which is communicatively achieved: the task would be that of establishing undistorted communication within family life. The critical role of welfare practitioners in their many guises is clear: the practitioner would work towards helping the client or group of clients to reinterpret socio-cultural realities and reframe their problems in terms of a critical perspective, perhaps confronting feminist ideas or notions of male authority within the household directly. Above all, the social structure of family relationships needs to be questioned and subjected to open and critical discussion. The interesting question which arises is to what extent do social workers and family therapists reinforce the prevailing models of family life through their modes of intervention? To what extent can they challenge dominant legal, welfare and medical discourses regarding family problems? These questions direct our attention to the empirical reality of a dualistic institutional structure in our society: a distinct separation of public and private spheres, which can either be confronted by social policy intervention or ignored and reproduced.

The role of the social worker, family therapist or other 'technicians of human relations' within this complex analysis can be made more clear. Wolfe (1989), for example, argues that the traditional institutions which grounded a sense of morality and normative certainty, such as the churches, government and families, are no longer capable of generating a consensus in modern societies about 'the rules of moral obligation'. Wolfe suggests 'that liberal democracies have neither done away with moral codes nor with institutions and practices that embody them'. He suggests that the 'gap between the need for codes of moral obligation and the reality of societies that are confused about where they can be found is filled, however uncomfortably, by the contemporary social sciences' (Wolfe, 1989: 221). Economics provides the moral grounding for the market system; 'that obligations to the self automatically cover obligations to others'. Political science provides the moral grounding for the necessity of a centralised coercive authority to ensure that people carry out their obligations to one another. And sociology provides the intellectual and moral grounding for social caring by emphasising morality as a learning process requiring the institutions of civil society. The division of society into these spheres of moral meaning is reinforced, of course, by their institutional and professional expression; the growth of the *social sphere* and, in particular, the rise of professional social work acting on and within the institutions of civil society, confirms and reinforces the view of family life and social problems as something intrinsic to private rather than public deliberation. However, statutory social work has become the public management of the familial sphere, especially in those circumstances when the character of private family life offends the economic management of the personal social services.

Social workers and other practitioners of the welfare state are professionally attached to an ethos of caring and social amelioration which is intellectually supported by sociology, albeit incorporating insights from psychology and social policy analysis, through professional education. Professional practitioners from the fields of health and welfare are, therefore, the modern-day carriers of a moral code which is oppositional to the market and the state. The growth of the social work profession has, at least at an ideological level, proclaimed an interest in empowerment of clients and, when appropriate, state responsibility for the weak in society. However, any attempt by welfare practitioners to establish as a basis for their work a moral economy founded on what Titmuss (1987) characterised as 'altruism' will, increasingly, be confronted by competing discourses grounded in managerialism, economic efficiency and traditional conceptions of family responsibility. In the 1990s the family is being asked to take on more responsibility for the well-being of its members as the state attempts to renegotiate its post-war welfare commitments legislation such as the NHS and Community Care Act 1990. while the question of the gendered nature of social policy rei unresolved as we embrace an increasing emphasis on commu..ity care, which as Finch and Groves (1980) rightly point out means care by women. Intervention into family life to reorganise relationships, instil social discipline or provide caring assistance as part of these broader economic and policy changes will have as its objective the control of family life so that private rather than public resources are employed. Family life will tend to be treated as a private matter, quite separate from work, predominantly concerned with caring, and managed by women, but subject to public supervision. Jordan's view of the social work role in terms of ensuring *the final distribution of welfare* in the private sphere of the family comes to mind (see Jordan, 1987). The evolution of the statutory caring professions has created a situation where control over family life is no longer assured for parents and relatives but is effectively licensed to them. The social worker *negotiates* with people in what Jordan (1987) calls their 'natural settings' about the things that they ought to do for each other, and importantly, sometimes uses statutory powers to reorganise families when the *negotiations* break down. It is in this sense that we describe social work and the caring professions more generally as grounding a particular view of moral obligation. The rise of the *social sphere* has meant that the clear boundaries between the public and private spheres are now mediated by professional practitioners who straddle those divisions and work at the interface between the state and the family.

One phenomenon which tends to reinforce these developments and encourages an inward gaze in those who are troubled is what Janice Raymond (1986) calls *therapism*. Raymond was addressing her remarks to women but their more general relevance is clear.

Therapism is an overevaluation of feeling. In a real sense it is a tyranny of feelings where women have come to believe that what really counts in their life is their 'psychology'. And since they don't know what their psychology means, they submit to another who purports to know – a psychiatrist, counsellor, or analyst. (Raymond, 1986, 23)

We can acknowledge the similarity between this observation and that made by Foucault that modern society is characterised by a need for self-disclosure: we 'confess' to a range of practitioners of the welfare state and increasingly equate disclosure with unburdening ourselves and with a sense of liberation. There are plenty of welfare agents willing to assist in this process. Therapism has become a 'way of life' in modern welfare society, supplanting the religious idea of confession with the 'sharing' of problems and worries with a professional counsellor. The growth of social work since the Second World War has reinforced this trend, particularly where psychodynamic casework approaches have been adopted with clients. The intimate one-to-one relationship between practitioner and client may result in a neglect of the wider structural forces such as gender, race and class which often limit the horizons of those seeking to bring about social change.

Raymond observes, for example, that *therapism* is obsessively introverted and inevitably preoccupied with people 'sorting themselves out' often at the expense of an outward public vision of their problems. Richard Sennett has made similar observations in his broader analysis of culture, history and politics leading to *The Fall of Public Man* (Sennett, 1974). The boundaries between what is intimate and what is public become blurred; 'the sharing of feelings predominates over the revelation of passionate truth'. It is the promotion of change in an individual's behaviour rather than in the social and political order affecting social problems which characterises *therapism*. Moreover, the refusal to make private feelings public either through the therapeutic or the social work encounter becomes reduced to an issue of the repressed individual or pathological family. Meanwhile the real problem is not that of publicising personal life but of *politicising* it. Raymond reminds us that an integral part of politics is reflection, which is aided by retaining a perspective on ourselves: 'privacy fosters involvement in the world because it adds a quality of reflection to life'. The Habermasian project of seeking to uncover the political and institutional foundations for open and democratic public space, where issues and debates can be subjected to discursive validation, is not far from Raymond's concerns. What needs to be stressed here is that the concept of the *public sphere*, as a distinct institutional space where the *social sphere* of welfare activity can be supervised and criticised, is very important for our sociological analysis of welfare intervention into family life. The controversies which have surrounded the interventionist role of social workers and health visitors in family life in recent years have pointed up the political nature of welfare work and the growing significance of the *public sphere* as an analytical category, especially in the light of growing numbers of public inquiries being held to examine allegations of professional incompetence in one form or another. I will return to this issue in Chapter 7.

For the multiplicity of practitioners, 'technicians of human relations', who intervene in family problems, the central issue is whether family life is to be seen as something 'normatively' or 'communicatively' based, to use Habermas's distinction again. This raises the question of how those professional practitioners charged with the responsibility of intervening in family life should be directed, and what discretionary authority should be delegated to them in the execution of their professional responsibilities. Managerialists concerned with efficiency and economy in case management will tend to view the family as not only a resource to be administered but also a defining institution of the *private sphere*. For the welfare practitioner to assist clients to engage in a critical discussion and reflection about family relationships and obligations may, in circumstances of fiscal restraint, be looked upon by managerialists within the social services and social work departments as encouraging disorder, expense and policy confusion; prompting people to treat family life as if it is a *communicatively secured institution,* and therefore something about which individuals might make deviant choices, will be considered disruptive, especially in an era where the policy emphasis will be on using family resources more and state resources less. Social worker discretion will increasingly be endangered by bureaucratic, legal and fiscal edicts.

Our attention is drawn at this point to the crucial area of interaction between professional practitioners and clients. The most important issue when considering intervention is how clients are to be managed. The context of social work with families may increasingly be shaped by issues of managerialism and the allocation of scarce resources, but how practitioner–client relationships form and develop is a complex matter. One thing which is very clear about them, especially those that form within the statutory sphere, is that they can never be completely determined by managerialism or bureaucracy. We bestow professional status by education and statute on social workers and so allow them to exercise judgement and discretion in fieldwork practice; the interpretation of the social work role will, inevitably, be subject to situational adjustment by both the practitioners and the clients. The relationships between social workers and their clients, or indeed between family therapists and their clients, will vary from one practice context to another.

The social work role and the post-structuralist critique

Ford (1988) observes that the process of 'negotiation' in social work practice described by Jordan is often augmented by the subtle skills of social workers striving to be 'ordinary in unordinary situations' or, put in another way, by social workers trying to harness what Pinker (1983) has called the 'normal skills of sociable living' to the professional execution of counselling tasks. A conceptual space is created here within which this widely shared view of social work as involving 'advocacy, counselling and negotiation' has led to the development of approaches to practice which seek to ground such notions in workable devices or tools that make professional–client relationships more open, more controllable in terms of setting and measuring objectives, and generally less inequitable with respect to the power resources available to the parties in professional–client relationships. The development of contracts and task-centred approaches to practice best exemplify this type of development. The mutuality which Maluccio and Marlow (1974) describe as a central defining feature of contracts in social work is contained implicitly in the views held by Jordan and by Ford. There has been a suggestion, for example, that the concept of the 'empowerment' of clients may be an ethical imperative imposing a professional duty on professional practitioners from the fields of health and welfare to ensure that their clients attain more control over their lives, even if ironically that is imposed on them by the professional practitioner (see Baistow, 1995). It is the increasing popularity of a more client-oriented, or consumerist, approach which distinguishes contemporary social work practice from more overtly authoritarian and didactic approaches of the past. However, this move towards more professional openness in welfare practice has been subjected to critical comment, especially by those informed by the theoretical insights of post-structuralism.

There seem to be two dominant themes which emerge from the post-structuralist critique of this more open vision of social work. First, the range of formal and informal resources available to social workers in terms of legal powers, knowledge and skills makes the social worker's relationship with clients inequitable, but those who favour contracts appear to believe that they can mitigate the effects of these structural differences in power through devices such as contracts and agreements about objectives and tasks. Secondly, the practice paradigms of contemporary social work wrongly assume that the meanings of language are fixed and definite. The common meaning which the social worker and the client read into agreements is illusory. Post-structuralist analysis of discourses has, as pointed out in Chapter 1, revealed that meanings are provisional and are 'assembled' or 'constructed' by the multifaceted ways in which institutional practices, professional language, technical processes and general patterns of behaviour produce and reproduce meanings (see Rojek, Peacock and Collins, 1988). The two themes are related to each other. We must acknowledge that discourses are constructed by clients as well as by professional social workers. The inequitable power relationship between the two social groupings often revolves around the competing nature of their discourses. The imposition of power by the social worker over the client can result in the client's refusal to accept priorities and solutions to problems offered by the professional, and can be conceptualised therefore as a conflict over the meanings, concepts, language and behaviour constituting the core of their respective discourses. Too often the sense of resistance, rejection and challenge offered by subordinate social actors to professional power is neglected in post-structural thought. All sense of the collision, transformation and modification of agreements through social interaction is therefore lost by treating discourses as unlocated universes of meaning. This point is revealed by the criticism of the underlying philosophy said to characterise social work discourse.

The fundamental issue is the charge made by Rojek *et al.* (1988) that all existing paradigms within social work are rooted in 'humanism'. They claim that the 'humanist' orientation of social work fails to acknowledge that concepts such as 'need', 'welfare client', 'human rights', 'human dignity', 'normal and abnormal', etc., are *constructed* or *assembled* by the theoretical language of professional social work. Indeed they maintain that 'humanism' is a flawed philosophy because it wrongly assumes that human beings 'make their own history'; like Foucault, they insist that history has no subject. Humanists, Foucault would argue, commit the error of essentialism in that human action is treated as transhistorical, timeless, innate or having an invariable essence. In similar vein, Rojek *et al.* argue that, along with medicine, religion, education and psychiatry, social work seeks to relieve people of their sufferings and to liberate their underlying and unrealised human potentials. This criticism applies equally to Marxist and feminist perspectives which also adopt a humanist position. However, Rojek *et al.* argue that the 'humanist' orientation to social problems overlooks the constructive and creative aspects of power; professional knowledge and statutory powers combine to create, or construct, 'pathologies' and deviant identities. Humanist orientations to social work also underestimate the potential dangers inherent in essentially utopian notions of emancipation: the realities of poverty and social disadvantage are too complex and entrenched to be adequately addressed by social work intervention, however well intentioned. As a counter to the misconceptions prevailing in feminism, Marxism and other radical paradigms in professional practice, discourse analysis points up the value of Foucault's project of 'accounting for the constitution of knowledge, discourse, domains of objects . . . without having to refer to a subject' (Foucault, 1980). 'Subjectless' social work and the archaeological method of analysis of how knowledges are constituted pioneered by Foucault, and drawn on by Rojek *et al.*, whilst stimulating, can lead us to imagine a world devoid of knowledgeable human subjects.

By way of underlining this point we can draw an important sociological distinction between the project at the heart of discourse theory, which tries to show the varieties of 'truths' that can be furnished by studying the constitution of different knowledges, and the ethnomethodological project of studying how knowledgeable human beings build up and negotiate meaning through social interaction (see Garfinkel, 1984). The former analysis is one that can inform the wider knowledge base of social work but is on a different level and timescale from the latter analysis which focuses attention on the everyday, taken-for-granted world of social interaction where distorted communication becomes solidified by the real material circumstances of poverty, class and racism, and needs to be dissolved by the social worker if any assistance is to be offered to overcome immediate problems. What we need, in short, is a discourse analysis grounded in social relationships.

I want to suggest that there is a sociological approach to understanding and describing practice which draws attention to the connection between discourse formation and social relationships formed as part of the practitioner–client association. That approach is the sociological theory of codes developed by Basil Bernstein.

Towards a sociological model of discourse in social work practice

In advancing our understanding of these issues I think that there is much to learn from the sociology of educational transmission developed by Basil Bernstein, particularly his theory of codes. Whilst it is not possible to provide an exhaustive description of Bernstein's analysis, it is necessary to clarify the central categories which underpin his sociological perspective in order to understand its relevance for social work practice.

The concept of code in Bernstein's work refers to 'the transmission of the deep meaning structure of a culture or subculture: its basic interpretation rules': it is an implicit principle which is acquired gradually, and tacitly (Bernstein refers to the use of Ralph Turner's concept of 'folk norm' in this context), perhaps through formal education and informal socialisation, and which assists social actors to react to, select and organise relevant meanings in a given context. The code regulates the social actors' perception of relevancy, speech, actions and reactions, in short their discourse, and regulates the context in which that discourse can be fully expressed and realised. Another way of conceptualising codes is to liken them to the notion of a paradigm or cosmology which Jewson (1976) usefully defines as 'conceptual structures which constitute the frame of reference within which all questions are posed and all answers are offered' (Jewson, 1976, 223). Codes, like paradigms or cosmologies, are 'ways of seeing', whilst simultaneously being 'ways of not seeing'. It is useful to continue to expand on this concept and its place in Bernstein's analytical system first, before exploring its relevance to social work practice.

Bernstein uses the concept of code in his analysis of educational systems to specify, in condensed form, two basic processes governing the boundary relationships between different spheres of knowledge and information and the relative power of social actors involved in manipulating and working with that knowledge and information. First, the relationship between the contents of different types of knowledge and information and between different statuses of knowing is described by the concept of *classification*. The classification of knowledge can be said to be strong where the degree of insulation between the contents of knowledge and the different statuses of knowing is rigid. In the educational sphere classification is strong when disciplines are taught in 'pure' form such as geography, economics and history, but weak when taught as something called modern or general studies in which all the disciplines focus on a relational idea such as industrialism. Further, the admission of non-academic information into the analysis of issues and the learning process would characterise a weak classification of knowledge. Secondly, the relative power and social control by social actors over the learning process is described as *framing*. The framing of knowledge and information can be said to be strong where there is a concentration of power and control in the hands of the teacher to determine the pace of the learning process, the sequence rules involved in establishing priorities for learning, and what counts as legitimate knowledge and the manner in which it should be known. Weak framing would allow students or pupils greater scope for amending or replacing the rules governing the pace, sequence and relevance criteria involved in the learning process. And, of course, weak framing enables the student/pupil to have a greater input into the process of determining the legitimacy of knowledge and information: it may mean the pupil insisting upon analysing the music of East 17 rather than that of Beethoven on the music curriculum!

In the comparative analysis of traditional and modern forms of educational organisation (specifically studying the shift from teacher-centred to pupil-centred education with the move away from selective grammar schools and rigid forms of classroom organisation) Bernstein has developed two additional concepts to describe the changing pattern of *classification* and *framing* of knowledge accompanying recent developments in schooling and the curriculum. The concept of *collection code* describes a situation where the contents of different knowledges stand in a closed relationship to each other. The idea here is that within this type of curriculum 'the learning has to collect a group of favoured contents in order to satisfy some criteria of evaluation' (Bernstein, 1977: 87). Bernstein had in mind the common practice of teaching 'pure' combinations of either science or humanities 'A' levels in traditional grammar schools. Juxtaposed to this concept is that of the *integrated code* favouring weak classification and framing of knowledge.

In translating Bernstein's concepts into terms which are meaningful for the analysis of social work practice, I have replaced the terms *collection code* and *integrated code* with those of *correctional code* and *appreciative code* to denote two generally distinct professional orientations or discourses about social worker–client relationships. Obviously the idea of a curriculum is not appropriate in this field. In making this distinction I have drawn on David Matza's conceptualisation of two discrete approaches towards deviance (see Matza, 1969). The notion of a *correctional* approach is rooted in a view which regards deviance as pathology in need of treatment. Social workers would act as mediators between the state and the individual to ensure that the 'abhorrent' behaviour is 'corrected'. The concept of an *appreciative* approach to deviance is firmly located in a naturalist, anti-positivist view of the plurality and diversity of human behaviour. The social worker adopting this stance would seek to acknowledge and understand the individual's unique qualities and problems without seeking to challenge them, at least not coercively. Instead the task of the social worker would be to shift attention to the wider society where labels are created and where the material conditions generating deviance have their origin. A *correctional code* tends to view problem populations as *being in society, but not of it* whereas an *appreciative code* tends to view problem populations as the *creation of society*. In a broad sense I am trying to acknowledge that there is a division within welfare and social work about whether the focus of practice should be on the individual or on the social structure. A psychodynamic approach to casework as opposed to radical community work might be one stark example where such differences emerge. In practice, social work efforts must move between the individual and wider systems in society (Pincus and Minahan, 1973). However, the more limited purpose of employing such concepts is to establish polar points on a continuum representing distinguishable configurations of power in professional–client relationships.

In terms of the *classification* and *framing* of the *correctional code* there will be strong insulation between the professional practitioner and the client in terms of status, relevant expertise and professional knowledge, and, with respect to social workers, the strong *classification* and *framing* will secure and reinforce their superordinate position as the gatekeepers to other benefits and services offered by the welfare state. In short, the strong *classification* and *framing* is rooted in a professionally supported pragmatic rather than emotional attachment to the client's needs. With respect to the *classification* and *framing* of the *appreciative code,* there will be weak insulation between the practitioner and the client or client group in terms of status, with greater stress placed on the organic links with the family. The role of the therapist will be as far as possible that of an equal participant in family development. Expertise and knowledge about welfare benefits and legal rights may be offered to the family, and theoretical knowledge bearing on the therapeutic needs of families will be employed, but the practitioner within this code will have a readiness to respond to client demands and initiatives in a way that statutory work concerned with correctionalism prohibits. In short, the weak *classification* and *framing* is rooted in a client-centred, and very often politicised, perspective on social problems rather than a pragmatic professional one.

It is important to stress that strong *classification* and *framing* enhances the degree of professional status of social workers in two ways. First, it lowers the visibility of their performance to those external to their work. Secondly, by basing their practice on a psychodynamic, expert-client relationship they both ape the established professions in their mode of work and claim privileged spheres of knowledge. Weak *classification* and *framing*, by contrast, leaves greater external visibility of performance. Expert knowledge, for example, is not privileged over 'common sense' in the determination of action, and as a consequence social workers within this *appreciative code* are unable to prevent clients from politicising issues by recourse to the typically 'professional' strategy of containing problems to the individual level. Attempts to practice feminist social work or therapy might be a case in point: feminism would encourage both practitioner and client to explore the patriarchal sources of family problems. In this manner, *correctional codes* are inevitably based on the isolated social worker–individual relationship, stressing psychodynamic and caseworker approaches, whereas *appreciative codes* are founded on a solidaristic social work–social group relationship, stressing the common structural origins of problems and encouraging, very often, collective rather than individualistic solutions. In the former relationship, remedy is sought by changing individual behaviour; in the latter relationship, remedy is inevitably sought through consciousness raising, lobbying and attempts to influence the policy process in political bureaucracies which distribute resources and rights. The principles of social control which shape social work action and the therapeutic context will therefore vary in different practice contexts.

Orientations to meanings in social worker–client relationships

At the level of inter-personal relationships between social workers and their clients, what becomes crucial for our understanding of social control is the identification of the principles of *classification* employed by the parties over their negotiation about the nature of and remedies for a personal or social problem, and of the relative strength of *framing* with respect to altering or influencing those principles of *classification.*

In examining the relationship between class and the process of cultural reproduction, Bernstein formulated the issue by enquiring 'how the distribution of power and principles of social control are transformed, at the level of the subject, into different invidiously related, organising principles, in such a way as both to position subjects and to create the possibility of change in such positioning' (Bernstein, 1981, 327). The answer he gives is that 'class relations generate, distribute, reproduce and legitimate distinctive forms of communications, which transmit dominating and dominated codes, and the subjects are differentially positioned by these codes in the process of their acquisition' (Bernstein, 1981, 327).

The social basis of classification is to be understood in terms of the subject's location within a division of labour and, more concretely, in relation to a specific material base. For example, Bernstein illustrates this theme (Bernstein, 1981) by reference to a study of the classificatory principles employed by two groups of children from different class backgrounds, when they were asked to group together different kinds of food. The children seemed to enunciate two kinds of principle for arranging and ordering the foods. Either the foods were grouped in terms of the children's own immediate experience – 'it is what we eat at home', or 'it is what my Mum makes' – or in terms which transcended their immediate experience, for example, 'these all come from the ground' when different types of vegetables are grouped together, or 'these come from the sea' when different types of fish are grouped together. Whereas the former classificatory principle bears a direct relation to a specific material base, the latter bears only an indirect relation. On being asked to repeat the exercise, it was found that many middle-class children were able to switch their principle of classification (in fact using the one commonly adopted by lower-class children) while the lower-class children repeated the classificatory principle which they had used before.

This type of analysis can be understood in terms of Bernstein's description of 'positional' and 'personal' family structures and the acquisition of restricted and elaborated codes (see Bernstein, 1973). I will comment further on this below. That earlier work undertaken by Bernstein demonstrated that orientations to meanings are the product of the subject's structural location within the broader social division of labour in our class society. The immediate experience of a subject's relative power position in relation to significant others; their perception of self-status in relation to a network of social and official relationships; their sense of what issues and problems are significant or less significant within a personal hierarchy of problematic issues; their sense of time in relation to what is past, immediate or in the future: these factors shape and determine orientations to meanings.

It is the fact that working-class people have no option but to tackle the day-to-day concerns of living without resources, with financial insecurity and with a sense of their relative powerlessness that generates principles of classification grounded in the material realities of everyday life. The centre of gravity of their interactional practices lies in dealing with what W.B. Miller's classic analysis calls 'focal concerns of the lower class community' (Miller, 1958). These 'focal concerns' were described by Miller as 'areas of issues which command widespread and persistent attention and a high degree of emotional involvement'. Negotiating a life centred around avoiding trouble with the law and authority; asserting autonomy in the face of official and external authoritarian constraints; being streetwise and overcoming boredom and passivity: these are the 'focal concerns' identified by Miller and which preoccupy many lower-class groups typically categorised as 'problem populations'. In terms of Bernstein's analysis such groups carry and reproduce their culturally subordinate position in their use of communication codes that orient them to concrete, context-dependent meaning. The social worker, however, is located within a set of interactional relationships whose centre of gravity is, as Bernstein would say, 'within a complex division of labour regulating practices with respect to a *generalised* material base' (Bernstein, 1981, 323). So the social worker may well try to introduce ideas which seek to open up wider horizons and possibilities for their client, but if that client is rooted in the daily anxieties presented by poverty, then that experience is what they will draw on to make sense of their situation. The question becomes one of whether the social worker has the political will to attempt to transcend that material reality in their relationships with clients or will use it as a legitimation for professional inaction. Orientations to meaning become a product of structural position. But they are crucially a product of the distribution of power in society and not of the position *per se*. Social workers are inevitably placed in a superordinate position over their clients, but how is that power used?

This latter point must be examined by contrasting the implications for social work–client relationships which flow from the two codes that have been identified. Of particular interest is the possibility that clients may transform the nature of the relationship.

Any social relationship, even that based on authoritarianism or sheer coercion, is capable of being transformed. From the side of social workers, either subjects in the superordinate position can question the basis of their own authority, as many social workers do, and attempt to democratise their relationship with their clients, or the ideology sustaining a *correctional code* in the administration and practice of social work can change through wider societal and/ or professional forces. From the side of the client, the subject can question the political or normative basis of the treatment received from the agencies of the welfare state and engage in forms of collective and political action to disrupt the individualised mode of problem resolution. This is highly likely if the client possesses an elaborated code, is middle class and is aggressively resentful of being brought within the purview of the social work department, as can happen in cases of child sexual abuse where offenders can be drawn from across the social class spectrum. Both the Cleveland and the Orkney child abuse controversies illustrate the mechanisms for politicising and broadening the issues. In both cases a combination of community mobilisation, legal threat and political manipulation destroyed the individualistic emphasis of the social work framework of the cases and transformed the controversies into issues of public debate and policy deliberation (see Black, 1993). I will return to

this issue in Chapter 7. However, if clients are rooted to a per-
sonalised and isolated view of their problems, in which they are
preoccupied with the 'focal concerns' of an immediate crisis, then
there is probably a need for a mechanism to open up wider possibilities to them. In order to achieve this, 'radical social work' has
encouraged an interest in community development strategies. However, Pinker (1983), in particular, has criticised social workers who
would provide that mechanism for disrupting the *correctional code*.
He has been highly critical of attempts to dilute the tasks of social
workers. He is, in general terms, against genericism and for special-
isation for social workers. He is opposed to those tasks 'which would
involve [social workers] in ill-defined community-based activities'
(Pinker, 1983, 162). His opposition extends to the 'patch systems'
operated by some social workers working in concentrated teams within
delimited geographical areas, and he is especially critical of that
'romantic illusion of the left to suppose that populist sentiment can
be harnessed and channelled by social workers through local communities to bring about radical change in the structure of society'
(Pinker, 1983, 162). Within any social worker–client relationship,
therefore, there is a dialectical tension between *individualisation* and
socialisation of a problem. The space created by that tension is the
one filled by modifications to the dominant code by both social
workers and their clients. In these circumstances social control often
operates to 'manage' the tendency of clients to seek wider referents
for their problems and to negotiate compromise in 'treatment'
strategies.

The negotiations that take place within inter-personal relationships between social worker and client, and the wider professional
climate within which social workers operate, may modify the codes.
The experience of education indicates that a number of possible
alterations can be made to the *classification* and *framing* of dominant codes (Smith, 1976). Whilst further empirical investigation is
necessary and will, through time, draw attention to subtle differences and emphases in the nature of power balances in social work/
counselling relationships, we can nevertheless suggest some patterns
of code modification that can be expected within the sphere of social
work, counselling and therapeutic practice.

Egalitarian correctional and egalitarian appreciative codes

The general thrust of the work is to enlist the co-operation of the client in the assessment of need and resolution of a problem by revealing the extent to which they have 'rights' to information or to be consulted or indeed to veto any proposals relating to how they will be treated. Within the educational sphere pupils and students have been involved in administrative decision-making through their participation in school councils, staff–student committees and the like. Similarly, social work clients can be drawn into what are, effectively, case conferences, and broader discussions about their social problems. The object might simply be to inform clients of their interests, but might also be to combine such developments with possible therapeutic objectives. The strength of classification between the 'relevant' expert knowledge possessed by the social worker and the absence of such knowledge by the client might weaken, but the objective of modifying the client's behaviour to a more 'acceptable' pattern would dominate the social worker–client relationship. The relative status of the parties, therefore, would remain characterised by professional hierarchy and propriety and hence would be characterised by strong framing which would be underpinned by a clear mutual understanding of the 'rights' which each party possesses. A counselling relationship in a non-statutory context, characterised above all else by a non-judgemental and non-instrumental approach by the practitioner towards the client, could be described as *egalitarian appreciative*. Marriage guidance work has developed in such a way as to emphasise the pragmatic and non-judgemental nature of conciliation services, as we will note in Chapter 3.

Coercive appreciative code

This is characterised by the social worker explicitly seeking to break down the strong classification and framing established by statutory and professional structures. It might describe attempts by some social workers to 're-socialise' clients into a new approach or experience with social work agents, especially if the client is more familiar with social workers working within the parameters established by a *correctional code*. Clients may have internalised the status of 'social work client' and be happily subservient to the implications of it; a variant form of welfare dependency can arise where clients' expectations are that social workers will use their statutory powers to threaten them and force compliance. This code is probably dependent on the social worker's ability to convince the client that they are being offered a new regime. Crucially the task will be one of encouraging the client to overcome tendencies toward introversion and self-blame and to take an expansively social and environmental view of their problems. Framing will be weak, if not the classification of knowledge.

Co-operative appreciative code

This particular code will characterise attempts to develop modes of intervention aimed at achieving recognition of an individual's particular needs through group work. Attempts at gender-sensitive family or group therapy work might provide an example (see Urry, 1990; Schneider, 1990). The orientation of therapeutic work will be exploratory, being concerned particularly with bringing about new levels of awareness and sensitivity among participants about a set of problems commonly left at a 'taken for granted' level. Most therapeutic encounters under the auspices of clinical but not statutory authority will tend to be of this type.

Co-operative correctional and coercive correctional codes

This code will, by contrast, characterise a situation where the work with a family or therapy group explicitly sets out to bring about change in behaviour because of the exercise of statutory powers which may be used to secure participation in the therapeutic encounter. Where statutory powers are employed to coerce participation then it might be possible to talk about a *coercive correctional* code distinct from a *co-operative correctional* code. Cases of domestic violence where the aggressive male partner voluntarily participates in a therapy group might be an example of the co-operative mode. An example of the coercive mode might be found in the approach described by Dale *et al.* (1986) in the context of dealing with 'dangerous families' involved in child abuse. The use of statutory powers becomes an integral part of the process of dealing with child abusing families and overcoming what has been called 'professional dangerousness' (Dale *et al.*, 1986). There may appear to be similarities between these codes and that which I have described above as *egalitarian*. The main difference that I wish to suggest is the language of client 'rights' implied by the use of the word *egalitarian* which contrasts with the language of statutory authority which demands either collaboration with or submission to legal powers prior to any therapeutic encounter commencing within the code under this heading.

Concluding remarks

A final observation needs to be made about the relationship between Bernstein's work on language and social class and the very enterprise of social work and therapeutic intervention into family life. Behind Bernstein's analysis lies the concept of *code* which perhaps requires the word 'behaviour' to be attached to it in order to express its purpose in his general analysis and approach; the *behaviour code* acts through the primary socialising agencies such as family, peer group and school, and controls the transmission of values, norms, priorities, even ambitions, in short the culture or subculture, by orienting people to particular meanings embedded in the social structures or structure of relationships which they inhabit. The close interrelationship between social structure and language use and the generation of meaning is fundamentally shaped by the structure of family relationships.

> A unique feature of Bernstein's work is that it suggests how the social structure is represented in linguistic interaction. According to Bernstein, the essential element governing access to codes is the ... system of role relationships within the family; and he finds two main types, the positional role system, and the personal role system. In the former the part played by the member (for example, decision-making) is largely a function of his position in the family: role corresponds to ascribed status. In the latter ... the status is achieved. (Halliday, 1978, 67)

Positional families will tend to predominate among social work clients, and very often it is the hierarchical nature and inflexibilities of the family role system which have given rise to violence and problems involving a breakdown in parenting. Bernstein's earlier work focused attention on the use of restricted language codes within such role systems. He found that meaning tended to be implicit rather than explicit, concrete rather than abstract and context dependent and local in order for meaning to be understood fully, reflecting the status-based and inflexible pattern of social roles. The close tie between the way language is used and the non-person-oriented nature of the social structure is significant. By contrast personal family types are characterised by elaborated language codes where meaning is explicit, more abstract and not context dependent, and is the linguistic expression of person-oriented relationships. The issue of family structures and their relationship to competing 'voices' within families about decision-making will be explored in Chapter 4.

The relevance of these observations for psychotherapy has been recognised by Bernstein (1964). Therapy of any kind, whether in a group, in a person-to-person context, or routinely as part of social work–client interaction, depends upon communication. Lower-working-class clients who have little experience of elaborated language codes by virtue of the social structure of their relationships within family and community may make bad therapeutic subjects. The therapeutic relationship involves the patient/client being able verbally to present and order their discrete experience; the authority structure within the therapeutic relationship can be ambiguous and social status differences familiar to the patient/client in the outside world serve badly as indications of how the encounter should be managed, hence greater reliance on language and communication will be called for. The working-class patient/client is somewhat artificially detached from her social background and becomes the focus of attention in a situation isolated from that which she normally relies upon to aid communication. The assumption in the successful therapeutic encounter is that insight into problems and the transcendence of their troubling impact on the patient's life will be achieved through the medium of communication, essentially through speech.

> The therapy relationship is based upon the belief that the conditions which brought the patient into the relationship may be ameliorated by communication in a context where the normal status relationships serve as no guide for behaviour in a context which involves a suspension of the patient's social identity and where the referent for communication is the discrete experience of the patient . . . members of the lower working class who are limited to a particular speech system are likely to find that requirement difficult to meet. (Bernstein, 1964, 55)

A similar observation is made by Meltzer (1978). Any form of intervention into problem families, or problem relationships, will confront the problem of therapeutic suitability and communication skills.

The use of a *correctional* rather than *appreciative* approach towards practitioner–client relationships may depend on the perception of the client's suitability for one type of intervention rather than another; statutory powers may be used more readily in cases where communication proves incapable of acting as a medium of problem solving. Again one sees that the exercise of power will vary from context to context.

The usefulness of the concepts of *classification* and *framing,* and the idea that their varying patterns coalesce into discrete *codes* which shape language and power relationships, can be seen to extend beyond the limits that Bernstein set for his analysis. As a general theme in the analysis of family life the concepts are useful; it will be shown that in the areas of marriage relationships and divorce the vocabulary of classification and framing can direct our attention to the changing capacity of people to negotiate and transform the nature of the marriage relationship not only as individuals but also with the support of the law which has become more *appreciative* of the tensions and complexities of marriage in contemporary society. Indeed an important feature of family life today is the tension between movements which would introduce a greater degree of *correctionalism* into family affairs and those which tend towards an *appreciative* perception of family life as an area which should remain unmolested by external interests. That tension can be expressed as an issue of perception by those who view the family as merely changing, while others point towards a process of deterioration which requires immediate *corrective* intervention. The relationship between the state, the social sphere of welfare intervention, and the private sphere of family life embodies this tension between benign neglect and social control.

A closing comment needs to be made here concerning the broader public debate surrounding family life, and particularly public anxiety about child abuse as expressed through instruments such as public inquiries. Grimshaw (1976) has acknowledged the similarity between the critical theory of Habermas and that of Bernstein with respect to communication and the distortions which impede it. I will suggest that Habermas's project of realising an open and authentically democratic public sphere, where something approximating to an 'idealised speech situation' may be given institutional solidity, is aided by using Bernstein's framework as a method of measuring the

distortions in communication and analysing the very processes of
discourse formation. It has been the core theme of this chapter that
we need to move beyond general theoretical formulations about the
use of power; we need always to be aware of the concrete situations where knowledge and power manifest themselves and, crucially, are negotiated and worked out in routine social interactions.
Bernstein's work provides this necessary link to the broader critical
theory of Habermas who seeks to connect issues of public discourse
to political relationships and empowerment within the public sphere.
I will explore this issue in Chapter 7. The large public inquiries
into child abuse illuminate better than anything else the sometimes
tortured relationship between the public sphere, the social sphere
and the state.

3

Marriage problems and the 'technicians of human relations'

Mention has already been made of the growing number of problem behaviours and interpersonal difficulties which can now be 'treated' or subjected to 'expert' knowledge, guidance and intervention. One area of particular growth has been that of marriage and conciliation services. David Morgan (1985) has described developments in this area as the 'medicalisation of marriage'. What this means is the application of medical models of intervention into family problems in clinical settings, often distinguished by the use of systems thinking. Lasch (1977) refers to this development in rather negative terms as 'the new religion of health' dominated by the 'technicians of human relations' which can include everyone from social workers, psychiatrists, psychologists and family therapists to marriage guidance counsellors.

These developments may be understood as an extension of the interventionist strategies begun in the nineteenth century to 'modernise backward sectors of society' through a concerted attack on public health and intemperance among the poor, and the bolstering of family life by an alliance between the medical professions, philanthropists and women alluded to in Chapters 1 and 2 in relation to the work of Donzelot (1980). Indeed the Charity Organisation Society in its more modern form of the Family Welfare Association and Family Discussion Bureau led eventually to the setting up of the Institute of Marital Studies in 1968, so linking the family focus of the nineteenth century with contemporary concerns about divorce and marital conciliation. For Lasch, the creation of the family as an asylum from the pressures of the outside world is compromised by interference which treats the family form as 'plastic' and 'amenable to therapeutic intervention'. Perhaps this can be interpreted as a further example of *the critique of therapism* discussed in Chapter 2. Lasch argues that the family has become dominated by experts external to it. The transferring of key functions of the family to the welfare state has been reinforced by the growth of professional experts in family problems, especially those relating to marriage and parenting. The family, according to Lasch, has become so dependent on external experts that parental confidence is weakened by the proliferation of psychiatric and medical advice offered through the growth in popular literature advising on a range of family problems. But the family is also undermined by the growing number of ways in which 'experts' on human relationships intervene into family life. The particular malaise which constitutes the focus of his analysis is the apparent tension created within modern family life resulting from the delegation of responsibility for discipline to agencies other than the family: the parents are undermined and left partly clothed, unwilling to impose values and authority on children who are actually crying out for a sense of boundary in their family life, a sense of social discipline and a sense that their parents rather than their peer group will provide guidance and moral judgement. The extension of this analysis into Freudian psychoanalytic theory need not trouble us here. It is a stimulating account of modern family life and a useful starting point to explore some of the issues raised about marital relations.

A recurring theme in contemporary political debate about family life is the extent to which the kinds of problems highlighted by Lasch are ultimately caused by or influenced by changes in the marital relationship. This issue will form the central focus of this chapter.

Without over-simplifying long running and complex social changes, I will argue that one useful way to view the changing pattern of intervention into marital relationships, both legal and therapeutic, is to draw on the conceptual vocabulary discussed in Chapter 2, that is, the language of the *classification* and *framing* of knowledge. Marriage as a social institution, and by virtue of being regarded as a social institution, was traditionally characterised by strong *classification* and *framing*. Our understanding of marriage has been shaped by ideas of convention and religiosity combined with taken-for-granted notions about family structure and authority. With respect to the issue of *framing*, the extent to which couples could tolerably amend the rules of marriage and their personal conduct in fulfilling the social roles associated with being married was, until the 1960s at least, very limited. This strong *framing* with respect to behaviour within marriage is a relatively modern phenomenon in that centralised state control of marriage stems only from the earlier part of the nineteenth century. Control of information about marriage was a product of nation-state building and the emergence of the bureaucratic conditions facilitating the recording and monitoring of marriage by the state, particularly among the lower classes (see Gittins, 1993; Barker, 1978; Smart, 1982). The fundamental legal requirement of marriage prior to the eighteenth century seemed to be that it was to be conducted publicly with witnesses, especially for those from the lower social orders. The church only gradually gained control of marriage, and the Marriage Act 1836 and the Births and Deaths Registration Act of the same year brought into being a centralised system of state registration of marriages (see Leonard, 1978; Helmholz, 1975). However, in the period since the end of the Second World War the *classification* and *framing* of knowledge regarding marriage has become increasingly weaker. There has been a passage from a *correctional* to an *appreciative* code with respect to the way in which marriage is commonly regarded throughout society and by professional counsellors, though some politicians and policy makers of the right regret this.

Clark and Haldane (1990) have characterised this in terms of two discourses on marriage. What I will call the *correctional* discourse is dominated by a view of marriage as an institution involving constraints, rules, prescribed social roles and penalties against those who would transgress the conventions and norms governing marital relations. The language is one of submission to one's partner and the culture and controlling powers in the wider society. In place of creativity in role-playing we see human relationships depicted in terms of conservatism, control and, above all else, order. By contrast the *appreciative* discourse emphasises choice, creativity and the social construction of human relationships. This code is informed by humanistic theories of social life, and presents the social actor as a rational person empowered to shape and mould social and family life in accordance with his particular life projects. These contrasting discourses are at polar ends of a continuum, and marriage and marriage conciliation operate in the space between these polar positions. Marriage in modern times has perhaps veered towards the *appreciative* pole, but the New Right is currently arguing the case for a more traditional and *correctional* code to guide policy and practice in family matters. There are two areas where we can observe the movement between the polar positions relating to marriage: first, the shift in legal control of marriage and divorce from negative and punitive control towards a more positive and welfare orientation, and second, the changing social conditions and social meanings attaching to marriage, motherhood and the welfare of children. As marriage has come to be regarded more as a matter of personal choice and individual self-fulfilment, a space has been created for new knowledges concerned with human relationships, sexuality and psychological well-being. The real tension has probably always been between those who advocate personal discipline and self-control and those who favour self-exploration and personal freedom as a means of managing these human issues. The shift to a more explicitly *appreciative* view of marriage and marriage problems creates the conditions of existence for the new 'technicians of human relationships', but it does not necessarily determine the content of their intervention. Theory and practice in this area of welfare are very pluralistic.

Family law and the regulation of marital relations

The concept of 'technician of human relations' used in the title of this chapter should be related to all third parties who intervene in family relationships by virtue of their possession of some recognised specialist knowledge deemed to be relevant to the ordering of family relationships. It obviously alludes to the counsellors and therapists who work with couples and their children in situations of marital crisis and family breakdown, but it also points to those who intervene into family life when family problems become a public issue. In the context of divorce, for example, it relates to the law and legal agents who contribute to a sense of the family as a beleaguered institution whose course is not entirely within the control of its members. The law has been the pre-eminent mechanism for regulating family life. The central purpose behind family law, and more particularly matrimonial law, is to maintain the institutional structure of the family based on lawful marriage. Historically the law has adopted a punitive stance against those who deviated from the expected pattern of fidelity and duty to the marriage relationship. Divorce law up until the first half of the twentieth century was based on the idea of punishing the guilty party because it had as its objective to identify and stigmatise the guilty spouse. This often meant that errant husbands were forced to pay maintenance to their wives whilst, of course, also losing their conjugal rights. Errant and adulterous wives were more harshly treated by losing rights to maintenance and property, even that which they had taken into the marriage (Brophy and Smart, 1981). And, of course, issues relating to custody of and access to children have often appeared to be tinged with vindictiveness against offending partners, particularly in those circumstances where the woman was considered to have been the guilty party. Having said this, it should be acknowledged that the law did bring about *formal* equality between the sexes in a range of legislative measures at the end of the nineteenth century and through the first quarter of the twentieth century, including the Married Women's Property Act 1882, the Maintenance of Wives (Desertion) Act 1886 and the Guardianship of Infants Act 1925 (see Smart, 1984). Smart observes that 'it is quite possible to depict these reforms as a natural process of liberalisation and enlightenment' (p. 28) but she also comments that 'much of the statutory legislation which was introduced during the late nineteenth and early twentieth centuries was simply counteracting the massively discriminatory tradition of common law' (p. 30). The emphasis should be placed on the formal rather than the substantive powers given to women in family law during this crucial period.

In the case of illegitimacy, once the bureaucratic means was available for the state to record births with some accuracy and so identify those who were illegitimate, the law placed full responsibility upon the mother rather than the father for bringing about the undesirable situation of illegitimacy. This was the case particularly with respect to poor mothers who would call upon public resources through the Poor Law. The workhouse was made available to those unable to provide for themselves and their offspring; deprivations were used coercively to discourage extra-marital sexual relations and encourage legally sanctioned marriage. Laws relating to illegitimacy were indicative of the negative and punitive approach to family regulation. It was not until the Legitimacy Act of 1926 that an illegitimate child could inherit from a mother who had died intestate (see Smart, 1982). The Act also permitted the legitimation of the child if the parents subsequently married and had not been married to another partner at the time of the child's birth. This signalled a changed legal stance. Carol Smart observes:

> In this way, the law could show a certain amount of compassion towards the child, which was in keeping with the emergent family law principle of safeguarding the welfare of the child . . . at the same time it could still discourage and punish adulterous relationships that resulted in the birth of a child. . . . In post-war Britain however the balance between these two principles of punishment and welfare altered. (Smart, 1982, 132)

Smart (1982) goes on to provide an interesting interpretation of the changing emphases in family law. The Royal Commission on Marriage and Divorce which reported in 1956 embodied most of the punitive and negative controls regarding divorce which had been a feature of family law in England and Wales since the mid nineteenth century; the policy was one of using 'deterrence to promote stable family life' by insisting upon the retention of the concept of matrimonial offence and seeking to identify and punish the guilty spouse. The balance between punishment and welfare changed rapidly, however, and within ten years there was a 'qualitative change in the mode of legal regulation'. Matrimonial law became less negative and punitive in its orientation, less aimed at deterrence. Instead it shifted towards a stance of positive regulation aimed at encouraging 'the formation of lawful family units by facilitating divorce, remarriage and the legitimation of children and by extending a certain degree of legal recognition, as well as duties and obligations, to the unmarried' (Smart, 1982, 137–8). Smart suggests that there were two axes of legal regulation of the family. The first was the abandonment of the negative and punitive approach to marriage breakdown. The 1969 Divorce Reform Act in England and Wales and the Divorce (Scotland) Act 1976 signalled this change. The grounds for divorce moved away from concepts of offence and guilt towards irretrievable breakdown, mutual responsibility and need. The underlying legal and policy stance was that problems of illegitimacy were best handled by making it easier for parents of such children to remarry; divorce was to be seen as merely a stage in a process of remarriage, or as part of a wider process of reorganising families, and so high divorce rates were not to be considered as part of a crisis in family life or as a symptom of the breakdown of the nuclear family. The second axis of regulation was the growth in welfare intervention into the family in order to supervise the well-being of children. I have already alluded to this issue in the broader welfare context, but in the case of divorce from the 1960s onwards priority was given to the interests of children, and their needs were used to justify extensive intervention in family life as an integral part of the legal process of divorce. Théry (1989) critically examines the concept of 'interest of the child' in the French context where shifts in divorce law similar to those found in the United Kingdom can be observed; the movement there has been towards a more liberal and pluralist framework of regulation which recognises the diversity of domestic situations and the need for law to acknowledge rights to free choice in matrimonial matters. The interesting insight made by Théry is, of course, that the concept of 'interest of the child' itself becomes a new principle for bringing about regulation of the post-divorce family. The reordering of family relationships is shaped and determined by how they relate to this important principle, which in turn is itself variously determined by the voices of parents, judges and social workers as much as by that of the child.

An integral part of the process of 'deregulating' matrimonial conflict, and of the movement away from a punitive stance, was the integration of medical and administrative structures within the judicial institutions which supervise marriage breakdown. Increasingly welfare reports on the family were gathered through home visiting by court welfare officers; invariably this meant probation officers in England and Wales, who would enquire into social relationships and also the financial standing of the family. Until the recent Child Support Act 1991 the courts were involved in the detailed settlement of a family's maintenance arrangements. Smart makes the extremely important observation that the power of the divorce courts to issue attachment of earnings orders 'is an indication that the hallowed principle of privacy has been overwhelmed by the need to reduce the financial burden of broken marriages on the state' (Smart, 1982, 143). This was written well before the Child Support Act 1991 created the Child Support Agency (CSA) within the Department of Social Security. Through a range of legislative changes, including the legal recognition of the housewife's right to a share of her husband's property on the dissolution of the marriage, family law has become more liberal in its attitude, and more benevolent because it is less punitive and glaringly patriarchal in its unfairness.

One contemporary manifestation of this apparently more benevolent approach is the sideways shift of state interference in the problem of family breakdown to the CSA, restricting legal jurisdiction to matters concerning mediation in problems of child custody, access to children and, of course, marital conciliation. One particularly interesting aspect of this sideways shift is that about 10 million people are for the first time subject to a Social Security formula which affects their behaviour and finances. The vast majority of those who will become subject to the CSA's scrutiny would not in previous circumstances have been forced to deal with the Department of Social Security. This change in the mode of regulation indicates that marriage matters in the 1990s and beyond are to be guided by more explicitly political dynamics. Questions of the economic and moral costs of divorce are currently at the top of the political agenda; the legal aid budget for matrimonial cases alone cost in excess of £200 million in 1994, a third of the total legal aid budget. Policy responses may have little to do with legal precedents and gender equality and more to do with political prejudice, especially on the matter of single parents. To return to the theme of the *classification* and *framing* of knowledge raised earlier, the law has gradually become more *appreciative* of the needs and problems surrounding family break-up. The harsh *corrective* code informing legal and moral thinking about marriage prior to the 1950s has been displaced. At the level of the law these shifts may be emphases rather than major transformations.

One particular feature of the shift in matrimonial law towards a 'no fault' basis for divorce, and the expectation that divorce should be based on the principle of a 'clean break' between parties (a principle rather belatedly acknowledged by the CSA in its amended procedures announced in early 1995), has been the increasing importance of solicitors as mediators shaping and directing the divorce process, especially with respect to the dividing of matrimonial property. For example, in a study of the impact of the Family Law (Scotland) Act 1985 on solicitors' divorce practice, Wasoff, Dobash and Harcus (1990) found that there were variations between solicitors in their handling of negotiations. The unfettered discretion of the courts has been replaced by a system of supposedly clear legislative guidelines setting out the principles upon which property should be divided between parties under the Family Law (Scotland) Act. However, the idea of a clean financial break between divorcing parties was found to be in conflict with notions that one party should retain the matrimonial home. The definition of what was and what was not common property, and the complexities of the legislation compounded by the numerous 'caveats, qualifiers and exemptions' which make the unambiguous applications of the principles of the legislation difficult, were frequently cited by solicitors as problematic features of the new law. In circumstances such as these the solicitors take over the direction of the process of divorce through their negotiations with and advice to their client. Whilst the 1985 legislation had 'reduced the scope for dispute', and was generally considered to be an improvement on what had often appeared to be the remote, harsh and vindictive practices of the courts in the past, 'it was thought to encourage voluntary agreements as a means of court-avoidance'. A negotiated settlement between what could be 'warring' parties in a divorce may not necessarily be in the best interests of the individual client with respect to their financial and property settlement if all that is being obtained is escape from the court system. As 'technicians of human relations' solicitors probably have few equals. Their access to the deep anxieties of people and their personal affairs is very great indeed. So the changes which have characterised the transformation in family law allow people only a partial increase in direction and control over their lives. The law remains a major structure filtering and ordering human affairs. The introduction by the Scottish Courts in 1990 of a 'Rule of Court' empowering them to refer parties to family conciliation services is a further example of the penetration of the legal system into the area of marital relations. This form of interference has, perhaps, altered rather than displaced the law's purview, but at least the shift has been a move towards an *appreciative* rather than a *correctional* stance.

The publication of a Government White Paper *Looking to the Future: Mediation and the Ground for Divorce* in April 1995 marked the final shift in matrimonial law in England and Wales towards 'no fault' divorces. The core themes of the White Paper are that marriage dissolution should be less acrimonious in order to protect children and that divorce should be made easier and less adversarial. To meet these objectives the White Paper suggests that couples seeking a divorce should attend an initial divorce information interview which would refer them to mediation services during a 12-month waiting period designed to allow for second thoughts about whether the divorce should be completed (the 'quickie' divorce based on the artificial attribution of blame to one of the divorcing parties will be abandoned). A national network of mediation services is envisaged but it is unclear whether the Government will be prepared to fund the necessary expansion of the service to meet the demands of its new divorce policy. The proposals which stem from the Law Commission report of 1990 are, perhaps, more concerned with limiting the amount of legal aid spent on divorces (£266 million in 1994–95) than with the rise in broken marriages. Despite a 'back to basics' tag attached to the approach set out in the original 1993 Green Paper, that section of the Conservative right most obsessed with the theme of family values, for example the Conservative Family Campaign, has criticised Lord Mackay, the Lord Chancellor, for proposals which the organisation believes will further undermine the family and marriage by simply making divorce too easy. Stephen Green, a spokesman for the Campaign, has gone as far as to say 'this is probably the most despicable proposal I have ever heard. What happened to values of loyalty and fidelity? Why are we proposing laws that will lead to more divorce, more single parents and more crime?' (*Observer*, 5.2.94). What is certain about this move towards 'no fault' divorces is that the role of conciliators and counsellors is bound to grow in importance as the approach becomes institutionalised in the coming years. However, the popularity of mediating services for governments may not lie in their role in saving marriages, but rather in their effectiveness in cutting the costs of divorce. The task envisaged for mediating services is to resolve issues of property, maintenance and custody at a cost of around about £550 rather than £1,565, which is the cost of the cheapest divorce under the legal aid scheme.

Despite a blatantly pecuniary interest in easier divorce, and the situational discomfort of the Conservative Government in controlling its right-wing pro-family 'back to basics' campaigners, the Conservatives have signalled a future shift towards 'no fault' divorces by the end of the 1990s. There is an inexorable movement towards further divorce reform. This merely reflects social pressures which have been building up since the 1970s; an open and creative approach to marriage at a social level may, therefore, be dragging legal structures into place which better reflect social practice. The law on matrimonial affairs is often perceived as being involved in a hopeless tussle with contemporary social conventions which have been evolving since the 1960s. Certainly in this area of human affairs it is the social forces which have shaped and altered law rather than the reverse. This will continue even though the White Paper on divorce may temporarily find itself politically at odds with the family values theme in Conservative policy.

Sex and marriage since the Second World War

In sociological terms the transformations which have characterised family life, particularly in the post-war period, are far reaching and quite complex. The fundamental shift which is often alluded to in popular as well as academic literature is from 'institutional' to 'companionate' marriage; this distinction draws attention to the popular conception that marriage is about personal and emotional relationships rather than economic calculation and property. Indeed a number of commentators have attributed the high divorce rate to the increased resolve of many couples to make marriage a more rewarding and fulfilling experience (see Berger and Berger, 1983; Fletcher, 1966). Underlying this notion is the view that what was known as institutional marriage involved relationships which were easier to manage because they were based on material rather than passionate attraction, such as the acquisition and exchange of economic resources, social status and domestic services. A marriage which raises issues of self-fulfilment and equal sexual gratification complicates marital relations to such an extent that high divorce rates are inevitable. But the idea of marriage nevertheless remains popular and indeed the convention. The rise of the emancipatory impulse amongst women, rather than the emancipation of women, also leads to marital relations which are characterised by friction rather than subservience. Co-operation and companionship are said to be the emerging features of the contemporary marriage, a response to changing interpersonal relationships founded on mutuality.

The marriage relationship has become what Giddens refers to as a *pure relationship* in his enquiry into *Modernity and Self-Identity* (1991). By this concept he means 'a social relation which is internally referential, that is, depends fundamentally on satisfactions or rewards generic to that relation itself' (Giddens, 1991, 244). Marriage has freed itself from the traditional influences which used to shape its conduct, such as kin bargaining, tradition, financial calculation and religious dogma. Giddens suggests that the concept of modern friendship clarifies the notion; 'a friend is defined specifically as someone with whom one has a relationship unprompted by anything other than the rewards that relationship provides' (p. 90). The relationship also becomes more intense, depending on the ongoing mutual reward and strength of the relationship for survival because no other supports bolster it. As soon as factors other than the 'love relationship' become significant in a marriage relationship, including the presence of children, a source of 'inertial drag' is introduced into the relationship. The desacralisation of marriage is a clear example of the way in which it has become a *pure relationship* in the period of high or late modernity. A further feature of the new 'purity' of the marriage relationship is the increased anxiety which characterises family life in late modern society; we are said to live in a risk culture whereby we are constantly reflecting upon our life projects, our successes and failures, and seeking to assess our day-to-day 'survival' in terms of our calculation of the varieties of futures open to us. We construct and reconstruct our self-identities through these reflections and through what Giddens calls self-narratives whereby we reflect upon the 'stories' and images surrounding our relationships and self-development. The formation of diverse family forms through divorce, and the embracing of homosexual identity, are undoubtedly products of the continual process of reflection which people embark upon in order to strive for self-identity and self-fulfilment in the rapidly changing social context of modern family life. The idea of marriage as a companionship between two people is an outgrowth of these social changes. I will return to this theme below.

Finch and Summerfield (1991) have traced the rise of the idea of companionate marriage in post-war Britain, locating it in the contradictory and confused ideas about family life during the period between 1945 and 1959 when readjustment to peacetime life provided the impetus for political and policy debate. There seemed to be three central themes circulating simultaneously. Concern was expressed about the low and falling birth rate and the most appropriate way to address the issue, at a time when more women were engaged in paid work and their labour considered essential in many areas of economic reconstruction. Allied to this issue was that of the motherhood role and how it could best be fulfilled. This became a particular issue in the 1950s when theories about maternal absence and childhood delinquency became a particularly active issue in public debate (see Bowlby, 1952, 1965). The concept of 'latch key kids' conveyed a strong public image of mothers abandoning their responsibilities to their children and, of course, the nation's future citizens. The third theme was that of the marriage relationship itself and how it could function in the midst of these modern-day tensions hitherto unknown, when marriage had, supposedly, little to do with emotion. In particular, much debate focused attention on the role of the father within the modern nuclear family. The issue raised by Lasch relating to the possible undermining of the patriarchal role and authority lay at the heart of this controversy.

The resolution of these contradictory impulses was sought through the development of social policy. Family allowances and family services, including childcare provision and housing policies geared to the needs of families, were considered to be ways of improving the problems of population decline. As Finch and Summerfield (1991) comment 'to summarise, post-war British pro-natalism was concerned with improving the material conditions of motherhood in order to promote it as a function' (p. 9). Companionate marriage was viewed by traditional opinion as something which would weaken the traditional role of the father and so undermine family stability. The concept 'companionate' was interpreted in terms of a functional view of the family division of labour where the husband remained the main breadwinner, but the wife contributed to household finances through part-time work which did not remove her from her primary duty of managing the domestic sphere and supervising her children. Finch and Summerfield comment that many of these issues changed once the question of population decline was resolved by the 1950s baby boom. At that point the marriage relationship itself, and its transformation into a partnership, was subjected to greater scrutiny.

The concept of companionate marriage was ideological in two general senses. First, it was compatible with ideas about modernisation and encouraged the abandonment of 'old fashioned' traditionalism regarding marital and sexual relations. It was ideological in the sense that it signalled a particular aspect of equality whilst ignoring the underlying gender structure to family life which remained, and remains. In a very limited way it was compatible with the rise of new images of the home cluttered with the new consumer durables which were marketed vigorously with the coming of television. Ideas about labour-saving devices too readily became associated with the distorted view of women as mothers and housewives with time on their hands. Secondly, it was ideological in that academic work also fed 'modern' images of the family by overdrawing the social changes which were taking place through urban renewal processes and industrial restructuring. The classic studies by Young and Willmott (1957) and Willmott and Young (1960) described the transition from the old extended family structures of the East End to the more privatised and consumerist orientation of family life in the Essex suburbs. The works of Fletcher (1966) and Bott (1957) represent further examples of classic family sociology of the late 1950s and early 1960s, in which greater co-operation and equality were deemed to be the main features of modern marriage. Combined with notions of the 'affluent worker', a rather short-term snapshot of post-war Britain became crystallised into a general view of modernity as encompassing a linear growth in economic well-being and growing equality in class and gender relations. These perspectives were also influential in the training of social workers and future family therapists.

The most obvious consequence of less rigid ideas about marriage was what I have called weak *framing*: despite the flow of largely ideological information about family life, the concept of companionate marriage reflected a cultural climate which encouraged creativity and negotiation between the sexes about what was considered to be tolerable with respect to sexual behaviour, childminding and other household and family responsibilities. The conditions existed for what Gramsci might have called 'contradictory consciousness': women were confronted by the material realities of family life governed by an entrenched gendered division of labour, whilst intellectually they were being bombarded by ideas, images and rhetoric seeking to reinterpret that reality in terms of the growing companionship which was said to define modern marriage. Women's sexuality and their employment became particularly controversial issues. Ideas of companionate relationships were invariably combined with debates about contraception and pre-marital and extra-marital sex. The fear that the family would become threatened and undermined by such developments was probably inevitable. The issue of divorce, therefore, has to be seen in the context of these wider sociological changes which were overtaking post-war Britain.

Guidance, counselling and therapy

The emergence of counsellors and therapists in the field of marriage was therefore very much an outgrowth of the changing ideas about marriage. Indeed it is possible that companionate marriage as an ideology contributed to divorce in many cases by fuelling a sense of disappointment, and indeed anger about marriage, especially when the legal shackles were removed by the 1969 Divorce Reform Act, and the corresponding Scottish legislation in the mid-1970s, providing an easier exit from unrewarding marital relationships. Given the changing social and moral climate surrounding marriage in the 1950s and 1960s, it is unsurprising that the modes of intervention into marriage and family life underwent their own transformation. The movement was characterised quite clearly as a shift from a *correctional* to an *appreciative* approach as the moral panic surrounding increased divorce in the years immediately following the Second World War, influenced by ideas from eugenics and religion, gave way to notions of non-judgementalism about marriage breakdown, as both legal and social attitudes to divorce, if not family breakdown, softened. The perception of divorce and family breakdown as discrete public controversies is probably worth retaining because a great deal of contemporary debate focuses attention on the consequences of unconventional family structures for society and children. Whilst these developments are often linked, in reality and discussion, to divorce, much of the contemporary 'moral panic' surrounding family life centres on female-headed single parent families where there has never been a marriage. I will say more about that contemporary debate in Chapter 6.

As Table 3.1 indicates quite distinctly, there has been an inexorable rise in the divorce rate since the early 1950s. Divorce rates doubled in the 1970s and have continued to be on a high plateau during the 1980s. Kiernan and Wicks (1990) observe:

> The speed of change is most clearly seen when one considers the divorce behaviour of people married in the same year. For example, 10 per cent of couples who married in 1951 had divorced by their 25th wedding anniversary. However, amongst those marrying in 1961, 10 per cent had divorced by their 12th wedding anniversary, whilst amongst those marrying in 1971 and 1981 the analogous durations of marriage were 6 and 4.5 years. (Kiernan and Wicks, 1990, 13)

The divorce rate has risen from 2.6 per thousand in 1951 to 12.7 per thousand in the late 1980s and has slightly increased to 13.7 per thousand in 1992, which means that the divorce rate in the early 1990s is six times higher than 1961 and more than double the rate

TABLE 3.1   *Divorces Granted in the United Kingdom 1951–87 (in thou sands)*

1951	1961	1966	1971	1976	1980	1981	1982	1983	1984	1985	1986	1987
31	27	43	80	136	160	157	159	162	158	175	168	165

Figures include dissolutions and nullity proceedings.
Source: Social Trends, 18 (HMSO and OPCS, 1988) and M. Robinson, *Family Transformation through Divorce and Remarriage* (London: Routledge, 1991).

of 1971. Britain has the second highest divorce rate in the European Community (EC) after Denmark, but also the second highest marriage rate at 6.8 per thousand of the eligible population. Only Portugal has a higher rate at 7.1. The number of marriages per year has shown a downward trend from approximately 405,000 in 1971 to 370,000 in 1980 to 331,000 in 1990. The last figure was a 4.5 per cent drop on the previous year.

The Scottish data indicate that since 1956 the number of divorce actions initiated per year has increased sevenfold from 1,600 to 12,479 in 1992, whilst the number of marriages per year has declined over the same period from about 44,000 in 1956 to 34,000 in 1991 (Morris, Gibson and Platts, 1993; Utting, 1995). With over two-thirds of 'fault'-based divorce actions raised by women, with behaviour (51.32 per cent) or adultery of the spouse (11.56 per cent) cited as the causes, there is a marked gender bias to the pursuit of the formal legal cessation of marriage. In general, the pursuers of divorce in Scotland are disproportionately women, with 60 per cent of actions for simplified divorce (where there are no children under 16 and the parties make no financial claims on one another) and about 80 per cent of actions raised for ordinary cause, which remains the standard procedure for divorce actions, being initiated by wives. This is a pattern which is likely to be found in other countries.

In the light of these statistical trends it was predictable that over the years there would be an increasing interest in family intervention, especially as the idea of the family remains both normatively and politically strong. The most recent information available from Relate (National Marriage Guidance Council) about its workload is for 1991/92. In that year Relate reported a 15 per cent increase in the number of cases dealt with to 70,000. The largest number of cases involve marriages less than five years old. The average length of marriage dealt with by Relate is 12.8 years, and 62 per cent of cases involve at least one child under 16 years of age (Relate, 1993). The National Association of Family Mediation and Conciliation Services representing 57 Out-of-Court Mediation Services in England and Wales reports that over 12,000 people made enquiries to its services in 1993. About 5,000 couples actually engaged in mediation.

To illustrate the movement in the style and modes of intervention in marriage conciliation alluded to above, I shall examine the marriage guidance movement in the United Kingdom. This account relies heavily on the valuable study of The Marriage Guidance Council (Relate) by Lewis, Clark and Morgan (1992).

The development of marriage guidance in Britain

The history of marriage guidance is a relatively short one. Lewis, Clark and Morgan (1992) and Chester (1985) have described how it gradually changed from a social movement with its origins in the 1920s to a social service providing guidance and counselling, often on a one-to-one basis, from the 1950s onwards. What was once work motivated by deeply held values about marriage and human relationships voluntarily given, through time became transformed by professionalisation and bureaucratisation; volunteers no longer gave of their time as amateurs but intellectually subjected themselves to rigorous training and organisational discipline. The shift can be characterised more broadly as a movement from the goal of *marriage saving* to that of *individual problem solving*. This change parallels the change in social attitudes to marriage and its transformation from being regarded as an institution to being seen as a social relationship. The interesting feature of these movements, at least with respect to the development of marriage guidance in the United Kingdom, is the way in which the mission of the National Marriage Guidance Council (NMGC) became less motivated by the need to reinforce a particular moral Christian view of marriage upon those seeking its help, and more inclined to assist the withdrawal from marriage of troubled clients, in short, more *appreciative* of the problems and needs surrounding the marital relationship.

The great force which marriage guidance sought to control or regulate was, of course, sex. Increasing medical and scientific knowledge about human sexuality, and public policy interest in demographic trends manifest through policies on population growth and control, conflicted with religious and moral views about how people should behave, particularly with that perspective which viewed all extra-marital sexual activity as sin. Contraception, for example, could be viewed as a necessary part of a rational public health policy, limiting the spread of sexually transmitted diseases, and regulating the reproduction of poor and physically weak human stock by those attracted to eugenics, but instrumental in encouraging promiscuous behaviour and marriage breakdown by those attracted to an uncompromising religious view of marriage. Early attempts to develop a marriage guidance movement, and indeed later policies too, sought to reconcile these two forces. Science and religion, or sex as physiology and sex as sin, had to be harnessed to a perspective on marriage which supported the institution whilst also allowing and encouraging the exploration of more modern attitudes to sex and reproduction.

This tension was clearly discernible in the aim of the Marriage Guidance Council, up to and during the Second World War, to base a societal morality on love rather than fear through the adoption of a positive view of sex within marriage. So the twin influences of religion and medicine dominated the early years of the Marriage Guidance Council. Herbert Gray, a clergyman and founding father of the movement, advocated the traditional marital virtues of chastity and fidelity, but he eschewed all notions of sex as sin as long as it was confined to marriage. Dr E.F. Griffith, a fellow founder, was attracted to marriage guidance through an interest in birth control and eugenics, and brought the influence of medical science to debates about sexuality, contraception and marriage breakdown. These two central figures shaped the early marriage guidance movement with the principle that 'the home was the pivot of social reconstruction' following the disruptive years of the war, and further, that those proposing to enter both marriage and parenthood should be properly prepared for it and be able to demonstrate evidence that they possessed knowledge and a responsible attitude to family life. It was the task of Marriage Guidance to provide knowledge and education about family life. Griffith's strong eugenic influence on the early formulations of the Marriage Guidance Council revealed a sinister potential. Lewis, Clark and Morgan (1992) quote from his book *Morals in the Melting Pot* (1948):

In a well organised, intelligent society there would be no need to have abortions, illegitimacy, VD and all the rest for the simple reason that society wouldn't tolerate that sort of behaviour.

Griffith goes on to discuss the category of people who would be termed 'failures': those lacking the knowledge and indeed physical and mental well-being to take on the burdens of marriage and parenthood, people who, in the view of many attracted to eugenics, would weaken the human stock of our society and who would inevitably experience poverty and engage in criminality.

I would like such people isolated from society and given a course of re-education and would not allow them to mix with the general public until they presented evidence of knowledge and stability. (quoted in Lewis, Clark and Morgan, 1992, 64)

The Government's decision that Marriage Guidance should fulfil a counselling role only perhaps curtailed the broader project of educating the population envisaged by the eugenicists within the movement as it became a federated national organisation in 1946.

A parallel but separate development in this area was the work of the Charity Organisation Society which became the Family Welfare Association in 1946 and later the Family Discussion Bureau (FDB). As the twin influences of religiosity and eugenics were working themselves out within NMGC, a more clinically based approach to family problems was developing. Lewis, Clark and Morgan (1992) make the point that in the period 1947–49 when there was active lobbying to secure government funding for marriage guidance work following the Denning Report on procedure in matrimonial causes (PP. 1947, Cmd 7024), the more clinically based approach of the FDB was looked upon with more favour in government circles; its psychodynamic casework approach appeared to be more scientific and more rational than that being provided by the NMGC. The emphasis on non-directive counselling within the NMGC was often looked upon as being too passive for those distributing grant monies; it smacked of amateurs merely 'listening' to personal problems without the underpinning of theoretical knowledge. When the Harris Committee (PP. 1948, Cmd 7566) eventually awarded grants to the NMGC, FDB and the Catholic Marriage Advisory Council it did so while signalling a greater respect for the clinical approach. Psychodynamic approaches informed by psychoanalytic and behaviourist theory attempted to work on the boundaries between social work and psychiatry, but when the FDB eventually moved into the Tavistock Institute in the early 1950s it was quite clearly no longer offering a non-medical form of social work. NMGC and other organisations working in the field stood apart with their moral framework. When the FDB eventually changed its name to the Institute of Marital Studies it signalled an explicit commitment to theoretical training in psychotherapy and therapeutic practice in a way lacking in the other organisations operating in the marriage guidance field.

The influence of the Institute of Marital Studies was significant, however, and the NMGC became involved with a variety of counselling and therapeutic methods from the 1960s onwards. Clark (1991) describes the NMGC model as an admixture of methods including non-directive counselling, psychodynamic approaches adopted through training contact with the Institute of Marital Studies, and behaviourism, as the NMGC engaged in marital sex therapy. A feature of the debates about therapeutic method and modes of intervention in the NMGC was the lack of a clear policy statement about what the organisation was seeking to achieve. So the movement away from the more fundamentalist perspective on marriage informed by Christian values, which had been a feature of the early years, led ultimately to a confusing eclecticism. The particular change which caused most confusion took place in the late 1950s when the idea of non-directive counselling was imported from America. This change ushered in an approach which was more person-centred, but it was at the expense of a focus on the marital relationship. The shift towards *therapism,* whereby the individualised problems of a particular client took precedence over other considerations, inevitably followed. The tendency to devalue wider structural factors involved in marriage breakdown is a consequence of this approach and something which I will discuss further below.

The concepts of *guidance, counselling* and *therapy* have all vied with each other as models in the field of marriage guidance, and continue to do so. Clark (1991), in assessing their relative significance, suggests that with respect to the NMGC there has been a general movement: guidance was dominant in the 1950s when the main form of assistance to couples was in terms of 'guiding' them towards appropriate expertise, whether that be legal, religious or medico-psychological; counselling replaced reliance on experts as the volunteers themselves engaged in training and became more actively involved with their clients, seeking to help them to 'get in touch with themselves' as part of a wider interest in self-reflection which matured in clinical circles in the 1960s; a more intense interest in therapy, in both psychodynamic and behaviourist forms, finally prevailed in the 1970s and 1980s. The current attitude to these modes of intervention remains pragmatic. However, the name change to 'Relate' undertaken by NMGC in February 1988 is interpreted by many, including Lewis, Clark and Morgan (1991), as quite clearly signalling a non-directive approach to marriage guidance aimed primarily at individuals rather than relationships. The shift from marriage saving to interpersonal counselling and therapy is transparent; the objective is to help people to cope with the difficulties of withdrawing from problematic and painful marriages and relationships rather than to mediate and conciliate in order to keep people together.

This picture of a pragmatic, secular and largely non-judgemental structure of marriage conciliation services needs to be qualified. Where individuals remain strongly and devoutly attached to a set of religious beliefs, the control exerted on their attitudes to marriage and divorce will be strong. The controlling impact of religious precepts on the marriage relationship is something which is perhaps prematurely rejected. The conception of marriage as a 'pure relationship' in the sense suggested by Giddens does not apply to couples who adhere to a deeply embedded belief system which regards reverence to God as inextricably bound to an acceptance that marriage is indissoluble. The Jewish Marriage Council, established in 1946, for example, has developed to the point where today they offer a comprehensive coverage of services aimed explicitly at defending the concept of the Jewish family and the role of Judaism in organising the perspective of Jews on moral questions relating to family life. The range of services offered extends well beyond the provision of conciliation and counselling services to encompass a telephone crisis line, home economics and the improvement of Kosher cookery, a Jewish Marriage Bureau, and an extensive educational programme which deals with matters as varied as sex and health for teenagers and living as a solo. The Get Advisory Service deals with the problem of obtaining a Get (religious divorce). Like the Catholic Marriage Advisory Council, the Jewish Marriage Council deals with the problems arising from the distinction between a civil divorce and a religious divorce. Where couples or an individual cannot countenance the latter, the issues surrounding family integrity and personal happiness can be wide-ranging. The role of therapeutic intervention in such circumstances can very easily become conjoined with the reinforcement of religious values and beliefs in what might be perceived by some, possibly clients, as oppressive ways. The Jewish Marriage Council, like Relate, stresses that its services are non-judgemental. However, the totality of their focus, combined with their exceptionally strong and religiously central conception of the importance of the family in Jewish culture, marks out the Jewish Marriage Council from the more secular organisations in the field. The organisation's standard introductory pamphlet *When a Jewish Marriage Breaks Up A Jewish Family Breaks Down* quotes from Chief Rabbi Dr Jonathan Sacks: 'No faith has invested marriage and parenthood with such significance, spirituality and beauty as has Judaism'. The clear moral and religious mission found here is reminiscent of the NMGC in its earlier years.

In concluding this chapter on intervention in marriage, the question arises as to why conciliation and marriage guidance services should have developed in the way they have since the 1940s. Psychotherapy has been called the growth industry of the 1990s; estimations from the British Association of Counselling suggest that about 30,000 people in Britain earn their living from counselling with a further 270,000 people in the voluntary sector providing counselling of one form or another (Persaud, 1993). Marriage conciliation and counselling have increased in tandem with other forms of counselling and psychotherapy. Marriage breakdown provides an impetus for many to obtain help with self-examination and ego building following bad relationships, especially those who can afford to pay for counselling privately. A purely functional answer as to why there are so many counsellors would be that such services fill a functional gap created by the declining influence of religion and traditional values; marriage conciliation is applied by practitioners committed to the concept of marriage as a form of social cement which facilitates necessary running repairs until a new stability in family and marital relationships can be established.

The post-structuralist argument draws our attention to the intersecting points of professional discourses, emanating mainly from psychology, social work and medicine, which make visible a host of family-related problems and bring about the increased professional expertise needed to respond to problems partly created and constructed by the 'technicians of human relations'. Such an account is only partially valid. We need also to acknowledge the dialectical interaction between the construction of social problems and problem behaviours by 'experts' and the lay individual's assessment of those problems and how they might relate to their own self-concept and life experience.

To mention again issues raised in Chapters 1 and 2, post-structuralism rejects the notion of the subject, what has been referred to as 'an ontologically real self', and focuses attention on the constitution of knowledges. In terms of the vocabulary of *classification* and *framing*, post-structuralism highlights the problem of the classification of knowledge because it has tended to have little to say about the problem of framing. Both dimensions need to be understood.

Why marriage guidance services?

In addressing this question, it is worth distinguishing between two discrete but undoubtedly related levels of analysis: marriage guidance and conciliation as a *societal* problem, especially its facility to prevent marriage break-up with all that entails for social order and welfare expenditure, and marriage guidance and counselling as an *individual* problem required by people to reinforce their self-identity at periods of anxiety.

First, we should acknowledge the wider political and policy movements which have helped to direct interest in marriage in the postwar years. To some extent I have already outlined the concerns which stimulated change within the marriage guidance movement. But we also need to trace the development of the wider structural framework within which marriage problems are perceived as problematic for society as a whole and not just for those individuals experiencing marriage breakdown. Social policies can assume a particular model of family life, with the commonly accepted and frequently reinforced nuclear, male-breadwinner model finding particular favour (see Van Every, 1991). Deviations from this model through divorce or single parenthood seem to have generated a sense of social alarm in contemporary Britain. And again marriage guidance and conciliation services can be perceived as instruments of social policy whose purpose is to control and rebuild the 'moral edifice' surrounding family life. Increasingly there are those who argue that the welfare benefits system in particular needs to be used to coerce people into remaining married, or indeed marrying in the first place (see P. Morgan, 1995). I will address this issue in more detail in chapter 6 when the issue of the 'underclass' family is examined. Not only does the distress of marriage breakdown have financial costs, both public and private, but increasingly research is demonstrating that the impact of marriage dissolution on children is devastating with long term societal repercussions (Langley, 1995). The expansion of marriage conciliation services signalled in the White Paper *Looking to the Future* is following an American pattern which is very rapidly becoming established. Since 1993, 12 American states have established compulsory seminars in which children of divorced parents describe, in detail and with frankness, their experience of marriage break-up to an audience of divorcing parents. The programme intends to encourage a greater degree of parental reflection on the implications of their actions. Under the auspices of the Association of Family and Conciliatory Courts, thousands of divorcing parents listening to the children's harrowing accounts of family break-up are subsequently encouraged to seek help from the expanding numbers of marriage counsellors. Divorce in the 1990s and beyond will involve more recognition of the needs of children by instituting such seminars and services as a routine element of marriage dissolution. In Britain, the Children Act 1989 in England and Wales, and the corresponding Children (Scotland) Act 1995, give priority to the interests of children in matters of marriage breakdown. Marriage conciliation will necessarily grow in importance as this principle shapes family law. A recent example which illustrates the changing emphasis in divorce matters has been the growth in the numbers of Child Contact Centres which enable fathers to keep in touch with their children following an acrimonious divorce. Such centres facilitate contact between children and a biological parent, usually the father, in spite of a desire by the other parent to exclude such contact; it is deemed to be in the best interests of children to maintain a level of knowledge about, and interaction with, both of their parents in spite of the unpleasant events which may have led to the marriage break-up. This may be an example where mediation and conciliation is replacing the coercive power of the law in the area of family life, especially in cases where a mother refuses to abide by a 'contact order' made by a court. The Child Contact Centre may be an alternative to coercing one parent into ongoing interaction with a former partner which she/he finds difficult for one reason or another.

Second, we need to address the issue of why people may feel that they need a range of counselling and therapeutic services. We must enquire into the condition of social existence in what Giddens calls high or late modernity. This requires the undertaking of a task which is generally spurned by the post-structuralist perspective, namely the examination of issues relating to self-identity. What is particularly interesting is the relationship between the constant construction and reconstruction of self-identity and the role of *therapism* in aiding, or indeed undermining, this personal project. It is this issue that I will focus on for the remainder of this chapter.

Modernity, self-identity and therapism

In seeking to illustrate the essence of 'high modernity', Giddens (1991) starts his analysis by discussing Wallerstein and Blakeslee's book *Second Chances* (1989) which is about divorce and remarriage. The particular feature of the divorce experience which he accentuates is the social and intellectual process of uncoupling from past commitments and relationships and the facing up to a future where new *opportunities* as well as *dangers* await the divorcee.

> The sphere of what we have today come to term 'personal relationships' offers opportunities for intimacy and self-expression lacking in many more traditional contexts. At the same time, such relationships have become risky and dangerous, in certain senses of these terms. Modes of behaviour and feeling associated with sexual and marital life have become mobile, unsettled and 'open'. There is much to be gained; but there is unexplored territory to be charted, and new dangers to be courted. (Giddens, 1991, 12–13)

The dual nature of living in a society where the pace of social change is fast, where *opportunities* and *risks* abound, like the divorce process itself, and where information about life experiences is constantly fed back to people through books such as *Second Chances*, characterises what Giddens calls 'high modernity'. We are reflexive about our needs, our projects, our problems at both an institutional and individual level. Whilst institutions are constituted by the need to constantly revise what information is available for their functioning, so too will individuals engage in the same process of reflexivity.

Whereas in earlier periods of modernity we were influenced by enlightenment views about rationality and the application of scientific knowledge to the control and predictability of all social and material life, in the period of late modernity we are less certain about this passage to progress. Science is based on what Giddens calls the 'methodological principle of doubt'. Gone is the certainty about the accumulation of knowledge and the gradual but inexorable completion of the picture which will reveal how all problems can be solved. Instead change and uncertainty seem to be built into the development of the three key features of modernity: *industrialism*, *capitalism* and what Foucault called *panopticism*.

The dynamic features of modernity which generate a sense of pace, change and uncertainty are, first, the development of technologies which separate time and space and facilitate relationships on a global scale and, second, the development of abstract systems which act as disembedding mechanisms, which literally enable relationships to be 'lifted out' of their locality. Giddens refers to two types: *symbolic tokens* which act as media of exchange, for example, the development of systems of credit which suspend time, enabling transactions across temporal and spatial distances without the parties involved ever meeting. Giddens draws our attention to another type of abstract system of what he calls disembedding mechanisms, that of the *expert system*. By this concept he wishes to point up the way time and space are *bracketed* through the deployment of modes of technical knowledge which are independent of both the practitioners and clients using them. He refers to relationships between doctors and their patients, and usefully points towards therapists and counsellors as further examples of where this disembedding mechanism is at work. For example, the heroic relationship between doctor and patient distinguished by the exclusive patron/doctor contract characteristic of medicine in the years prior to the nineteeth century (see Jewson, 1976) has been replaced by universalised abstract knowledge, information and data which enable the development of shared technical knowledge acquired through the established channels of professional education and training. Any properly trained practitioner should be able to minister to any suitable client well understood, licensed and standard treatments. A distinctive feature of modern information systems is that they provide wide access to data emanating from the scientific research community in both complex and uncomplicated formats. Health data relating to body image, nutrition and the psychology of coping with the stresses of modern life are examples of the type of 'expert knowledge' which typically filters through to lay people through a constant and well established system of information distribution.

The desacralisation of social life has been a prominent feature of modernity, but the failure of science and technology to replace the certitudes of religion with a new framework for generating social meaning has resulted in what a number of social commentators have called 'the privatisation of meaning'; inner exploration of what constitutes the 'self' has become an increasingly common personal project, assisting individuals to make sense of what often looks like a senseless world. Giddens maintains, therefore, that issues relating to self-identity have become of particular significance in the late modern world.

The concept of self which emerges from this analysis is one which entails an active component: the narrative of the self requires the individual to be conscious of his place in the social world, his relationship to time and space and, crucially, his involvement in self-actualisation. Again, by drawing on an illustrative study, Janette Rainwater's book *Self-Therapy,* which stresses the pro-active nature of building self-identity, Giddens highlights the similarities between the pursuit of self through self-therapy and the pursuit of self-identity in the 'real' world. In self-therapy the accent is very much on the need for people to confront *risks* and novel situations in order to escape from past doubts and oppressions. The importance of being able to build personal integrity is emphasised by seeking to reconcile, or 'integrate', life experiences with the individual's self-narrative (dialogue with oneself about goals, fears and aspirations). The very idea of therapy arises because of the pursuit of meaning and self-knowledge in a complex and changing social environment. For example, people are increasingly regarding their body as representative of their sense of self. The popularity of 'body regimes' whereby exercise and diet become instruments to shape the body in accordance with the person's self-narrative might be an indication of a growing sensitivity towards a sense of self (see Shilling, 1991, 1993). The constant dialogue involved in making and remaking the self is a product of a world in which choices are many. The *risks* and *opportunities* are great, but, without pre-established patterns and traditions to follow, the selection of criteria to adopt when making choices can be unclear. The consequence of this, according to Giddens, is that we are forced to select a 'lifestyle'. The concept of 'lifestyle' has no place within traditional social orders because patterns of behaviour and life plans are pre-determined by social convention, but in high modernity it is suggested that we are forced to construct 'lifestyles' to try and give material form to our narratives of self-identity. The idea being expressed here is that we are constantly seeking to adjust our material existence in line with what we want to achieve for ourselves and with how we see ourselves. Importantly, this idea is not confined to middle-class and affluent people only. Lifestyle is shaped by material realities including poverty and powerlessness. But creativity and self-identity are not simply the products of middle-class achievement. Life in the ghetto or a deprived peripheral housing estate determines the content of what Miller (1958) called *focal concerns,* which may be different from the affluent suburbs, but they do not shield the poor from the 'institutional components of modernity' and do not obliterate self-identity:

> in some circumstances of poverty, the hold of tradition has perhaps become even more thoroughly disintegrated than elsewhere. Consequently, the creative construction of lifestyle may become a particularly characteristic feature of such situations. Lifestyle habits are constructed through the resistance of ghetto life as well as through the direct elaboration of distinctive cultural styles and modes of activity. (Giddens, 1991, 86)

The current controversy about unconventional patterns of family living, especially among the poor, or the 'underclass', can be conceived of as an outgrowth of the processes described here by Giddens. The rejection of marriage, commitment and a sense of responsibility to children produced by a 'lifestyle' centred on hedonism may be the product of the anomic effects of modernity on communities and social relationships as experienced from the bottom of the social hierarchy. I will return to this theme in Chapter 6.

The complex interdependence characterising high modernity enforces upon everyone high levels of *trust* and *commitment* in order to lubricate the socio-economic existence of modern life and make any form of economic development possible. This is very similar to the *trust* and *commitment* required within modern marriages. The emergence of the phenomenon of 'pure relationships' is a direct by-product of the forces driving modernity. Marriage and marital relationships are disconnected from tradition and from extraneous influences and affected only by the intense intimacy between two people. Within marriage self-identity has to be a negotiated product of two people engaged in mutual exploration of themselves and their partnership. It involves high levels of trust, commitment and *risk*. What is the role of therapy, or indeed marriage counselling, in this context? The term *therapism* is a shorthand for all counselling relationships in this context. I am suggesting that the post-structuralist vision is only partially valid. Practitioners from the fields of psychotherapy, medicine, social work and a host of other related disciplines do indeed construct problems, pathologies and treatments through their various professional discourses. Through professional practice and language, problem individuals, problem families and problematic relationships are given a visibility which would not exist without the specific focus of the therapist, social worker or marriage guidance counsellor. Professional discourses describe behaviours in such a way as to make them appear problematic; they provide an interpretation of behaviours and relationships which demands intervention and correction. On the opposite side, the client actively makes sense of his problems and how they relate to a particular life experience or lifestyle. The self can be conceptualised in terms of an active construction of identity rather than merely as the residual element remaining after the practitioner has delineated the parameters within which the individual must act. Therapy is a product of the emergence of 'expert systems' which have arisen in modern society because of the need to develop social control over problematic social behaviours, but it is also a response to the need expressed by individuals for support and guidance regarding their 'self narratives', their life plans, and their desire for a more coherent and positive sense of self. Both the *classification* and *framing* of knowledge are involved here; individuals are active in *framing* during interaction in counselling and therapy. Therapy is increasingly something which people actively engage in and initiate for themselves. Perhaps there is a class distinction that does need to be made at this point. Middle-class and affluent individuals seeking aid in the construction of their life plans will voluntarily seek out the particular brand of psychotherapy which suits their needs. Working-class individuals invariably only encounter therapy through its imposition on them by statutory powers. They are required to examine their behaviour, their values and their personal and family goals in terms of some perceived failure to function effectively in a complex and changing society. Where it is not overtly imposed on them it may be subtly employed through the setting up of facilities which have as their object the monitoring and supporting of families in trouble, whilst appearing to be community facilities such as family centres (see Cannan, 1992). Ironically access to counselling and guidance about the personally worrying matters which surround divorce may be very limited for the less affluent. It may only be through referral from the divorce court at the time of marriage breakdown that those who are neither affluent nor considered potential social work clients will receive any of the forms of counselling and therapeutic help which the affluent middle classes are increasingly seeking out and paying for themselves. But irrespective of the context, I am suggesting that the importance of what Giddens has to say about self-identity must not be overlooked. As I was at pains to emphasise in Chapter 2, the particular practice code determining the *classification* and *framing* of knowledge in a given practitioner – client relationship will vary. But the object of the therapeutic relationship, whether that be in the context of marriage guidance or some other problem situation, is to encourage the client to articulate his anxieties and build a more assured self in the face of threatening challenges.

The increasing attraction to and the growth of marriage guidance and conciliation services in contemporary society is therefore inextricably bound up with the multiplying number of risks involved in marriage as a 'pure relationship'. The combination of both legal and social *appreciation* of the difficulties involved in establishing a successful and rewarding relationship has undoubtedly created a space for social intervention. And just as the quest for self-identity has created strains in human relationships, the legal and social constraints which prevented people from expressing their sense of self have been relaxed, allowing them the possibility of exploring the self through a series of relationships where hitherto only one would have been tolerated. Social existence in the period of high modernity will surely mean that the institution of marriage will increasingly bend to accommodate the plurality of ways in which self-identity will be expressed and family life established. Such a state of affairs will lead inexorably to an increase in the numbers of 'technicians of human relations' assisting the vulnerable to negotiate the *risks* and *opportunities* involved in this process.

One final issue that ought to be addressed before leaving this subject concerns the wider social and political implications of what Raymond (1986) calls *therapism*. As discussed in Chapter 2, Raymond raises the question of whether a concern for the self, more specifically the exploration of self-identity through therapy, results in what she calls 'an overevaluation of feeling'. In common with Foucault and Lasch, Raymond raises a critical question mark over the purpose and influence of the therapeutic movement. Certainly her particular concern is with the consequences that an overly introverted community of women may have for a publicly oriented feminist movement. *Therapism* creates what Rieff (1966) called in his book *The Triumph of the Therapeutic* 'the sane self in a mad world'. The individual pursues personal well-being but at the expense of a sense of wider responsibility, concerned with keeping the self intact in order to ensure modest functioning in a stressful world. Reiff, of course, attributes this growing amoralism to the secularisation of society. Without religion, it is argued that in place of a larger morality outside of the self there is only self-indulgence and the quest for personal happiness.

Two further popular concerns are expressed about the rise in *therapism*. The first is that therapy leads to a form of dependence on experts. The second concern is one already touched on: the extent to which therapy which seeks to mediate between conflicting interests, such as one might encounter in the divorce situation, resolves that conflict by employing essentially precipitate, unfair and frequently sexist solutions which fail to address the fundamental imbalances of power within family relationships. Both themes can be illustrated by reference to the behaviour of divorce lawyers. I have referred to research on solicitors' practice in implementing the Family Law (Scotland) Act 1985 above. What seems to happen is that conflict management can often lead to unfair solutions and compromises aimed at nothing beyond avoiding court. A great deal of what is called mediation and conciliation in the divorce context is not therapy in any sense that Raymond would recognise. The proliferation of terms seeking to describe mediating processes only serves to confuse. A distinction should be made between conflict resolution as part of a legal 'quick fix' and the active engagement between client and counsellor to understand and explore the potential for self-development which typifies the therapeutic context. In the context of divorce actions, lawyers provide a technical service which creates dependency on the part of vulnerable clients who lack the 'expertise' of their legal counsellor. Issues of law very often conflict with issues relating to self-identity and in the divorce situation legal matters predominate at the expense of personal well-being.

However, one characteristic which the 'technicians of human relations' share, whether they be clinicians, social workers or lawyers, is that they are all implicated in what Giddens describes as the 'sequestration of experience':

> The separation of day-to-day life from contact with experiences which raise potentially disturbing existential questions, particularly experiences to do with sickness, madness, criminality, sexuality and death. (Giddens, 1991, 244)

Therapism may well increase the thickness of insulation between couples facing marriage problems and the plethora of 'real' choices that can be made. The guidance offered by counsellors may be based on abstract knowledge which has little relevance to the material circumstances and moral obligations of everyday existence. One facet of living in the period of high modernity where 'expert systems' proliferate is that commitment to one particular form of therapy, or mode of counselling, may close off the possibility of seeing problems from an alternative perspective. At this point Foucault and the post-structuralists may be correct when they point to the essentially problematic nature of practitioner – client relationships in those contexts where knowledge is imperfect and possessed overwhelmingly by the 'expert'. A commitment to sexual therapy may close off consideration of the possibility that two people really should not be together because of incompatibility. A commitment to simple legal forms of mediation which eschews all forms of psychological counselling may be equally disastrous. But the interplay of *trust*, *commitment* and confusing choice often means that selecting one's 'technician of human relations' in modern society is an act of faith guided more by instinct than by reason, and that having one imposed on oneself may be a matter of good or bad fortune.

4

Family structures and the moral politics of caring

The popularity of community care for the frail elderly and the mentally ill and handicapped has never been higher among policy makers. Since the early 1970s successions of Government Committees of Enquiry into the role, tasks and problems of the personal social services have been pointing insistently towards the community as the main site where personal social care should be organised. Furthermore, Seebohm (1968), Barclay (1982) and Griffith (1988) have successively signalled a shift in policy thinking by advocating a more explicit community orientation for professional social workers. This gradual movement in thinking changed the social policy agenda for the 1990s, culminating in the National Health Service and Community Care Act 1990. As local authorities and health boards take on the responsibility for planning and administering the new framework for community care, particularly the planning, co-ordinating and assembling of 'care packages' through a system of case management, it remains to be seen whether this new public commitment to community care at both a political and a practitioner level will fundamentally alter the underlying realities of this type of policy strategy.

The patchy but dogged history of community care as a policy idea has been well documented and need not be discussed here (see F. Martin, 1984; Higgins, 1989; and Finch, 1990a). The main interest of this chapter is in the acknowledged reality of what community care means: care by the family, which means disproportionately care by women. Finch and Groves (1980), Lewis and Meredith (1988) and Ungerson (1987), to name but a few, have all revealed evidence of the gender bias inherent in the caring relationship. Finch (1989) has in addition provided a useful discussion of the question of 'obligation' in families, especially as this relates to caring tasks and responsibilities within family networks. What this interesting literature has made visible, through working at the interface between sociology, social policy and social work, is that there are important issues to be addressed concerning what Clare Ungerson calls 'the moral politics of caring'. Whilst the selection of a daughter or daughter-in-law rather than a son as a primary carer should not surprise anyone, it is less clear why one particular daughter should emerge as a carer rather than her sister, or, indeed, why an elderly mother should be cared for by her daughter-in-law rather than her own daughters. Focusing on such cases is fascinating, and the studies by both Qureshi and Walker (1989) and Ungerson (1987) detail examples of different caring patterns. However, to dwell on the phenomenon of the moral politics within specific families, which will be influenced by a host of situational factors, without also attempting to understand the influence of family structure and functioning in shaping those factors, would be inadequate. For example, do criteria typically drawn on to make caring decisions vary according to family type? It is clear from the empirical work already undertaken by Qureshi and Walker (1989), Ungerson (1987) and Finch (1989) that families arrive at decisions about caring for a variety of reasons: some are founded on notions about obligation, duty and necessity, whilst others may be based on a vocabulary of love and even distributive justice. The interesting, yet neglected, issue which concerns this chapter is the relationship between family structures or types, and the 'political style' used within families to engage in bargaining about caring issues. The search for a theoretical understanding of family caring must be pursued. Is it possible, for example, to arrive at a broader sociological understanding of the social mechanisms within families and identify structures which might allow a less legitimate place for sexism in a family's moral calculus about caring responsibilities? This type of question, I would argue, must be addressed because not only is it sociologically interesting but it is also of practical importance at a time when social policy and social work are acknowledging the pivotal place of informal family care within the emerging public policy strategies for the elderly and mentally ill in the 1990s. We therefore need to know more about the intimate social and political processes which determine how families decide what to do about caring responsibilities and, importantly, how those decisions interact with new developments in community care policy.

One of the persistent ideas emerging from advocates of more welfare pluralism throughout the 1980s (Hadley and Hatch, 1981) and from recent research on social care (Challis *et al.*, 1990; Challis *et al.*, 1989; Challis and Davies, 1980) is that social work agencies should operate as co-ordinators and managers of care packages for individuals in need rather than being the direct providers of care. Such arguments were picked up first by Griffith (1988) and eagerly adopted by a Government suspicious of the effectiveness of statutory social work and concerned about the costs of residential solutions to caring needs. This has meant that relatives and neighbours are increasingly being thought of as resources to be used by policy makers and social workers in order to keep people in need of personal social care in their own homes. So through this type of community care initiative social workers are increasingly going to be involving themselves with 'normal' rather than with 'deviant' families. In place of action initiated by a breakdown in family relationships, the social worker's task will be that of lubricating contact between neighbours and relatives, or of helping to foster friendships between people in order that they might assist each other. Given this entrepreneurial and management function envisaged for social workers and case managers in the new community care framework, the questions arise as to whether such case managers will simply utilise social resources which are available, and therefore inevitably reproduce and reinforce gender inequalities and personal burdens in caring responsibilities, or whether they might contemplate intervention in the moral bargaining of family politics to challenge those inequalities in some way. Without doubt the broadening of the scope of social workers' duties to promote change in the behaviour of families and people not defined as being 'deviant' is ideologically as well as professionally contentious. Nevertheless, given this potential development in social policy, it is incumbent upon social scientists to address the large issues about power and injustice within families, and the exploitation of people who presently lose out in the moral politics of family living. The contemporary policy emphasis on community care demands a sociological analysis of its realities beyond those identified so far by the research literature in social policy.

The explicit purpose here is to advance our understanding of the moral politics of caring by bringing together analyses of the structure and functioning of different family types, especially that research which has studied how families construct their realities and organise their decision-making, with work in social policy on gender and caring.

Family types and family functioning

My main concern is with the structure and processes which exert an influence on the feelings which people have about bonding with each other and the implications that this has for their feelings of obligation to each other. I am therefore intent on seeing family structure in a rather Durkheimian way as something which varies and so affects people differentially. The questions at issue here are: what types of family structure shape members' feelings of attachment and obligation, and how might such structures influence the moral politics within families about caring, particularly in periods of stress, crisis, or rapid social change?

The amount of published work on families and family structure is quite extensive, ranging over psychiatry, social psychology and family therapy as well as sociology. The methods used to study social behaviour in families also vary widely, with much of the research in psychology and psychiatry being based on laboratory investigation of families where one member has some clinically defined problem such as schizophrenia. Despite the differences in methodology between these branches of knowledge and the classic work in the sociology of the family of Bott (1957), Rosser and Harris (1965), Bell (1968) or Firth *et al.* (1970), there are a number of common threads. In particular, the concepts of 'cohesion', 'adaptability' and 'communication' seem to be a focus of most sociological and psychological perspectives on the family.

Given the vast amount of work in the field of family studies, I have selected three pieces of research which seem to focus on family structure in an analytically useful way. First, the work by Olson and McCubbin (1983) has been based on what they call a circumplex model of marital and family behaviour. This model is based on relating the variations in patterns of cohesion to family adaptability in the face of problems or stressors. This research is based on analysis of what the authors call 'normal' families. In other words, it is not laboratory-based research on families defined as having some form of 'pathology' and does not have a clinical or therapeutic objective, although they do seek to provide theoretical and analytical guidance to those involved in family therapy. By contrast, a second piece of research which I will discuss, by David Reiss (1981), did grow out of laboratory research on families with schizophrenic members. The analysis offered by Reiss, however, has wider sociological validity because his main interest was in the social processes involved in the way families build up shared constructs or paradigms. Reiss refers to this as 'the family's shared construing of problems'. As the subtitle of the book indicates, the analysis focuses on 'what makes families work' and as such is extremely interesting for the issue under consideration here, that of the better understanding of the 'moral politics of caring'. A third piece of research which I will describe is that undertaken by Kellerhals, Coenen-Huther and Modak (1988) on 107 Swiss couples. More conventionally sociological, though it uses the vignette technique in survey research (see Finch, 1987), the objective of the study was to understand more about the relationship between norms of distributive justice and types of interaction in family groups. It is useful not only for bringing out this relationship, but also because it makes some tentative observations about social class differences in family interaction. These pieces of research will therefore be used to highlight important issues relating to the social processes of family decision-making and 'moral politics'.

Family structure and family dynamics

Olson and McCubbin (1983) conclude, following an extensive review of the literature in psychiatry, family therapy and sociology, that 'family cohesion, adaptability and communication are three dimensions of family behaviour that emerge from a conceptual clustering of over fifty concepts developed to describe marital and family dynamics' (p.47). Whilst these concepts may be given a variety of names depending on the theoretical vocabulary of different disciplines, they commonly direct our attention to the degree of connectedness within families (cohesion); the ability of family systems to respond flexibly to change (adaptability); and to the levels of competence or skill which family members may have to speak and listen to each other in a precise, clear way, with an ability to empathise and be reflective about what is said (communication). Whilst Olson and McCubbin consider communication as a facilitating dimension which they recognise as being 'critical to movement on the other two dimensions', they give it less detailed analysis than I think is required. In particular, I am unhappy about seeing communication merely as a 'facilitating dimension' which allows movement in the structure of family bonding and flexibility. To be able to speak, to make objections, or to enter arguments and negotiations, is as much about being in a *position* within a structure of power and authority as it is about the possession of communication skills. However, I will concentrate on the two dimensions of family structure given most emphasis by Olson and McCubbin. The underlying issue at the core of my analysis is the tension between individuality and collectivism in family living: what autonomous space is left to individual family members to exercise choices within different types of family?

Family cohesion, which Olson and McCubbin (1983) define as 'the emotional bonding family members have towards one another' (p.48), can be observed and analysed through a variety of social processes. Inferences can be made about the degree of connectedness or separateness between family members through such things as the amount of time they spend with acquaintances outside the family circle; whether they express feelings of closeness or affective indifference to each other; the way they experience leisure and recreation, either typically with their friends or with relatives or siblings (see Olson and McCubbin, 1983, 48). Through observation of decision-making processes in the laboratory it was possible for Olson and McCubbin to note whether coalitions formed in situations of stress and conflict, or whether typically consensus was sought on all or most matters. Finally, it is significant if a family expresses or lives with strong boundaries between who is or is not part of the 'family'. Family adaptability, which Olson and McCubbin relate to the ability of a marital or family system to change its power structure and role relationships in response to situational and developmental stress, can also be observed through a variety of concepts. The way a family allows *assertiveness* to be expressed is one indication, and acts to *control* and *discipline* its members is another. These processes will be related to whether the legitimacy of authority within the family is positional and status bound or negotiable and person centred.

The concept of family cohesion is differentiated by Olson and McCubbin into four levels, indicating either that a family's relationships with each other are characterised by 'connectedness' in which family members do a great deal together and reciprocally help one another, or 'separateness' which specifies a situation where individual family members tend to pursue their own projects and activities, and where there is a social expectation of individuality rather than communality finding expression. In both cases, Olson and McCubbin specify more extreme forms. With respect to 'connectedness', they conceptualise a dimension which they call 'enmeshed' which describes a case where family togetherness becomes overweening and perhaps stifling of individuality and the individual pursuit of projects. With respect to the dimension of 'separateness', they refer to a situation of 'disengagement' where the ties of cohesive bonding between family members are very loose.

The dimension of family structure referred to as 'adaptability' similarly can be differentiated into four levels, ranging from 'flexible' forms of adaptability to what Olson and McCubbin call 'structured' forms of adaptability. They also specify more extreme forms of adaptability. One form is described by the term 'chaotic', to denote a situation presumably of uncontrolled change where family members may feel like billiard balls being propelled by the social forces around them. The other extreme form is described by the term 'rigid' which might denote a situation where families display intransigence and perhaps an unwillingness to change. By crosstabulating these dimensions of family structure, Olson and McCubbin are able to classify sixteen types of marital and family systems. Based on their degree of empirical frequency, they further classify the family types into what they call *balanced, mid-range* and *extreme* (see Figure 4.1). The *balanced* and *mid-range* types occur most commonly. *Balanced* family systems can function at the extremes when necessary but do not do so for long periods. *Extreme* family systems function only at the extremes and family members are incapable of changing or find it difficult to change their behaviour.

Having developed their circumplex model, Olson and McCubbin are able to apply it to describing and predicting how different marital and family systems might respond to stresses. The structural features of family relationships will therefore equip people to respond differentially to crises and strains confronting them. The central hypothesis offered by Olson and McCubbin is a simple one: families of the *balanced* or *mid-range* type (see Figure 4.1) will have a greater number of strengths and fewer weaknesses, which will enable them to survive a variety of stresses and strains over the family life cycle.

The empirical research seems to point to fluctuations in the levels of cohesion and adaptability over the family life cycle. Cohesion is typically highest among families in the early stages of the family life cycle, but drops to lower levels as children reach adolescence

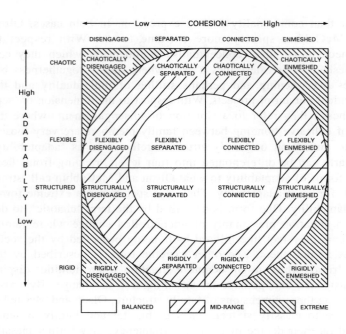

Figure 4.1   *Circumplex Model: Sixteen Types of Marital and Family Systems*

Source: D. Olson and H. McCubbin, *Families: What Makes them Work* (London: Sage), p. 50.

and experiment with more freedom and autonomy, reaching its lowest point at the 'launching' stage when they eventually leave the family home. The particular point of interest is the fact that cohesion within families typically rises again at the 'empty nest' and the 'retirement' stages, although not to the same levels as during the early stages of the family life cycle. Adaptability similarly follows a pattern of steady decline from the early stages and increases again slightly at the 'empty nest' and 'retirement stages', often when problems and decisions about caring and family obligation are having to be confronted.

With respect to the ability of families to adjust to problems such as ill health and ageing, there will be a variation in their capacity to draw on family support in times of trouble. Whilst the variables relating to the demographic, economic and occupational changes affecting social care in our society are well documented (see Bulmer, 1987; Finch, 1989; Chapter 3), the sociological work on family structures seems to suggest that, even if these variables are controlled, there will still be variations between families in terms of their cohesiveness and adaptability, and therefore in the willingness and capacity of family members to help one another. As the pattern of structural features described by Olson and McCubbin will vary between families, it follows that families will also vary in their ability to sort out interpersonal problems such as those regarding obligation to discharge welfare responsibilities to each other. Family strengths which Olson and McCubbin suggest are characteristic of *balanced* family types, such as a strong sense of family unity, loyalty and inter-family co-operation, but with flexible role performance and sufficient individuality allowed to members to maintain constructive relationships outside the family, may best enable families to make 'supportive' decisions about caring needs.

However, what normative yardstick must we apply to the notion of 'strong' rather than 'weak' family structures, and what counts as a 'good' or 'successful' adaptation to a caring crisis within a family? Are Olson and McCubbin perhaps leading us into a traditional sexist view of families? It seems to me that the norm that generally women should do the caring, in particular women without responsibilities to a husband and children or women without jobs, may only be challenged within family types that are *not balanced* in the sense suggested by Olson and McCubbin's analysis. One way of looking at this is to accept the idea that within the family there will be a variety of voices and discourses vying with each other. Within families high on the cohesion dimension but low on the adaptability dimension (bottom right quadrant of Figure 4.1) the space for competing voices and discourses may be minimal. By contrast, families low on cohesion but high on adaptability (top left quadrant of Figure 4.1) may allow a greater diversity of discourses to enter discussions and decision-making by virtue of the absence of a consensual ethos. Families high on both the adaptability and cohesion dimensions (top right quadrant) may also allow a greater latitude for behaviours which are 'deviant', but only if family solidarity is not threatened. Feminism as a discourse which questions the domestic and traditional role for women in the caring relationship may have a greater chance of being voiced in some particular 'extreme' family structures described by Olson and McCubbin. The possibility arises that feminist ideas on caring may be made to compromise to the point of losing their distinctive voice within *balanced* family types or families with a strong consensual ethos. I am, of course, making the assumption that ideas which challenge the conventional view of the woman's caring role are potentially subversive to unitary concepts of families based on a traditional domestic division of labour because they are not supported by common custom and practice. To continue with the idea of competing discourses, Carol Smart (1989) interestingly points out, in a discussion of feminism and the law, that the law as a body of knowledge, anchored in an edifice of institutional and professional power in the courts and legal profession, systematically disqualifies feminist discourse because of its method of reasoning and definition of relevance. Similarly within the family structure, based on notions of co-operative living supported by the institutions of religion, welfare, law and socially constructed morality, feminism can be systematically disqualified. It can be seen as a set of ideas and a voice which endanger the cohesion and functioning of the family system by drawing its knowledge and power, its 'truth' in Foucault's terms, from outside the moral economy of family living. It is likely to be perceived in this way by both men and women wedded to a view of motherhood involving filial duty. For this reason communication cannot be seen as merely a facilitating medium, but is shaped and determined by the structures which organise what can and cannot be said. Mostly the idea of women not accepting caring responsibilities is excluded intellectually by patriarchal discourse because it seems 'natural' for women to be carers.

I want to develop this argument by examining the work undertaken on the ways in which families construct their paradigms or realities, before focusing more specifically on the relationship between family structure and 'political styles'.

The family's construction of reality

Family paradigms are 'an extended and dependable repertoire of background understandings, shared assumptions, traditions, rituals and meaningful secrets' (Reiss, 1981) that make it possible for the family to function implicitly. The paradigm is a 'fine texture of implicitly understood features and codes'. It is woven gradually and individuals carry some features with them as they leave one family to marry into another. The paradigms therefore specify how the social world is to be interpreted and how it works.

The tension inherent in all family life between individual autonomy and collective family identity will be particularly marked in the way in which families build up and sustain their shared constructs. When Janet Finch (1989) discusses power and negotiations in families in relation to the selection of who does the caring, and rejects the idea of a 'battle of interests' in favour of a view which sees family negotiations as a prolonged and subtle process, she is alluding to the building up of a family paradigm. Family members come to implicit understandings about roles and obligations. Legitimacy is sought and created for certain actions which family members may take and there will be manoeuvring of position by individuals within the family over a number of years so that 'by the time the elderly person actually needed to be cared for . . . the shared understandings which had been developed in the kin group ensured that the eventual carer did feel quite genuinely that no one else was available' (Finch, 1989, 200). So understanding power and negotiation processes within families may require less of a teleological view of power and more of a communication or discourse perspective (see Habermas, 1977).

Initially, Reiss (1981) arrived at the notion of a shared family construct through laboratory observation of families' problem-solving behaviour. Inferences about family paradigms were made on the basis of observations both of how families responded to the specific problems set for them within the experimental setting and their perceptions and mastery of the laboratory environment. The question of methodology and the research objectives of working with families in a laboratory study are less interesting here than the insight that families seemed to develop shared constructs.

Based on the pursuit of knowledge about families as unitary groups through the application of laboratory research, Reiss concluded that, as well as properties of the social world, such as class and culture, shaping the family's transactions with its social environment, there were 'factors intrinsic to families that shape their modes of perceiving and interacting with their social milieu' (Oliveri and Reiss, 1981, 392). From the observation of families' variations in dealing with problems and working collectively to find solutions, a theory of shared family constructs was developed.

The premise of the theory is that individuals develop their own 'construct' of social phenomena and that this, in general, constitutes a theoretical guide to how the social world works, particularly in novel situations. Further, the theory assumes that 'lengthy, intimate, face to face relationships cannot go forward without a reconciliation, integration, and shared development of the basic premises of individuals' personal theories' (Oliveri and Reiss, 1981, 392). So it is the emergence of a collective view or collective synthesis of individual perceptions that Reiss and his colleagues call a construct or paradigm. The construct guides the family and provides a stable family view of any new situation. From the laboratory situation it was possible to observe that families seemed to differ in their capacity to 'master their world or be overwhelmed by it'. The theoretical model of family paradigms specifies three concepts to describe these different orientations to problem-solving and family members, perceptions of the social environment more generally. Reiss calls the concepts *configuration, co-ordination* and *closure*. The notion of *configuration* conceptualises the degree of 'patterning and organisation in family members' solutions to laboratory puzzles'. Families high on the *configuration* dimension 'view the environment as composed of many elements with intricate but essentially patterned and understandable relationships' (Oliveri and Reiss, 1981, 393), whereas families low on *configuration* seem to hold to a 'conviction that principles underlying environmental events are hidden; not open to influence by the family' and as a consequence of this they tend to 'impose simplistic and obvious problem solutions rather than attempting to grapple with and master the more intricate and challenging possibilities inherent in the task' (Oliveri and Reiss, 1981, 392). *Co-ordination* conceptualises the levels of collaboration between family members during problem-solving. Families varied on this dimension between those that developed a 'uniformity of outlook and values' and those that tended towards dissidence, with each member viewing the problem and the environment as having a differential impact on family members. The third concept of *closure* describes the variations found among families with respect to the length of time they remain open or alive to new information as it accumulates during a problem-solving task. Some families seemed to want to arrive at quick decisions and were uninterested in new information, others delayed their decision-making. Families who adopted *early closure* were dominated by the view that past experience furnished them with readily available interpretative frameworks for understanding and solving problems. By contrast, some families set aside past experience and interpreted and reinterpreted information as it became available and so *delayed closure*. From this empirical research Reiss has so far been able to identify three family types: *Environment-sensitive, interpersonal distance-sensitive* and *consensus-sensitive.*

Environment-sensitive families recorded high scores on all three dimensions. They tend to see problems as being solvable by identifying and applying general principles of logic. The family jointly seeks as many cues as possible, taking account of individual differences within the family. The sensitivity to both the wider environment and possible individual differences of perception means that closure is delayed. *Interpersonal distance-sensitive* families tend to favour the resolution of problems through independent individual efforts. Collective effort is possibly seen as a threat to individuals' mastery and decisiveness. Problems are therefore seen to be solvable by individuals who interpret them as uniquely part of their personal universe. Closure is often premature as individuals seek to emphasise their independence by demonstrating an ability to make quick decisions. *Consensus-sensitive* families are intolerant of dissent, however momentary, and the wider environment beyond the family is seen as potentially harmful to inter-member ties. Ideas and opinions are, therefore, quickly surrendered; early closure occurs in the pursuit of internal consensus.

Environment-sensitive families would appear to equate with Olson and McCubbin's concept of 'balance', having a flexible relationship between individual and family. *Interpersonal distance-sensitive* families come close to the concept of 'mid-range', but could conceivably take an 'extreme' form (top left quadrant of Figure 4.1), with a greater latitude given to individual effort at the expense of a collective family endeavour. *Consensus-sensitive* families come closest to the 'extreme' family types (bottom left quadrant of Figure 4.1) with individual identity submerged in the pseudo-mutuality of family consensus (represented by bottom right quadrant of Figure 4.1).

It is not possible to say whether Reiss's classifications accurately match those of Olson and McCubbin, although both pieces of research are concerned with the way behaviour patterns coalesce into structural properties. The central point which I would wish to make is that the tension between individual autonomy and collective family obligation should be the dimension for comparison. To what extent do the family structures described by Olson and McCubbin, and the patterns of family constructs or paradigms described by Reiss, help us to understand how families enlarge or constrict individual autonomy? As well as viewing power within the family in terms of coercive forms of control (the issue of domestic violence directs us to the material and institutional supports of male violence within the family), we should also be sensitive to the ways in which the normative and discursive practices of family living close down space for certain individuals' autonomous action (see Scanzoni, 1979; Cromwell and Olson, 1975). The analyses by both Reiss and Olson and McCubbin are informative about this question.

Whilst I acknowledge that the conflicts inherent in the moral politics of caring will reflect the relative importance placed upon material issues (job, career and the financial costs incurred in caring) and normative issues (obligations to spouse and children relative to obligations to the person needing to be cared for) in confirming or avoiding caring obligations (see Qureshi and Walker, 1989, ch. 5), the structures of family relationships will have an important determining effect on how these factors enter into family negotiations and politics. The process will involve a tension between relationships established over the family life cycle which will more or less integrate or bond the individual to the family group, on the one hand, and the resourcefulness of individuals in their use of ideological, normative and expedient arguments in family negotiations and bargaining, on the other hand. The positioning of the individual within the social structure of the family will therefore influence and in turn be influenced by what the individual says. However, the long-term development of family structures will create a formidable constraint on what can be said, on which voices will be influential and, crucially, on the way in which family decision-making is conducted.

Family decision-making and political styles

It is perhaps incumbent on me at this point to make some general connections between the analyses offered by Reiss and by Olson and McCubbin and the moral politics of caring. I will make some broader remarks about the social policy implications below, but with respect to the specific issue of the moral politics of families, very distinct political styles might be expected. A preliminary and speculative observation is that families which are described as *environment-sensitive* may conduct family politics with more regard for normative understandings that have currency in the wider society. More stress will be placed on collective efforts to resolve caring problems, and principles, rather than custom and practice, may have a more significant role. The particular emphasis I would wish to give is that some families of this type will lay particular stress on communication about family issues as a means of resolving conflicts rather than relying on generally understood explicit rules about divisions of labour and responsibilities. They will conduct family affairs through a 'discursive politics'. However, the thrust of that 'discursive politics' may nevertheless be aimed at reconciling the demands of individual family members for an escape from caring responsibilities with social expectations in keeping with notions of family duty. Families that are described as *consensus-sensitive* may conduct family politics in such a way as to minimise deviance. There will be less reference to wider, socially established normative principles and perhaps more stress on custom and practice. The emotional bonding between family members will have a greater determining influence on family decision-making than belief in more abstract principles about what is fair or unjust. They will conduct family affairs through a 'politics of mores'. *Interpersonal distance-sensitive* families may well adopt a style of politics based on the comparison of individual virtues and efforts. If normative considerations are to be influential, they will typically impact on an individual's contribution to a caring problem rather than be effective at a family level. Family affairs will, therefore, be conducted through a 'politics of individual virtue'. To return to my observations about Olson and McCubbin's concept of *balanced* and *extreme* family types, it seems plausible to expect that ideas and norms which challenge conventional sexist views about caring will have greatest impact in the *interpersonal distance-sensitive* family. The stress on individualism rather than collectivism may offer a better context within which ideas considered deviant in terms of the moral bind of conventionality might flourish.

To reinforce these insights about political styles and family structures we can consider a study concerned explicitly with individuals' perceptions of justice within families. Based fundamentally on classifications of family types similar to those used by Olson and

McCubbin, and Reiss, the research by Kellerhals *et al.* (1988) sought to explore the influence of family interaction patterns on the way issues of distributive justice are resolved. Using what they call 'an interactive test of self-definition of the family', 107 Swiss couples were requested to select and agree upon the characteristics which in their opinion described their relationship and family most accurately. Deriving very similar types of family structure to those already described by the American sociologists, the Swiss authors constructed two typologies to illustrate differences in the patterns of *integration* and *adaptation* within the families.

The integration typology is derived by crossing or relating 'cohesion' (i.e. whether families insist on *fusion,* or similarity, between members or insist on *autonomy*, or difference) with 'integration' (i.e. whether the family relates to the outside world in an *open* or *closed* way, where contacts are restricted). The adaptation typology is derived by this time crossing cohesion with 'regulation' (i.e. whether members insist on formulating precise rules of functioning relating to tasks and responsibilities or instead are communicative and negotiate situational meanings in changing circumstances).

The conclusion arrived at by Kellerhals *et al.* was that three family types emerged from the *integration typology:*

(*a*) Cohesion by fusion and being closed to the outside;
(*b*) Cohesion by fusion and openness to the outside;
(*c*) Cohesion by autonomy and openness to the outside. (Autonomy and closed to the outside was not found.)

And three types emerged from the *adaptation typology:*

(*d*) Cohesion by fusion and normative regulation;
(*e*) Cohesion by fusion and communicative regulation;
(*f*) Cohesion by autonomy and communicative regulation.

By employing the vignette technique (see Finch, 1987) they set decision-making problems involving issues of justice and fairness for the couples to resolve. A distinct pattern emerged between couples classified as lower-middle class and those classified as professional by socio-economic status and household income. With respect to the integration typology, 45 per cent of lower-middle-class couples and 17 per cent of professional couples were characterised by (*a*).

By contrast, 18 per cent of lower-middle-class couples and 37 per cent of professional couples were characterised by (*c*). On the adaptation typology 50 per cent of lower-middle-class couples and 19 per cent of professional couples were characterised by (*d*). By contrast 18 per cent of lower-middle-class and 37 per cent of professional couples were characterised by (*f*). The conclusion arrived at was that lower-middle-class families tend to expect and insist on members being consensualist in their behaviour and views and are more likely to set down explicit, even rigid, rules about roles, responsibilities and general behaviour. The principle of justice seemed to be based on what Kellerhals *et al.* describe as the 'intrinsic evaluation of contributions'. Decisions are typically reached rapidly. Professional or upper-middle-class families seemed to allow and expect individual family members to express their differences and discuss and negotiate about roles and responsibilities. The principles of justice are more often related to the idea of a contract and 'external criteria of evaluation of acts are accorded more legitimacy, persons are compared more on an individual than on a categorical or a statutory basis' (Kellerhals *et al.*, 1988, 125).

This type of research reinforces the general pattern described in the work by Reiss, and Olson and McCubbin. Whilst it is insufficient either in scope or sophistication to reveal conclusively that family structures and decision-making processes follow a clear differentiation along class lines, it is nevertheless very illuminating. It demonstrates empirically a pattern that might be expected, but class is perhaps less significant than the structural patterns of relationships in family life. Decision-making outcomes seemed to be more or less related to variations in family structure, so constituting what I would call family political styles. The moral politics in some families will therefore be concerned with duty, obligation and convention, while in others the emphasis will be on equity in the distribution of responsibilities.

With regard to the particular issue of identifying a structure of family relationships which would be capable of allowing more legitimacy to non-conventional patterns of caring duty, it is clear that the less bound by custom and social prejudice family members are, the less likely it is that the conventional sexist solutions will be sought. A capacity for genuinely open communication between articulate and sensitive family members creates the most favourable conditions for the acceptance of novel solutions.

The conceptual framework which I set out in Chapter 2 can again be referred to in order to underline the general differences between family types and political styles involved in decision-making. The weaker *classification* and *framing* characteristic of Bernstein's concept of 'personal' family types may be more likely to tolerate flexibility and novelty in caring solutions, whereas those families described by Bernstein as 'positional' will have strong *classification* and *framing* and will be characterised by rigidity in decision-making.

Family therapy as social policy: the issue of elder abuse

To return finally to the social policy context in which I located my analysis, when does the moral politics of the family become an issue of public policy? This question is not new. We have already acknowledged that the work of Donzelot (1980) and Lasch (1977), for example, has provided us with an account of the growing encroachment on the family by those who have variously been referred to as 'social pathologists' and the 'technicians of human relations'. The growth of the caring side of the welfare state in the twentieth century has, according to their analysis, been paralleled by the growth in the disciplinary state, as the management of problem populations by professional social work has focused increasingly on the institution of the family. Squires (1990) refers to this development as the growth in 'anti-social policy'. This disciplinary practice has been concerned mainly with the issue of child welfare. My argument is that the issues surrounding the family's responsibility to provide informal care encouraged by the Government's welfare pluralist policies may increasingly force us to transfer our focus from what we regard as the typical clientele of the welfare state, the 'deviant' family, to the 'normal' family who may be grappling with the difficulties of the caring burden with resentment and anger. That anger may require to be managed and attenuated by new social work strategies (see Finch, 1990b).

The possibility of family therapy moving beyond its traditional domains in order for social workers to tackle 'family dysfunctions' in the wider community has increased with the importing of the American concept of case management into British social work planning. Whilst the main responsibility of case management will be that of *planning* care packages, the social worker's role in the field will inevitably be that of *constructing* care packages by encouraging family members and neighbours to care for each other, especially in those circumstances where the state will no longer guarantee to subsidise home help or provide care in residential settings. In fact, the change in orientation required by statutory social work to engage in this wider responsibility is not great.

Jordan (1987) argues that the primary task of the social worker is to ensure fairness in 'the final distribution of welfare' within the private sphere of the family. Negotiating with people in their natural settings about their failure to do the things that they should do for each other is what gives social workers their distinctive professional role. If such a notion is accepted by professional social workers, then the challenge of fighting sexism and unfairness in informal caring through mediation in the moral politics of the family is still to be faced, and will confront social workers more than ever now that the new framework of community care has been brought into being. As already alluded to, that challenge will bring social workers into contact with families not considered to be deviant. Social workers and case managers may face the choice of ignoring the structure and pattern of family relationships which may lead to a debilitating burden for some, mainly female, individuals, or supporting and reinforcing the conventional sexist solutions to informal care through case management, or, alternatively, of developing strategies to intervene in families to assist and support equity in the family. It is the last option and its implications that must be examined, given the possible future expansion of community care.

There seem to be two related policy issues that must be addressed. First, it is not always self-evident that informal care by relatives and neighbours is the best form of care that could be provided for elderly and mentally distressed people. My analysis has suggested that the empirical evidence about family structure and functioning indicates variation in the capacity and willingness of families to care for their members in periods of stress, irrespective of their geographic and financial abilities. Indeed Qureshi (1990) and Qureshi and Walker (1989) document many instances where a history of ill-feeling between mother and daughter, or a carer's feelings of resentment about caring responsibilities, meant that bad rather than good informal care was provided. Qureshi (1990), commenting on the innovative Kent Community Care Project, states that one in ten of those receiving family assistance with no home help said that they wanted a home help because the burden of practical caring placed upon their relatives was destructive of their emotional relationship with them. Some carers commented about feelings of loathing or dislike of an elderly parent. In the case of mental illness and handicap, the suitability of community care as a general policy strategy has been questioned by Goodwin (1990) and Hawks (1975) among others. Medical care and nursing knowledge offered in a warm but structured institutional environment may well be preferable to the hostile, prejudiced and uncaring realities of community care for mentally distressed people. The recent accent on community supervision orders is just a belated acknowledgement that neither community nor family can cope adequately with patients suffering severe psychotic conditions, especially if there is no reliable way to ensure the administration of medication (see Bean and Mounser, 1993, 1994). However, if there is a growing need for social care within the community at a time when the trajectory of public policy is leading inexorably away from state provision or state subsidised provision by the private or voluntary sector, then the task of case management may well be to engage more expansively in what amounts to a *family therapy* role for social workers in order to ensure a wider supply of informal carers.

Secondly, if the social worker's role in dealing with 'the final distribution of welfare' effectively involves a *family therapy* strategy, then the controversies about the expansion of social work control beyond dealing with problem populations become a reality. The 'dispersal of discipline' process described by Cohen (1985) and referred to in Chapter 1 may yet develop further than we have so far considered. The analysis of family structure and functioning which I have been discussing in this chapter gives an indication of what that *family therapy* might have to tackle, namely the securing of the co-operation and involvement of male as well as female family members, friends and neighbours in caring responsibilities despite poor, badly developed feelings and relations with the person needing care. A sketch of a *family therapy* approach can be suggested.

Broderick (1975), for example, sees a parallel between Kohlberg's (1964) conception of a universal hierarchy of modes of moral reasoning found in children and similar processes of development in what he calls 'the governance of families'. I have already indicated through my discussion of the work of Olson and McCubbin, Reiss, and

Kellerhals *et al.* that there are distinct differences to be observed
between family structures and their functioning and the fact that
families draw on diverse criteria for arriving at decisions. Indeed a
general class pattern is evident, with middle-class families being
more environment-sensitive in Reiss's terms, more balanced according to Olson and McCubbin, and, according Kellerhals *et al.*, more
likely to decide on issues of fairness in the family on the basis of
communication, and more ready to negotiate on the basis of principle rather than simply adhering to fixed, non-negotiable roles. Such
characteristics are, according to Broderick, a manifestation of the
highest level of moral reasoning. The two lower levels of moral
reasoning are based, first, on 'hedonistic zero-sum power confrontations' and, second, on 'conventionality and obedience to rules'.
Whilst zero-sum confrontations are likely to lead to a disregard for
the views and feelings of weaker family members, the recognition
and acceptance of negotiated rules may act as a check on arbitrary
power and are often the focus for family and marital therapists, and
could be the focus for social work intervention. The use of the contract in social work which is also aimed at bringing about rule-
bound negotiations between parties is now generally established in
social work practice in Britain (see Corden and Preston-Shoot, 1987).
The extension of that practice approach into dealings with non-deviant
families to bring about solutions to case management problems in
community care will evolve gradually as the practice of care management expands and, increasingly, has to be based on hard economic criteria. The phenomenon of middle-class and middle-aged
carers 'dumping' elderly people in casualty departments and daycare
centres and literally abandoning elderly relatives to the care of anyone other than the family is now a daily experience. Such behaviour, in the absence of a coherent social policy for an ageing society,
will perhaps require social workers to mediate and resolve family
caring difficulties directly rather than seeking beds or custodial care
in institutional settings which will become increasingly scarce.

One emerging issue confronting policy makers and social work
practitioners is that of violence against elderly people by their carers
(see Decalmer and Glendenning, 1993). This is a problem that is
likely to increase as the policy accent remains on community and
family care rather than on institutional solutions to care difficulties.
The pattern of violence against the elderly is different from that of
child abuse, or indeed that of domestic violence by males against

LACK OF
POWER
CAUSE

their female partners. Whilst the class distribution of child abuse is mixed, a disproportionate number of cases are being found in the lower sectors of the social structure (I will discuss this issue further in Chapter 7); elder abuse is less clearly structured by social class, although a lack of resources and power may exacerbate the causes of violence by carers against their elderly charges. The challenge of dealing with an extremely difficult and sensitive problem is growing at a time when more emphasis than ever is being placed on community care solutions for the frail elderly.

There are undoubtedly barriers to finding solutions for this problem. The very idea that a carer might be systematically and frequently subjecting an elderly charge to physical beatings and sexual abuse is one that appears to have been denied for many years. Whilst the issue of child abuse was being discussed and investigated in the 1960s, it was not until the 1980s that the phenomenon of 'granny battering' began to be aired in the academic and medical literature (see Cloke, 1983; Eastman, 1984). The widely accepted view of the family as a private sphere which should not be exposed to outside interference by practitioners of the welfare state has probably had a debilitating effect on professional practice. But as Penhale (1993) observes, the very factors which make the family a 'private affair' and the source of intimacy 'may also make it prone to conflict and ultimately, if the conflict is not resolved by negotiation and compromise, to violence' (p. 98). The intensity of involvement between relatives in a caring context may well exacerbate this problem. The responsibility of the social work agencies for dealing with this issue is becoming clear. It requires intervention into the moral politics of family life, perhaps in a more intrusive way than has traditionally been the custom of social work practitioners. That intervention will not be confined to the 'deviant families' well known to the social service and social work departments. Instead the clients of the welfare state will be, and are increasingly, drawn from the middle-class suburbs, indeed, from any section in the social structure where the resources to buy caring services are insufficient.

There are similarities between elder abuse and child abuse, although the legal, economic and emotional independence of adults also points to important distinctions (see Penhale, 1993). The particular points of similarity all indicate the importance of family structures for generating the conditions in which abuse is likely to occur. Abuse occurs in families which are socially isolated and lack financial and social resources; 'familial roles seem to be distorted and disturbed within both types of abusive families (families in which elder and child abuse occurs) and clarity of roles becomes less distinct or even obscured' (Penhale, 1993, 102). Research also points to the transmission of violent tendencies across generations. Whilst the expression of violent tendencies between the sexes may be different, with males perpetrating physical abuse, and females more likely to commit acts of neglect, the underlying conditions for the presence of violence and abuse in a caring context seem to be generated by the type of family structure which underpins the relationships.

The causes of elderly abuse are many and complicated. Zinn and Eitzen (1990) suggest that parents living with their adult children can cause special problems in those contexts where questions relating to their earlier relationships remain unresolved. The accumulated hostility towards and resentment of a parent can find expression in violence. A number of commentators and researchers have pointed to the danger of taking a narrow resource-based approach to this issue, of seeking to resolve the problem of abuse and violence against elderly people by their carers through the allocation of more money into the community care system in order that more care assistance may be provided. Often by focusing on the problem of care-giving the more deep-seated and problematic nature of the social relationships between carers and the cared for is overlooked (see Bookin and Dunkle, 1985; Homer and Gilleard, 1990). The central argument of this chapter is that an understanding of the way families are structured is the key to understanding this complex issue. Returning to Figure 4.1, we might expect a higher incidence of the mistreatment of elderly people in caring contexts where the carer and the cared for are from the extreme types of family structure, particularly from family types described by the top left quadrant and bottom left quadrant of the typology. The rigid cohesion of the family types, characterising a situation where family members, and particularly children, are rigidly or chaotically enmeshed, may possibly build up a sense of resentment and desire for escape which the imposition of a caring burden for adult children in later life undermines. A similar sense of resentment may well characterise individuals whose experience of family structure is represented by the extreme types in the top right and bottom right quadrants of Figure 4.1. A lack of social cohesion in family life described by these types may result in feelings of distance and lack of commitment to the family member requiring care. Violence and abuse may be more likely where bonds of affection are poorly developed or lacking altogether. Clearly these issues require empirical investigation. However, this work does suggest that case management is not just about the manipulation of material resources and the application of administrative adeptness, but is also concerned with the development of interpersonal and counselling skills to deal with problems which are, at best, ignored by the community care policies currently being implemented, and, at worst, exacerbated by a system of resource use which burdens women and families without thought for their capacity to cope.

Whether recognised as such or not, the National Health Service and Community Care Act 1990 ushered in a system which effectively constitutes family therapy as a social policy. By this I am suggesting that the use of what Pinker (1983) has called the 'normal skills of sociable living' within a framework of professional practice and authority defines the core activity of social work despite the rhetoric of the Griffith and Barclay Reports which cast social workers in the role of *social care planners*. In the context of the community care legislation this binds social workers and clients into a configuration of negotiated compromise about the distribution of scarce caring resources. A central strategy of this policy, and one recognised in both the White Paper *Caring for People* (1989) and the 1990 Act, is the involvement of clients and their carers in the decision-making processes surrounding their own case management; with respect to the typology of social work codes described in Chapter 2, carers and clients are to be involved in an *egalitarian correctional* approach. The rhetoric is very much that of consumerism, choice and rights to information and participation, but the objective is ultimately to secure a caring solution compatible with the economic and material resources at the command of the care managers. Social work skills will, in that context, be used to encourage people to do for themselves what the state is no longer prepared to be responsible for. This constitutes a broad conception of family therapy but one which has similar connotations to the more typical encounters within the clinical setting: it encourages self-reliance in place of dependency and more effective family functioning within the private sphere in place of reliance on public expenditure or public institutions.

Finally, Janet Finch (1989) draws attention to an important distinction between 'what we think' and 'what we do' in the context of family policy. She continues:

> Clearly it is important to distinguish between the effects of government policies upon people's lives in practice, and the extent to which such policies can and do shape the political, intellectual and moral climate in relation to beliefs and values about welfare. (Finch, 1989, 162)

Governments can constrain people seeking public assistance for their caring problems by financial cutbacks and tax disincentives. Indeed the current policy approach is forcing people back on to their private resources to meet family obligations. However, this is not the same as converting people to the view that the state has a minimal responsibility to help with welfare. The historical precedent for the current situation to which Finch draws our attention was the tactic employed by the nineteenth century Board of Guardians of exerting pressure on families to look after their own elderly in order to avoid resorting to Poor Law help; the result was the abandonment of their elderly relatives by the young prospective carers within the family. Similar examples can be found in other countries, for example, the principle of *right of recovery* which remained on the statute books in the Netherlands well into the twentieth century (see Cox, 1990). There too, families distanced themselves from their dependents to avoid obligation. Attending to the problem of families' reluctance to shoulder welfare responsibilities seems, inevitably, to be a central task of the social worker's role in the future if the community care policy now being developed remains unmodified.

5

Social policy and family life

The emergence of a discourse on poverty, emanating mainly but not exclusively from right-wing government circles, has distinguished single mothers and the principle of universalism in social policy as particularly serious problems threatening the post-war conception of the welfare state. The financial costs of both have served to draw attention to, and possibly to scapegoat, unconventional patterns of family life, transforming them into *a major social policy problem*. There appear to be two distinct areas of social policy debate which serve to underline family relationships as *the problem* in the welfare state. First, there is a debate which is less concerned with matters of principle and more to do with the *interpretation of the quantitative facts* of welfare state development. Having experienced a long period of consensus about welfare expenditure and priorities since 1945, it now appears that there is a growing international acceptance that the new agenda for all welfare states in the twenty-first century will centre on the issue of how to limit state obligations at a time when the population is ageing and the productive population available to pay for welfare through taxation is contracting. Second, there has arisen a *conceptual debate*, clothed much more in the vocabulary of principle and morality, about the proper division of responsibility between the state and the family in the provision of welfare, with the shift in government policy since the 1980s to an explicitly welfare pluralist approach to the delivery of services. A greater burden has been placed on the family, and especially women, as part of a wider and long-term strategy of cutting back state responsibility for welfare provision in a host of areas including pension provision as well as the more commonly understood areas of community care of the elderly and the physically and mentally handicapped. At the centre of these concerns is the construction of a discourse on poverty which is fixated with the problem of 'welfare dependency'. The elderly and single parents seem to be two categories of people causing particular anxiety to those who wish to renegotiate the state's commitments in the area of welfare. I will examine these two issues separately.

The public expenditure issue in Britain

The British Government's expenditure plans for social security to 1996 indicate an increasing financial burden which is considered to be unacceptably high. Social security is set to rise from £74.2 billion in 1992/93 to £79.8 billion in 1993/94. The projected figures for 1995 and 1996 are respectively £83 billion and £87 billion (Social Security Department, 1993). Following the November budget in 1993 the Chancellor announced that the figure is set to rise to £92.4 billion by 1997. In addition the statistical projections indicate that increasing numbers of people will be claiming benefits. The numbers claiming child benefit, for example, increased by 170,000 in 1992 and now 12,291,000 people claim a universal benefit which has been subject to a public debate which questions whether the principle of universalism in welfare benefits can be allowed any longer (Commons Social Security Committee, 1992). Similar debates are taking place about the elderly in modern society. The generational contract whereby the younger and productively active generation pays for the pension benefits of the elderly in society seems to be subject to critical review for the first time since the universal old age pension was established by the National Insurance Act of 1946. Just over half of all social security expenditure in 1990/91 went to people aged 60 and over; the figure was £28.5 billion. The current issue relating to pensions is whether universalism can be tolerated, given the large amounts of public expenditure committed to paying out for a benefit which is not financed by an accumulating fund but drawn directly from the state's resources. Demographic trends point to an ageing population: between 1991 and 2001 the 75+ age group will grow from 44 per cent of the elderly population (65+) to 48 per cent. The 85+ age group will, in the same period, rise to constitute 13 per cent of the elderly population (Family Policy Studies Centre, 1991, p. 2). It is this group which draws heavily on social care and health care services. The best projections for the future indicate that in the UK by the year 2027 all those aged over 65 years will amount to 19.2 per cent of the population or nearly 12 million people (Family Policy Studies Centre, 1991). Over 10 per cent of the population at that time will be in the 75+ age group who draw most heavily of all on the health and social care budget. The Policy Studies Institute (1991) observes that by the year 2000 it will cost the NHS an additional £400 million per year, with larger sums being required as the first decades of the new century progress. To put these figures into perspective, it should again be emphasised that over half of the social security budget goes to people aged 60 and over, a figure in excess of £30 billion by the end of 1992 and set to rise inexorably as the 1990s proceed.

The considered solution to these perceived problems of an ageing society is for families to do more for their own elderly members and the state less. The principle of universalism may well be modified in the not too distant future: governments may well intensify their encouragement to people to make private provision for their pensions through a host of fiscal and ideological devices, whilst at the same time reinforcing these incentives with a policy of targeting pensions at the most disadvantaged elderly. Taxation mechanisms could be established to claw back state pension money from those mainly middle-class elderly with moderate savings and moderate occupational pensions who are deemed not to need a state pension. Indeed there are already signs that these policy developments are being legitimised within the Organisation for Economic Cooperation and Development (OECD): the Conservative Government in New Zealand in the early 1990s has acquired the dubious status of being the first government in modern times to oversee the creation of what has been described as the first 'post-welfare society'. Welfare benefits have been cut to the bare minimum; old age pensions are taxed and *all* the resources of an aged person are confiscated by the state to pay for social care. Prime Minister Jim Bolger revealed his attitude unequivocally when he questioned the logic of allowing people to bequeath capital resources to their heirs whilst their neighbours pay for their current welfare needs through higher taxation (BBC 'Newsnight', 20 October 1994). Other countries within the affluent OECD are now actively examining these policy concepts. The exploration of these policy ideas in the United Kingdom was revealed in November 1993 when the *Observer* published details of a leaked Government communiqué between the Department of Social Security (DSS) and the Treasury which indicated that seven committees had been established to examine a range of ways in which the social security budget might be 'restructured'. The remit for one of those committees was 'to examine the scope for extending opting out of contributory benefits, and the greater use of private provision for contingencies, including unemployment, sickness, invalidity and, in particular, *retirement* [my emphasis]' (*Observer*, 21 November 1993). The same communiqué made it clear that universalism in social benefits remains a major anxiety for governments. The Child Benefit review committee within the DSS set itself the target of reducing the £5.8 billion child benefit budget by exploring ways of taking the benefit away from middle-class families on higher incomes. What income threshold will be considered by future governments to be liable for taxation remains unclear, but the principle of universalism in the area of family policy is now under radical financial attack.

The increasing cost to the taxpayer of an expanding social security budget has also accentuated an issue regarding the balance of obligation for family maintenance between the state and errant or absent fathers. Whilst 86 per cent of two-parent families derive their main source of income from earnings, 67 per cent of one-parent families rely on the social security system for their main source of income. Only about 4 per cent received regular income from maintenance payments before the introduction of the Child Support Act. About £219 million was paid out in one-parent benefit to around about 700,000 lone parents in 1991. Something in the region of £9.2 billion or 18 per cent of the total social security budget is paid out to families; around £5 billion of that is paid to single-parent families. Lone mothers have an extremely low level of employment when compared with women in a similar position in Europe (see Lewis, 1992). In Sweden, for example, 87 per cent of lone mothers are in the labour force and when not working full-time hold jobs which provide the legal entitlement to work three-quarters of the normal day (with all the occupational benefits accruing to full-time employees) while their children are small. In France 95 per cent of 3–5 year olds have places in publicly funded childcare facilities. Consequently ten times as many French women work through their childbearing years as their British counterparts. The United Kingdom is the only country in Europe where lone mothers have a lower employment rate than mothers in two-parent families (see Lewis,

1992). However, the current debate in the United Kingdom is not focused on finding mechanisms to assist entry to the labour market for lone parents, such as better childcare facilities, but rather about the need to find savings in the social security budget. There appear to be two strategies aimed at securing this goal. First there is a *moral campaign* initially organised around the theme of 'back to basics' but now more generally referred to as 'pro family' and against the notion of 'welfare dependency'. It evokes an image of a past society characterised by stable monogamous marriages, and is intended to encourage a radical transformation in the sexual behaviour of young unmarried men and women. The specific focus of this approach is to offer a strong condemnation of men who fail to fulfil their parental obligations. I will say more about this below. The second tactic is to pursue an *administrative campaign* through the Child Support Agency (CSA), created within the Department of Social Security, to reduce the social security costs of child maintenance by forcing absent fathers to contribute substantial resources towards the upkeep of their children. The CSA has attracted criticism for ordering its priorities in an attempt to achieve a £530 million benefits-saving target for its first year of operation in 1993/94 (in fact the Annual Report of the CSA revealed that it had saved the Treasury only £418 million and instead of over 60 per cent of maintenance claims being converted into arranged payments the proportion was only 31.5). The relish with which the new Agency set about increasing maintenance payments previously set by the courts led to controversy and the organisation of resistance in the form of the Network Against the Child Support Act. Faced with the difficulties in tracking down absent fathers who had never contributed towards the upkeep of their offspring, the CSA inevitably compensated for the financial shortfall by overburdening those partners who were known and had been paying regular amounts, albeit often very insufficient sums. The decision at the end of 1994 to suspend dealing with thousands of outstanding cases was a signal that the original strategy of the CSA would be radically amended. The decision in early 1995 to introduce an appeals procedure which would allow fathers to contest CSA orders, and have previously agreed 'clean break' settlements taken into account, highlighted the weakness of seeking a purely administrative solution to the issue of single parenthood and pointed towards the significance of waging an ideological and 'moral' campaign to underpin social policies. It could be said that the failure of the CSA to impose financial and moral order on the complications of family breakdown has resulted in policy confusion in Britain in the mid-1990s. This confusion has manifested itself in the increasingly polarised debate about social policy and family life.

Family policy or moral regulation?

The changing composition of the poor throughout the European Community indicates a decline in the proportion of people who are poor and on social assistance because of old age or large families, and an increase in the proportions who are in poverty through unemployment, low pay and, of course, single parenthood and marriage breakdown. The shifting pattern of poverty from old households to young households is a further expression of these more general movements in the patterns of poverty. Young households are forming in increasing numbers around a young single woman. More generally the breakdown of marriage is contributing to the phenomenon of the 'feminisation of poverty' and is directing policy debate towards what is called 'new poverty' (see Room, Lawson and Laczko, 1989). What is becoming clearer is that growing numbers of political parties throughout Europe as well as in the United Kingdom are taking the view that the family's functional importance in the welfare equation of the future is such that the declining trend in 'conventional' family formation and structure (interpreted as family living arrangements based on a male breadwinner model) is a problem requiring an urgent solution. It is a problem because of the increasing cost of divorce and welfare maintenance for fatherless children, certainly, but also because welfare strategies geared to alleviating child poverty (partly related to the increase in one-parent households) and developing community care require ordered patterns of family life in order to stimulate greater financial responsibility on the part of families and facilitate case management. I have already hinted at this issue in the previous chapter. It is in the area of single parenthood, which has become a particular public issue in the 1990s, that the family has become the centre of a broader debate about social and moral behaviour. The model of the single-female-headed family does not fit well with the policy profile of an autonomous and active familial unit which can be relied upon to be the foundation of community care policies in the coming years. It is the fear of a possible trend towards unconventional family forms which disturbs social policy planners. Indeed one of the pressing problems of modern welfare systems is how to provide for the welfare interests of children from single-parent households without simultaneously undermining the conventional two-parent family model desired by many social policy planners in government. Patricia Morgan (1995) addresses precisely this dilemma and points up the perverse incentives which have become established in many European welfare systems whereby lone parents are actually financially better off than low-paid married fathers. She cites the example of the Child Care Allowance introduced in Britain in October 1994 whereby a lone parent with two small children can work for 20 hours at £4.00 per hour and end up with a net income of £163.99 after deductions for rent and tax. A married father of two small children working for 40 hours at the same hourly rate would take home £130.95.

The demographic trends have been indicating significant social change in family life. The General Household Survey for 1991, for example, reports a decrease in the proportion of households matching what is commonly regarded as the 'traditional' family structure of a couple with dependent children: the proportion of families meeting this norm was 31 per cent of households in 1979 but declined to 25 per cent in 1991. The proportion of families headed by a lone parent increased from 8 per cent in 1971 to 19 per cent in 1991. The fact that the United Kingdom has one of the highest rates of lone parenthood in Europe has added to the local debate if not the international assessment of the issue. A figure of 1.5 million one-parent families in the United Kingdom by the year 2005 has been estimated, compared with a figure of 570,000 in 1971 (Family Policy Studies Centre, Factsheet 3). Between 1976 and 1986 the percentage changes in the numbers of one-parent families indicate that there was a 78 per cent increase in numbers due to divorce, and I have touched on some of the issues surrounding this particular area in Chapter 3, but there was also a 77 per cent increase in the numbers of never married. It is this group in particular which has become the centre of the current debate about 'the underclass family'. Nearly a third of all lone-parent families were headed by a never-married mother: there were around 360,000 never-married mothers out of approximately 1.2 million single-parent families in 1989 and they are growing at a rate of approximately 17 per cent per year (see Burghes, 1993).

Whilst some social commentators have been interested above all else in highlighting the appalling poverty and social deprivation which afflicts family life, not only in the third world but also in the affluent western nations making up the OECD, and have argued that all governments should develop integrated social policies aimed at alleviating family poverty (see Hewlett, 1993), many political analyses of family life in the 1990s, especially those by writers publishing under the banner of the Institute of Economic Affairs (IEA) (see Murray, 1990, 1994; Dennis, 1993; Dennis and Erdos, 1992; Davies, Berger and Carlson, 1993), emphasise the 'moral' malaise underlying changes in family structure and call for a greater recognition of individual rather than state responsibility for maintaining the institution of 'the family', despite the absence of effective government policy. The continuing interest in the idea that there exists a set of fundamental moral precepts which should guide both policy and practice in all matters relating to family life is evident from the Government's occasional infatuation with the theme of 'back to basics', a theme which encapsulates the notion that family obligations and responsibilities are the basis for sound policies in a whole range of areas including childcare, community care and social security. It is evident that, in the midst of an increasing volume of written commentary on family life, there are two discourses emerging: one emanating from the political left, and underwritten in the EC by the Social Chapter of the 1991 Maastricht Agreement, expresses an interest in the development of an integrated package of social policy measures aimed towards supporting the responsibilities of family life such as childcare, care of the elderly and the physically and mentally disabled, the other from the right focuses public attention on matters of individual morality and family structure because they are believed to be foundational for a less welfare-dependent and more market-oriented society. The political right, at least in Britain, have clothed their rejection of welfare state development in terms of their hostility to Europe and the Maastricht Treaty which seeks to impose economic and monetary union and the adoption of social policy commitments on the member states of the Union (see Burkitt and Baimbridge, 1995). Given this broader European context, the distinction between *family policy* and *moral regulation* may well represent competing welfare strategies within the EC for dealing with family and childcare issues as we approach the twenty-first century: the former appears to be anchored firmly in an approach to social welfare which emphasises continuing state intervention to effect the conditions of existence of family life; the latter is concerned pre-eminently with encouraging conventional family relationships based on a two-parent model in order to better facilitate increased family and market provision of social care. The concept of *family policy* as it has developed elsewhere in Europe, most notably in those countries influenced by Catholicism and Christian Democracy, has certainly retained an element of social regulation through the assumption of the woman's homemaking role, but more generously it can be interpreted as seeking to empower people by augmenting the resources available for family living and facilitating higher levels of participation in social and economic life for those members of society, mainly women, burdened by the obligations of caring and childrearing. The idea of *moral regulation* has its roots in American anti-welfare discourse and in this context relates to a society-wide project aimed towards establishing a broad acceptance that less state welfare requires more family, and possibly community, responsibility for social care, and that this goal will dictate that more conventional sex codes and lifestyles should be adopted by those who might make claims upon the state. It is quite clearly a social strategy less concerned with empowerment and more preoccupied with what Foucault might have called the 'disciplining of social bodies'.

The anxiety about single-female-headed families has been couched very much in behavioural terms. The summer of 1993 saw a particularly active campaign by the Conservative Government to set out the parameters of their policy concerns. Welsh Secretary John Redwood and Social Security Secretary Peter Lilley both gave speeches deploring the increase in numbers of teenage single mothers and the increasing phenomenon of families without fatherhood. The nature of those speeches seemed to obscure the real interest in cutting back state responsibilities in social policy by clothing the rhetoric in the principles of 'morality' and 'family values'. The underlying model of 'the family' at the heart of British social policy has been well established, particularly since Beveridge, and it has served as an instrument of social control since the 1940s. Government rhetoric, therefore, does not represent a significant departure from an established and institutionalised policy position. It merely reformulates the rhetoric in a slightly modified ideological framework in keeping with popular policy perceptions that the welfare state is indeed in need of a radical fiscal overhaul. Van Every (1992) argues, for example, that the model of the family in British social policy is one which has four elements: it is heterosexual, built around a married couple, with their own genetic children, conceived naturally without the use of reproductive technologies. The model serves as a powerful force shaping popular conceptions of what constitutes a 'proper' family, but more importantly, it serves as a yardstick by which deviations can be measured both by policy makers and at the level of common sense. Deviations from this model often appear to be difficult to accommodate within the strictures surrounding social service provision. Housing policy is geared towards the housing of families more or less meeting the model; a single mother with too many children of the wrong ages and sexes can cause problems. Single mothers who wish to express their sexuality within a gay relationship similarly cause anxiety amongst the social services. The traditional allocation of responsibilities and expected pattern of relationships is reinforced by the social services. It is assumed that men will support their wives and children financially, that women will be responsible for emotional support, that the children will be regarded as the property of the parents and the man will be actively powerful while the woman remains generally passive.

In dealing with these issues there has arisen a confusion between what I will call the 'supporting of families' and the 'policing of families'. This distinction, as with that between *family policy* and *moral regulation*, is used for analytical emphasis here. In practice many aspects of what might be called *family policy* contain a correctional as well as an emancipatory stress: policies on contraception and abortion or access to family centres may appear to be part of a family policy strategy aimed at tackling gender and poverty issues but can easily be preoccupied with the monitoring of families and women considered to be 'dangerous' by social workers (see Cannan, 1992). The underlying assumption of my argument is that in Britain in the 1990s social and public policy relating to family life has been increasingly preoccupied with issues of *moral regulation* and what Donzelot (1980) would call the 'policing of families' and less concerned with *family policies* which 'support family life'. This conceptual distinction can be illustrated by examining British 'family' policy in the wider context of Europe.

The concept of family policy: comparing Britain with other countries

It is apparent that countries vary with respect to their policy commitment to family life. Whilst most affluent countries within the OECD have developed a range of social policies geared towards supporting children and family life to some extent, countries have differed with respect to the degree of their explicit commitment to the concept of 'family policy'. Hantrais (1994a) has argued that France, for instance, has a more explicit family policy than Britain. This policy is manifest in a more comprehensive provision of public childcare facilities combined with a social security system which prioritises horizontal distribution from the unmarried and childless to the married (or cohabiting) with children (see Lewis, 1992; Lenoir, 1991). Scheiwe's (1994) enquiry into mothers' poverty through a comparative analysis of labour markets, welfare provision and family institutions in Belgium, Germany and Britain again underlines a very weak commitment in Britain to what might be regarded as the building blocks of good family policy: strong institutional support for mothers' labour market chances, socialised childcare facilities, cash benefits subsidising the costs of rearing children and, importantly, a welfare rather than punitive response to the breakdown of marriage. Scheiwe argues that the institutional arrangements in different societal spheres such as employment, social security and family and marital law structure the choices that can be made by women about family, marriage and employment matters. The pattern of arrangements throughout the EC is complicated, and Scheiwe rightly cautions against assuming uniformity across a country's institutional spheres. Nevertheless, when compared with the leading position of Belgium, France and Denmark with respect to child allowances, public childcare services and parental leave, Britain appears to be a welfare laggard. Childcare in Britain is privatised: 'labour market institutions grant employed mothers/ parents hardly any general rights that enhance compatibility of childcare and employment' (p. 210). Women are forced into part-time work, so losing earning capacity and occupational benefits. Child allowances and maternity benefits have been eroded and, of course, the Child Support Act 1991 was introduced to substitute private transfers for public transfers, rather than augment family income for impoverished lone-parent families. The Act has a clear disciplinary intention behind it aimed at absent fathers and single mothers.

Following Finch and Groves (1980), I am assuming that for the notion of 'family' we can substitute the term 'woman' because of the pivotal role assigned historically to women within western family forms. So an analysis of women's, or mothers', access to childcare services, employment chances or risk of experiencing poverty, will be illuminating for the more general task of assessing the extensiveness of the family policy component of a welfare system. The European Commission Childcare Network (1990) has assembled data relating to a range of policy areas including parental employment, employment rights and public and privately funded childcare services throughout the European Community (EC). Accepting that caution must be taken when comparing statistics compiled in different ways and relating to factors that may not be comparable, general trends in childcare provision and family policy emerge. Regarding places in publicly funded services as a proportion of all children in the age group (a good index of government commitment to assisting lone-parent employment), differences between countries within the EC were evident. In particular, Britain compares unfavourably in the provision of publicly funded pre-school care and education (see Table 5.1).

TABLE 5.1   *Places in Publicly Funded Childcare Services as per cent of All Children in the Age Group*

Country	Year of data	Under 3	3 – compulsory school
France	1988	20	95+ (school begins 6 yrs)
Belgium	1988	20	95+ (school begins 6 yrs)
Italy	1986	5	85+ (school begins 6 yrs)
Germany	1987	3	65–70 (school begins 7 yrs)
Denmark	1989	48	85 (school begins 7 yrs)
Spain	1988	–	65–70 (school begins 6 yrs)
Britain	1988	2	35–40 (school begins 5 yrs)

Source: Adapted from European Commission Childcare Network, *Childcare in the European Community, 1985–1990*, Women of Europe Supplement no. 31 (Brussels, 1990), p. 10.

With respect to maternity leave, the Childcare Network report shows that Britain has a good profile when compared with other countries in the EC, allowing the longest period of absence from work (11 weeks before the birth and 29 weeks postnatally). Many countries, including Germany, France, Belgium and the Netherlands, only allow

between 14 and 16 weeks in total. However, Britain's policy lead
was somewhat compromised by the fact that Britain used to be the
only country in the EC which applied a 'length of service' condition to maternity leave (employment with the same employer for 2
years full-time or 5 years part-time). Since October 1994 this no
longer applies. Parental leave points up the limits of policy commitment to family support in that it entails granting leave to mothers
to care for a sick child or relative, and, in some cases, to fathers
who wish to assist with the care of a newborn baby. Whilst Britain
has no entitlement to parental leave, and has refused to comply with
the EC Directive on this matter because of the decision by the Conservative Government to opt out of the Social Chapter, seven countries in the EC offer parental leave of some kind. In France parental
leave from work can be taken by either men or women until a child
is 3 and can extend up to a period of 3 years, although payment is
restricted to parents with three or more children. In practice leave
is often shared between parents who both continue to work part-
time. Other countries allow periods of leave varying between 10
weeks at 90 per cent of earnings in Denmark (where parental leave
is a statutory right) and 24 months of unpaid leave in Portugal.
Many countries operate a payment formula: Germany allows 18
months' leave but pays a low flat-rate payment for only 6 months,
and Italy makes payments at 30 per cent of earnings for 6 months.
An interesting, and often neglected, issue relating to family welfare
is identified by Scheiwe (1994) in her discussion of Belgium, where
individual rights to welfare support attaching to children have been
institutionalised. Whilst Britain is not alone among OECD countries in not having such a right, the presence of such entitlements
elsewhere in Europe indicates a strong commitment to a concept of
family policy which is glaringly absent in Britain. The personal claims
of children to public and private transfers makes them less dependent on the economic and family status of their parents.

   The varying pattern of provision of family support within the OECD
countries requires an explanation. Lewis (1992) provides some insight in her analysis of gender in the development of welfare regimes. Comparing Britain, France, Ireland and Sweden with respect
to their varying commitment to a male-breadwinner model of welfare, Lewis also indirectly points up variations in the degree of
commitment to a concept of family policy in these countries. My
assumption is that the greater the reliance of a welfare system on

women fulfilling a conventional homemaking role, where the male is treated as the main breadwinner and women work, at best, only part-time, the less developed its concept of family policy will be. Britain and Ireland have historically developed strong male-breadwinner models of welfare, remaining the only countries in the EC which do not allow parental and paternal leave from work, so encouraging conventional domestic arrangements. Beveridge's vision of the British welfare state assumed that women would be dependent upon their husbands to maintain them (see Wicks, 1987; Roll, 1991; Colwill, 1994), but long before Beveridge the foundations of a male-breadwinner model of welfare were being established. Lewis (1992) points to the marriage bar that operated in the professions during the inter-war years, combined with the public education efforts to school working-class wives and mothers in household management and infant welfare. Similarly in Ireland a marriage bar operated in the civil service to prevent women from working. It only ceased to operate in 1977. Ireland has the lowest level of childcare services in Europe and until 1984, when EC policy pressurised reform, women received lower rates of benefit, shorter length of payment of benefit and were ineligible for unemployment benefit. By contrast in Sweden, which effectively has a dual-breadwinner model of welfare with exceptionally high female labour-market participation, and in France, which has what Lewis calls a 'modified male-breadwinner' model of welfare which supports family life by the provision of generous family benefits and good publicly funded childcare services, the traditional gender roles for women are de-emphasised. Historically women's labour-market position has been strong in both France and Sweden when compared with many other OECD countries, and the assumption of policy planners in Sweden is that women will work full-time and so require a full range of welfare supports to facilitate this. The return of a Social Democratic Government in Sweden in September 1994 after three years of a right-wing coalition seems likely to consolidate the advances in women's welfare. Indeed the rejection of Carl Bildt's Conservative Coalition Government appears to be founded on a desire in the country to halt the welfare erosion initiated in 1991. The swing to the left in the 1994 election was in fact the biggest since the Second World War.

Whether a country embraces the concept of *family policy* as a tool of intervention to shape the material circumstances of family life or instead seeks to influence behaviour by moral persuasion and the statutory powers of the social worker is fundamentally a political and ideological choice. This observation is underlined by Irene Wennemo's comparative study of family benefits and tax reductions for families in 18 OECD countries (Wennemo, 1992). The analysis is located in the wider debate about what determines welfare state growth and policy commitments. The terms of that debate have been established, on the one hand, by those who would seek to explain social policy development in terms of *structural* variables such as demography, the logic of industrialism and the level of economic development and, on the other, by those who counter that 'politics matter' (see Pierson, 1991; Castles and McKinlay, 1979; Uusitalo, 1984; Pampel and Williamson, 1988; Kangas, 1991). Wennemo's conclusions point towards support for the 'politics matter' school. The explanation for this lies in the way that the state's welfare obligations are structured. The division of the component parts of a welfare system into its structural and variable features is widely acknowledged: the former are subject to little political adjustment because of historically well-established principles of entitlement and imperative social obligations which must be met by the state, such as pensions, sickness benefit, unemployment benefit and chronic poverty, and the latter are those parts of a system subject to incremental adjustment through political pressure. What first establishes rights to welfare is in itself a large and complex issue. Lockhart (1984) argues that the crucial timing of the introduction of key policy measures is determined by 'pre-eminent political elites', and that the incremental enhancements to those initial welfare entitlements are determined by a combination of political mobilisation and the decision-making of what he calls 'lesser elites'. Other theories emphasise the 'political business cycle' where policy developments are closely related to impending elections or other major political events (see Griffin, Devine and Wallace, 1983). Lenoir (1991) draws attention to the social and political struggles rooted in Catholic philanthropy and technocratic demography which gave birth to a strong tradition of family policy in France. I am suggesting, therefore, that the area of *family policy* falls into that category of welfare effort influenced by political choice which in turn determines whether a minimalist or maximalist commitment is underwritten by the state. So Wennemo has been able to show that there is a positive correlation between left-wing political party strength in a country and high levels of cash benefit for families and children; *structural* variables such as gross domestic product, 'level of industrialism', 'modern-isation', or indeed demographic data relating to fertility rates have been shown to have only an indirect link to the development of family policies. Britain's historically weak commitment to *family policy* has been reinforced by Conservative social policies and ac-centuated in the 1990s by an overt combination of moral censure against lone parenthood and financial stringency in the field of welfare. *Family policy* appears to be driven less by the necessity of meeting human need and more by an ideological compulsion to cut public expenditure, exemplified by among other things the public expenditure *savings* target of £530 million set for the inappropriately named Child Support Agency in 1993/94. Hantrais is therefore able to ar-gue with conviction that in comparison with France with its familialist orientation and explicit set of policies aimed at affecting demographic trends and family life, Britain 'lacks an explicit family policy' to the extent that 'the family is not given "official" recognition' (p. 155).

The political dilemma confronting British policy makers within the EC in the 1990s is that the distinctive movement towards a 'mixed economy of welfare' in the form of community care requires a more fully formed view of the place of family life in the organ-isation and delivery of social care. Countries like Holland, France, Belgium and Denmark already possess a clear conception of the state's responsibilities for family well-being, mainly because of the influence of Christian Democracy in many of these countries (see Van Kersbergen and Becker, 1988) and, of course, their broad ac-ceptance of the Social Chapter which the Maastricht Agreement established. In the absence of a social policy tradition of collective obligation towards the economic support of families, the British Government have been resorting to a strategy of social censure against those whose patterns of family living would appear to impose a charge on the public purse and disrupt social care planning. By focus-ing obsessively on matters of *family structure* (whether the family form is single parent, intact or reordered following divorce) rather than on the *quality of family relationships* the real agenda is re-vealed: family care provision in a welfare pluralist society is best supplied by first-married and never-divorced nuclear family forms. The policy clearly juxtaposes family and state as alternative sources of social service provision in the mixed economy of welfare. Whether one thinks of the crucial role given to social workers and care man-agers by the Community Care Act to construct packages of care using family and friends rather than local authority resources, or the frequent public pronouncements about the sanctity of marriage and the two-parent family by Government Ministers as part of their 'pro-family' theme, the pivotal role of 'family' in the social care equation has been clearly marked out. The terrain chosen by the Conservative Government to wage what was effectively a nineteenth-century 'moral purity campaign' was that of social and sexual behaviour, with little public acceptance of a collective obligation by the state and society to 'support families' through an integrated *family policy*. As the 1990s progress and the usefulness of that strategy is questioned, the imperative will be to harness the moral constructions surrounding the family debate more closely to the administrative task of reducing welfare expenditure. With such a clear practical as well as public cost-cutting role assigned to 'family living' and 'family relationships', acceptance of, rather than deviance from, the nuclear family structure is now being demanded by a wide range of policy makers and opinion formers. Family structure has become the main issue for social policy debate: it is the apparent breakdown of the two-parent nuclear family either by divorce, illegitimacy and/or promiscuous male irresponsibility that is said to lead to a range of social problems, of which the formation of 'an underclass' appears to be the most convenient and most alarmist shorthand way of conceptualising the parameters of public debate. It is too much welfare assistance that is said to cause family problems and provide perverse incentives for people to abandon their family obligations. Given this diagnosis of the problems confronting family life it would seem that *moral regulation* rather than *family policy* is logically called for.

The point to be underlined here is that the model of a nuclear and patriarchal family structure, enshrined in the benefit system and the principles of social policy formation, acts as a powerful ideological reminder of what should constitute order and deviance in family life. However, it might be argued that any perspective on the contemporary strains of family life which does not pay attention to the conditions of its existence, that is the economic and social well-being of all family forms, but instead accentuates the benefits of traditional nuclear family structure as somehow being uniquely beneficial to people's well-being, is flawed. It is precisely this issue which lies at the heart of the debate about 'the underclass family'. This issue will be the subject of the following chapter.

6
Models of the 'underclass family'

The focus of this chapter is the social analysis of the phenomenon called the 'underclass family' which, in the context of this discussion, means family forms and patterns of family life which are perceived to be highly deviant, particularly by the opinion formers in politics and the social services. Associated with the use of the label of 'deviant' for patterns of family life which are not built around marriage, there has been the expression of social anxiety, mainly through popular journalism, that the very institution of 'the family' is under threat in some communities and that the socialisation role of the family is failing, especially among some sectors of the welfare-dependent poor.

From the midst of contemporary public debate competing models of the 'underclass family' have emerged, reflecting the competing political and social analyses of what constitute problematic patterns of family life. These models I will identify as the *structured underclass family*, *the fatherless underclass family* and *the criminal underclass family*. They are imprecise labels but serve the purpose of pointing up the key features of explanatory emphasis in different theories of 'underclass' formation. The first approach stresses the impact of economic restructuring on patterns of family life, the second stresses the absence of fathers and the growing phenomenon of female-headed single-parent families, and the third points to the historically well-established connection between family relationships and delinquency. Each model implies different social policy responses to marginalisation.

The supervision of families considered to be anti-social has been a characteristic of most welfare systems. In nineteenth-century England the work of the Charity Organisation Society ushered in the concept of the caseworker, normally a middle-class lady, whose responsibility it was to monitor and assess the behaviour of the deserving poor within a given urban space designated by the Charities as worthy of help. An essential aspect of this type of surveillance was the creation of classificatory criteria whereby models or types of family could be constructed to aid social diagnoses and intervention (see Stedman Jones, 1971; Dean, 1991). Van Wel (1992) provides an extremely interesting and graphic account of how this process was applied in Holland. Family policies in Holland in the twentieth century have been based around the idea of socially segregating problem or anti-social families. The Dutch approach was to place problem families in what was called a *residential living school*. The allocation of families to spatially as well as socially remote living areas was aimed at resocialising families into what would be considered acceptable patterns of behaviour regarding such things as the proper maintenance of their property and the prompt payment of rent, as well as the display of a range of other behavioural characteristics deemed socially acceptable. In selecting and assessing families for this type of treatment, social work agents constructed what Van Wel calls a *problem figuration* which consisted fundamentally in the professional and social fabrication of models of family life considered problematic by the policy makers and therefore in need of intervention; the intervention goals and the type of social work solutions adopted to deal with problem families were inextricably bound up with the type of label used to define discrete types of family. The models of problem families represented both rational and fictional caricatures which reflected the professional prejudices of the time: models variously labelled the inadmissible family, the socially ill family, the maladjusted family, the deprived family and the symbiotic family were constructed, mirroring the changes in social work thinking over time from ideas rooted in eugenics to more contemporary perspectives anchored in systems theory.

The current anxiety about problem family structures is therefore not new. Mayo (1994, 170) describes similar strategies in Britain, especially in hard-to-let council estates like Ferguslie Park in Paisley. Ideas similar to those described by Van Wel were common in the inter-war years when opinions influenced by eugenics vied with social concepts from the emerging professional discourses of social work (see MacNicol, 1987; Oakley, 1991). And it is possible to construct distinct models of the 'underclass family' from *problem figurations* in the 1990s.

The structured underclass family

Social and political analyses which emphasise the creation of marginal or underclass status as the end product of social, economic and historical processes tend also to deny human culpability in bringing about marginalisation. There are a number of distinct themes within this broad approach. The *structured underclass family* emerges as the product of changing economic conditions leading to unemployment and welfare dependency, but the pattern of family life may well remain 'conventional'; there is not a necessary link between 'unconventional' patterns of living and 'underclass status'. The causal relationship is, therefore, one where the wider structural forces in economy and society shape behaviour.

Buck (1992) concentrates his analysis of underclass formation on the unit of the household; he maintains that family units which have no stable relationship with legitimate employment, either historically or prospectively, form the nucleus of the underclass. Using this framework, groups such as pensioners would be excluded because they have had an historic relationship with employment even if their condition is one of poverty in the period of retirement, and students would also be excluded by this classification because in their case an assumption of prospective employment can be made. By focusing on the household, rather than the more problematic concept of family, Buck highlights the economic forces which work towards marginalisation of household units. The long-term unemployed, including many single-parent households, would be included within this definition of the 'underclass', not because of behavioural traits, but rather because of wider labour-market processes. Pahl (1984 and 1988) provides more insight into how the household unit itself can become subject to systematic exclusion from not only the formal but also the informal economy. His analysis of the Isle of Sheppey observed that those households which experienced the long-term unemployment of their main breadwinners were also less likely to be involved in informal economic activity (casual work in return for goods or money to augment household income). Households with one or more full-time workers tended also to be the households most actively engaged in informal economic activity because they had the resources to buy the basic materials needed to engage in informal work, such as painting and decorating materials or building materials, and they also had more contacts than those who were more socially isolated because of long-term unemployment.

This type of analysis connects to broader descriptions of economic restructuring, particularly in the economically more peripheral regions, where dual labour-market processes and deskilling are exacerbating processes of social polarisation (see Gallie, 1988 and 1991). The division of the workforce into core and peripheral workers, the former representing highly skilled workers with comparatively secure employment and the latter the increasingly unemployable workers with outdated skills or no particular skills at all seeking intermittent and insecure employment in industries with a static or declining wage level, operates to fix the casual worker in a marginal position in relation to secure employment and packages of occupational welfare. Payne and Payne (1994) have undertaken research into the impact of recession and economic restructuring on the work chances of the unemployed, and related their findings to the underclass debate. In particular they examine trends between 1979 and 1989 in the work chances of the unemployed relative to those with jobs. The concept of 'work chances' in this context should be interpreted as the acquisition of secure employment with an opportunity for advancement and a real increase in long-term income: it points to the competitive advantage of those already in work in obtaining 'good' jobs from a point of relative security. Examining data on the relative work chances of different categories of worker in periods when the economy was emerging from recession in the early and late 1980s, Payne and Payne found that the work chances of those over 45 'did not improve at all', and whilst young unemployed men and women obtained work relatively quickly after the early 1980s recession, those aged 25–45 saw their work chances improve only towards the end of the decade. The tentative conclusion from this piece of work is that evidence for an emerging underclass structured by disadvantageous economic forces may be emerging in the 1990s.

William Julius Wilson (1985, 1987 and 1989) develops a similar focus on economic restructuring to explain the emergence of the phenomenon of the 'ghetto underclass' in the major American cities. In particular he cites the declining economic fortunes of what he calls the 'frostbelt' cities. Deindustrialisation in the major urban centres in the Northeast and Midwest of the United States has resulted in a decline in inner-city manufacturing and consequently lower levels of employment for inner-city residents. Middle-class blacks have moved out of the inner cities as they accomplish both social and geographical mobility, leaving behind a residue of residents with low skills and high levels of unemployment in areas where employment opportunities are declining rapidly. The formation of what is referred to in the American academic and political context as the 'underclass family structure', essentially single-parent female-headed households, is not explained primarily in behavioural terms but is presented by Wilson as the direct consequence of changes taking place to the industrial structure of the American city and the operation of labour markets. Behavioural adjustments to deindustrialisation and rising unemployment are therefore an effect rather than cause of marginalisation for inner-city residents.

Elsewhere I have drawn on the Weberian idea of closure theory to provide a theoretical framework for describing these processes of marginalisation (see Rodger, 1992). Using Murphy's (1988) notion of rules of exclusion, specifically the classification of the rules into *principal*, *derivative* and *contingent* forms, it is argued that the abandonment of a policy of full employment as a *principal* goal of economic and social management by many western governments from the 1970s onwards has contributed to social division by closing off access to *derivative* forms of welfare such as occupational pensions, health insurance and fringe benefits to those not in secure employment. In this way, I have argued that what Titmuss (1958) and Sinfield (1986) call the *social division of welfare* leads to 'employmentship' rather than citizenship access to welfare, and is inextricably linked to the structuring of marginality or 'underclass' status for those who are systematically excluded from the fruits of welfare society because of long-term and entrenched unemployment. A number of commentators have observed a failure of orthodox economic theories to explain the international pattern of unemployment. Therborn (1986), Webber (1983), Scharpf (1984) and Korpi (1991) have argued that the only way to explain the low levels of unemployment in countries such as Sweden, Austria and Norway is to focus attention on the 'strategic choices' taken by the governments of these countries to follow policies of full employment through active rather than compensatory labour market policies. By ensuring full employment, access to the full fruits of society and economy is assured, and social division is minimised. The idea of *contingent* exclusion in this context relates to those situational factors which may be used to marginalise people further by the attachment of cultural and behavioural labels to those differentiated by long-term unemployment.

The central theme being developed here is that marginality is structured by the economic and public policy choices made by governments and not simply a by-product of human frailty, fecklessness or behaviour. The model of family structure which emerges from the analysis of economic restructuring is not one necessarily considered to be 'deviant'. The *structured underclass family* may well have a conventional nuclear and patriarchal structure and is the victim of wider forces for economic and social change which effectively marginalise the family unit by excluding it from full participation in the average activities of society. Jordan and Redley (1994) provide a helpful link between those analyses of the underclass which focus on economic restructuring and the world of welfare benefits experienced by the poor. They draw attention to what they call the 'divergence between better-off and poor people's practices over work and welfare'. Whilst the better-off direct their efforts towards securing economic advantage in the worlds of property and secure employment, the poor are trapped by the 'hypercasualisation of unskilled work' which interacts with means-testing 'to produce a culture of undeclared cash work which is increasingly acknowledged by claimants themselves' (p. 172), although, as the research by Pahl (1984) has shown, even casual work is difficult for the long-term unemployed to find. The attitudes and values of poor people grow out of the necessity constructed by economic forces and the shortcomings of the welfare state.

Whilst economic and social forces *structure* marginality, the erosion of welfare benefits and what Dahrendorf calls 'social citizenship' reinforces the family unit's marginal position. In the United States the real value of social insurance benefits, paid to those with an employment record, has increased, especially since becoming index linked after 1975 (see D. Hill, 1992). However, means-tested benefits aimed at the very poorest have been cut, with reductions to programmes ranging from 11.7 per cent to Aid to Families with Dependent Children (AFDC) after 1981 to an 18.8 per cent reduction in the value of food stamps during the Reagan Presidency, whilst at the same time eligibility rules were also tightened (see Stoesz and Karger, 1992). The significance of welfare state support for the very poor and vulnerable needs to be stressed. Hanratty and Blank (1992) have undertaken comparative analysis of poverty rates in

Canada and the USA during the 1970–79 and 1979–86 periods. Their conclusions support the view that the sharp divergence in poverty rates between Canada and the USA in the 1980s is almost entirely due to the Canadian transfer system and the simultaneous contraction of welfare support to the poor in the USA. Differences between the countries in economic growth rates and demographic changes were insufficiently pronounced to explain the divergence. What is clear from their analysis is that participation rates in unemployment insurance schemes and social assistance/AFDC schemes increased in Canada along with rising benefit rates, whereas they declined in the USA. These policy differences meant that poverty levels after transfer payments declined at a much faster rate in Canada, reflecting the success of welfare benefits in removing basic poverty. The actual increase in poverty rates in the USA, especially among the non-elderly population, reflects the parsimonious levels of benefits and tighter eligibility rules introduced there. Single-parent families most dependent on transfer payments were hardest hit in the USA and much better off in Canada.

Similar shifts have been observed in the United Kingdom, particularly with the less than proportional growth in the value of pensions, unemployment and social insurance benefits in the 1980s, coupled with an increasing emphasis on targeting. The social insurance component of the total social security budget has been declining, from 83.3 per cent of the budget in 1949 to 65.4 per cent in 1985, while means-tested benefits increased from 16.7 per cent in 1949 to 34.6 per cent in 1985 (Jordan, 1989). The House of Commons Social Security Committee report, *Low Income Statistics: Low Income Families 1979–1989*, published in December 1992 recorded that the numbers living on a lower income than that provided by basic social security benefit rose by 37 per cent to 4.4 million in the 10-year period examined. The report also notes a 46 per cent increase in the numbers living at or below basic income support levels, which means that 11.3 million people are now reliant on a source of means-tested income which has been subject to a decline in its relative value when compared with the incomes of those in employment. Salaries and wages increased their value by a third in the 10-year period examined by the Social Security Committee, but the social security rises of 15 per cent are acknowledged as modest by comparison. John Hills (1993) provides a more detailed breakdown of the development of the changing pattern of income share between 1979 and 1991; 'examining the difference between the real incomes (after housing costs) of the individuals placed in successive tenths of the population in 1979 and 1990/91', he goes on to observe that 'while average income for the population as a whole rose by 36 per cent, the real income of the bottom tenth *fell* by 14 per cent. Meanwhile the incomes of the top tenth rose by 62 per cent' (Hills, 1993, 37). The gradual erosion of levels of welfare support, it is argued, especially by Field (1989), fixes the family unit in what amounts to an 'underclass status'. The need to examine the relationship between economic structuring and the erosion of social citizenship arises because many governments within the OECD are attempting to tackle the problem of economic under-achievement by cutting back on the welfare state; the aim is to lower the reserve price of unskilled labour and to reinstate the family unit as the *principal* source of welfare. Both processes contribute to *the structuring of the underclass family*.

Dahrendorf (1985 and 1987) too has contributed to our understanding of the interconnection between structural forces and the erosion of social citizenship. This latter concept is derived from T.H. Marshall's classic analysis, *Class, Citizenship and Social Development* (1965), and refers to the right to enjoy a minimum standard of welfare, security and education. Marshall believed that the development of social citizenship would contribute towards social integration and the reduction of social divisions in twentieth-century industrial societies. Dahrendorf, however, observes a tendency towards the erosion of these welfare and social rights as modern industrial societies grapple with their declining economic performance in an increasingly competitive global market. Cuts in welfare programmes and the decline in the real buying power of benefits have systematically created a situation where households weakened and depressed by long-term unemployment and the impact of economic restructuring also find themselves subject, increasingly, to market principles rather than state or collective support for maintaining their minimum standard of living: an era of commercialism, welfare voluntarism and minimum state responsibility has forcibly redrawn the boundaries of social citizenship. The exclusion is explained primarily in structural and institutional terms, although, in common with a great deal of work in this vein, displays of behavioural deviance said to be associated with 'underclass' status are identified. The behavioural deviance is not used as the defining characteristic of the 'underclass'. Dahrendorf's perspective on 'underclass' status shares many similarities with Field's (1989). Both emphasise the significance of the erosion of welfare benefits and social citizenship rights for 'fixing' people into a marginal position at the bottom of the social structure. However, as Heisler (1991) suggests, the extent to which marginalisation of sections of society will be reinforced by the erosion of social citizenship rights will vary. She correctly points out that different sections of society will be exposed to marginalisation to varying degrees: the elderly possess a normatively greater power than young unemployed people in acquiring economic resources. Family units which correspond to conventional structures may be less subject to stigmatisation, and hence to financial cuts in their welfare benefits, than those deviating from convention. Heisler also draws attention to the other dimensions of T.H. Marshall's concept of citizenship, namely civil and political rights. Immigrant groups, for example, may experience a more extensive erosion of their civil and political rights than other economically weak groups in society. The conclusion that an 'underclass' is forming in industrial societies must, therefore, take into account the extensiveness of the exclusions experienced by different sections of society.

From a structural perspective, therefore, a social phenomenon such as single parenthood does not define the *structured underclass family* but instead may be a consequence of the financial and social pressures created by economic restructuring. Sexual codes among young unemployed males are a reflection of their difficulties in fulfilling a conventional breadwinning role in areas distinguished by deindustrialisation and a declining demand for unskilled and semi-skilled workers (see E. Anderson, 1989). In the absence of an extensive and active labour market policy, such as that developed over many years in Sweden, family formation based on the norm of a married or cohabiting couple with children will be hindered by the weak financial foundation of family life dependent upon a welfare state based on principles of self-help and economic parsimony. The erosion of social citizenship, rather than addressing the problem of welfare dependency, may exacerbate an already bleak situation for those on the margins of social and economic activity. Maintaining a conventional male or dual-breadwinner structure for the family unit is ultimately dependent upon the availability of employment and other sources of income. Indeed, the rejection of unemployed, and often unemployable, young males by single women, in circumstances where employment opportunities are few and unemployment high, may in some situations be an act of economic rationalism.

The fatherless underclass family

The abandonment of active research in the area of family life and poverty by liberal social scientists in America following the publication of Daniel Patrick Moynihan's *The Negro Family* (1965) led to the appropriation of the field by the political right, according to William Julius Wilson (1985). The consequence of this uneasiness with an issue that seemed to be overly preoccupied with the behavioural and racial variables associated with family poverty is that the ground upon which research and debate takes place today has been chosen by the political right. The politicisation of 'the underclass debate' has meant that arguments such as those I have just described which stress the structural underpinnings of poverty and marginalisation are increasingly being cast as politically left, whilst those analyses which focus on the behavioural and cultural antecedents of 'deviant' or unconventional social patterns are increasingly viewed as being politically of the right. The understanding of the concept of *the fatherless underclass family* must, therefore, be seen in this politically acrimonious context. This is, perhaps, unfortunate if it prevents a proper understanding of significant changes in family structure, including the quite marked increase in the numbers of lone female-headed households in Britain and the United States. It should be understood at the outset that the most crucial distinction between those who are writing about family life and changing family patterns from the political right and those of a more liberal disposition is that the former stress the culpability of those said to belong to the 'underclass'. Their view is that the poorest and most disadvantaged contribute to their own impoverished position. As I have outlined above, those who stress the structural determinants of 'underclass' formation are less concerned with behavioural and cultural variables, arguing that their causal influence is of secondary importance: behavioural and cultural practices are viewed as an adjustment to lowered expectations about employment, housing and a better quality of life.

In a series of publications sponsored by the Institute of Economic Affairs (IEA) the central problem of 'underclass' formation is reversed. In a brief theoretical excursion from the task of defending the concept of the 'bourgeois family', Brigitte Berger sets out the premises of her analysis and critique of those who might subscribe to the notion of the *structured underclass family*:

> if one is to understand the political, economic and cultural institutions of modern society, it is not enough to think of systems, structures and the like. One must look 'behind', or 'beneath', these artifacts in order to perceive the living human beings who make these artifacts work. To put it differently, this is a perspective 'from the bottom up' – the 'bottom' being the everyday reality of living human beings. That reality ... is defined by the ways in which individuals in families embedded in their communal structures try to give purpose to their actions and make sense out of human life. (Davies, Berger and Carlson, 1993, 13)

Berger's conception of the 'bottom up' takes seriously the 'common-sense' view that, despite being 'an object of ridicule' for the 1960s' counter-culture and often 'maligned' by liberal intellectual and political elites today, the 'bourgeois family' remains firmly accepted 'by far the majority of ordinary people' who, she argues, 'continue to be guided in their daily lives and their hopes for the future by bourgeois norms' (p. 13). Consequently the yardstick used by those writing under the banner of the IEA to measure deviant family patterns is the norm of the patriarchal nuclear family which is believed to be the source of social and psychological well-being. Deviance from this norm is a matter of individual choice rather than structural determinism.

It is social behaviour, particularly in the areas of sexuality, work and crime, which is of fundamental significance for Murray's analysis of the underclass. Having identified these three areas of concern, he suggests that illegitimacy is the best single predictor of underclass family formation. And so the concern for *families without fatherhood* is the strong analytical theme running through a number of studies of poverty (see Dennis and Erdos, 1992; Segalman and Marsland, 1989; Davies, Berger and Carlson, 1993). It is the 'dismembered' family which leads inevitably, indeed inexorably, to welfare dependency. The issue of crime is undoubtedly linked to the phenomenon of lone-parent families in this writing (see Dennis, 1993), but it seems to be a derivative occurrence rather than a defining feature of 'underclass' family life. I will examine the relationship between crime and the family separately below.

Segalman and Marsland (1989) provide a good example of a

perspective on family life which focuses attention on the impact of welfare state growth on families' effectiveness in fulfilling their socialisation function. The preparation of children for social life depends, they insist, upon the presence of a father to provide the appropriate guidance and role model, especially for young males. The growth of welfare programmes since the 1960s is held to be responsible for damaging the willingness to work among a particular set of the unemployed. The 'primary arena' in which 'long-term damage is done is the family'.

> For the family is the crucial – indeed indispensable – mechanism in producing autonomous, self-reliant personalities, capable of resisting the blandishments of welfare dependency. It is apparently only in the context of loving support and rational discipline which the family offers . . . that children can be reliably socialised. . . . anything at all which weakens the fabric of families inevitably generates and escalates welfare dependency. In particular, social policies which make the role of the father redundant, or weaken the legitimate authority of parents in the socialisation of their children, are likely to create environments in which only exceptional children are capable of growing up into genuinely mature and autonomous adults. The vast majority of children reared in broken or inadequate families are headed for welfare dependency (Segalman and Marsland, 1989, 121).

Much of the argument and analysis of the IEA writers concentrates on the *quality of the family experience*. As the quote from Segalman and Marsland shows quite clearly, a poor experience of family life is regarded as having a widespread and negative impact on society. The empirical research undertaken to sustain this conclusion is not, however, based on a methodology geared to qualitative analysis; instead great reliance is placed upon the longitudinal statistical analysis of what can best be described as human development studies. This type of work is by its nature most meaningful when describing statistical correlations between family background, life chances and social outcomes as individuals pass from childhood to adulthood rather than complex social interaction, which is what would be needed to arrive at a fuller understanding of the *quality of the family experience*.

The most sustained argument in this vein, and critical of the growing numbers of *families without fatherhood,* is provided by Norman Dennis (1992 and 1993). The IEA writers in general, and Dennis in particular, focus on the 1960s as a watershed period, locating many of the contemporary problems of welfare dependency and illegitimacy in the cultural and value pluralism which originated then. The longitudinal research is used to ground a more basic argument. Dennis argues that the 1960s was a period which encouraged an attack on the idea of lifelong monogamy, and so encouraged an attitude to sexuality and procreation which privileged the rights of individuals over the responsibilities, disciplines and compromises which constituted the foundation of stable family living. Family as a lifestyle choice rather than a social and moral responsibility is, therefore, subject to severe criticism. The 1960s in particular was a period when there was, according to Dennis, a discernible decline in collectivity or other-regarding attitudes, coupled with low levels of far-sightedness and self-restraint. This assessment is anchored in an appreciation of Adam Smith who, despite the free market legacy that his economic analyses left to modern society, viewed 'public spiritedness' in a positive light. This line of Dennis's argument is especially relevant for an understanding of his analysis of the rising crime rate which I will discuss below.

Dennis does address the difficult issue of how data and research on socialisation and changing family patterns can be obtained and interpreted. His analysis, whilst attempting to uncover the available empirical evidence on this difficult issue, has a preference for large-scale statistical data. Reference is made to selected longitudinal studies which point towards a marked difference between families with what Dennis describes as *publicly committed fathers* (through formal marriage) and families with *publicly uncommitted fathers*. In particular, Dennis pays attention to a study undertaken at the National Children's Bureau into the social and economic implications of illegitimacy. Begun in 1958, the study included periodic follow-up investigations of a representative sample of over 600 children from the 16,000 born in England, Wales and Scotland between 3 and 9 March 1958 (Crellin, Kellmer-Pringle and West, 1971). There is also discussion of a more recent follow-up study undertaken in Newcastle upon Tyne of 264 men and women aged 32–33 originally studied as babies, infants and adolescents (Kolvin *et al.*, 1990). By its nature such data requires to be gathered in a controlled way over time in order that the effect of family patterns on future life chances and social behaviour can be better isolated and observed.

These studies point to well established correlations between lone parenthood, deprivation and maladjustment in child behaviour. The

Newcastle study (Kolvin *et al.*, 1990) used indices of deprivation such as parental illness, poor physical and domestic care of children, unemployment, overcrowding of the dwelling, and the degree of competence displayed by mothers, to classify families into three groups: those who suffered none of the deficiencies, those who suffered one or more, and those who suffered three or more. Families who were classified as not deprived at all had fathers who had been present since the birth of the child in 83 per cent of cases. With respect to families suffering multiple deprivations, 53 per cent had fathers who had been present since the birth of the child. Cases where fathers had been absent for 15 years or more were three times more likely to be found in multi-deprived families than non-deprived families. With respect to a more qualitative and subjective factor, namely, the grading of fathers in terms of their effectiveness as fathers and their levels of kindness and consideration, the Newcastle study reported that 53 per cent of fathers in the non-deprived group exhibited these qualities whereas only 7 per cent of fathers in the multi-deprived category were considered to be effective, kind and considerate by the children and their mothers. Other differences were recorded with respect to things such as height and weight of the children, speech defects and accidental injuries in the home. There is an established pattern and widely accepted social class difference in these matters.

Dennis is at pains throughout his analysis to stress that he is concerned with what is called the frequency distribution: 'the set of children from one domestic situation do well with greater frequency than the set of children from other domestic situations' (p. 47). The difficulty with this large-scale comparative analysis of family types is that there is an inevitable overlap between the distributions found in lone-parent families and two-parent families: 'the better end of the worse distribution did better than the worse end of the better distribution'. In other words research has found that children from some lone-parent families actually out-perform children from two-parent families in some instances and on some measures. Dennis is right to caution against drawing the false conclusion that there is no difference, therefore, between lone-parent and two-parent families. The real focus of attention is in any case not lone parents *per se* but rather the subset of never-married lone parents with *publicly uncommitted fathers*. Charles Murray (1990) specifically highlights this subset of lone parents who, he argues, are feather-bedded by welfare state support which discourages a responsible attitude to pregnancy and childrearing among both single mothers and wayward males. At the heart of his analysis Murray maintains that there is a clear distinction between *primary* poverty and *secondary* poverty: the former is caused by low-paid work, the latter by behavioural deviance (see D. Anderson, 1991). It is the behavioural deviance facilitated by welfare dependence which causes the poverty of the never-married lone-parent families. Murray's most recent excursion into British social policy analyses has elaborated the thesis he first offered in 1989. A distinction is now drawn between 'the New Victorians', with above average earnings who embrace religion and traditional family virtues of fidelity, self-restraint and concern for children and the community, and 'the New Rabble', who are inclined towards welfare, criminality, sexual indiscipline and single-parent families as their norm. The economic and cultural divide between those in secure employment and those outside it is acknowledged by Murray but the fundamental cause of the growing 'incivility' which accompanies this social division is the collapse of the family and marriage as socialising forces, for young men at the bottom of the social hierarchy especially.

Without accepting the premises of the IEA perspective, other research has produced findings which tend to reinforce the general thrust of Dennis's view, if not specifically about fatherless families, then at least about the importance of intact families. A recent study by Cockett and Tripp (1994) of children living in reordered families showed that those children whose families experience a series of disruptions and changes through separation and divorce are more likely than children from intact families to have suffered problems in five areas: they had low self-esteem, had difficulties with friendships, problems with school work, behavioural difficulties and health problems, including both functional illnesses, such as stomach-aches, feeling sick and bedwetting, and illnesses thought to be psychosomatic. The significance of their study was to isolate a growing subset of children who experienced a series of disruptions in their lives, sometimes three or more family structures, and who suffered even more than children living with a lone parent. It is the phenomenon of repeated disruption of family life that is crucial. The value of this piece of research is that it focuses attention on the children's experience: 152 children in late childhood and early adolescence were interviewed along with their parents. Half the children were living in intact families, the other half of the sample had experienced their parents' divorce. Children preferred their parents to remain together, even if they were constantly warring. The common assumption that children are happier living with separated parents who are not in conflict than in a household characterised by constant acrimony was found to be contrary to what children wanted (see Whitehead, 1992).

Feminist research on the domestic division of labour and the gender pattern of ill health has produced data which indicate quite clearly that lone parenthood is a stressful experience (Hardey and Crow, 1990 ; Glendinning and Millar, 1993). Women coping with the material and emotional strain of breadwinning and childrearing unsupported by a partner undoubtedly risk the possibility that their children will experience deficiencies in a range of areas. The feminisation of poverty in particular is a phenomenon that feminist analyses of social policy are subjecting to critical scrutiny. However, whilst making similar observations about the life chances of single-parent families and the increasing deprivation experienced by children in such situations, feminist analyses of social policy arrive at different conclusions from those advanced by Murray. Deprivation in female-headed single-parent households in the United States, for example, is due to the absence of a strong European-style welfare state rather than an overgenerous package of welfare benefits (see Norris, 1984). The weak labour-market position of women is a major obstacle preventing them from overcoming the deprivations associated with lone parenthood. The feminist position on these matters might be to argue the case for a positive range of family policies, such as can be found in France or Sweden, as I discussed in Chapter 5 (see Lewis, 1992; Hantrais, 1994a, 1994b; Lenoir, 1991).

Recent analysis of data from the American National Survey of Families and Households by Acock and Demo (1994) points towards greater variation within different family types than between them. Their study set itself the explicit objective of comparing four family types: *first marriages* in which both the mother and the father are in their first marriage with one or more biological child under 19 living at home; *divorced* families consisting of a mother who has divorced and has at least one biological child under 19 from a previous marriage living at home; *stepfamilies,* where the mother is married for at least the second time and has at least one biological child under 19 from a previous marriage living with her and her current husband; and *continuously single* family types consisting of a mother who has never married and has at least one biological child under 19 living at home. The study focused attention on mothers' rather than fathers' perceptions to aid comparability. Women also tend to be most involved in childrearing and to provide the best information about their children.

Two areas of Acock and Demo's analysis are worth accentuating: parent–child relations and children's well-being within the four family types.

Parent–child relations

The common assumption, made by Dennis and by Murray, among others, has been that the two-parent model of the family is essential for the normal development of children (see Segalman and Marsland, 1989, in particular). A central theme in the New Right's recent analyses of family life is that a mother's values and expectations for her children will vary by family type; deviations from the two-parent family structure are understood in terms of a socialisation deficit model of family life. Acock and Demo examined the data relating to childrearing values for children under 5 and 5–18, comparing the responses of mothers from the four selected family types. Their strong conclusion was that parenting values held by mothers do not vary by family type; all family types had mothers who stressed the importance of following culturally valued guidelines for behaviour. Although there was variation noted with respect to parent–child interaction, particularly a difference in the frequency of enjoyable times spent by first married mothers with their children compared with mothers from the other family types, the differences across family types were small. A similar pattern emerged for first married fathers, especially when compared with stepfathers. This finding directs our attention to the qualitative nature of family relationships. There was no statistically significant difference across family types for parent difficulties with children. Whereas first married mothers were twice as likely to be involved in school activities as continuously single mothers, there was little difference in maternal interaction across family types for children under five, or in mothers' involvement in the leisure activities of their children in the 5–18 age range. An interesting finding drawn from the data is that single parenthood is less stressful than pre-divorce parenthood when acrimony and conflict are at their worst. Divorced women living as single parents report an improvement in their parental status and functioning. Overall the data point to evidence of what Acock and Demo call 'technically present but functionally absent fathers'. Parental neglect appears to be paternal neglect. The argument advanced by Dennis (1993) and Dennis and Erdos (1992), that it is specifically the phenomenon of *families without fatherhood* which accounts for a range of social problems including juvenile delinquency and a decline in civility, is flawed because the absence of *fathers* as active participants in family life is a feature of all family types.

Children's well-being

There were few statistically significant differences across family types on measures of the 'socio-emotional' adjustment and well-being of children. Controlling for social background, the data discussed by Acock and Demo produced no significant differences across family types in academic performance. It is the variation within family types rather than between them which is commented upon; family process variables relating to the quality of family relationships rather than family structure alone are highlighted as important. There was support for the view that conflict within an intact family can be more harmful than living within a divorced family, although this finding is not consistent with new British research by Cockett and Tripp (1994), which argues the contrary case: children prefer their warring parents to remain married rather than to separate. There is evidence from Acock and Demo's analysis that there may be an optimum level of conflict which can sustain a lively, but harmonious, family life. The conclusion drawn by Acock and Demo is that:

> teachers, politicians, and popular commentators are simply wrong if they assume that single mothers do not value their children's education, do not have high educational expectations for their children, or do not impose family rules. What is needed to support these families is not rhetoric but changes in social policy and the provision of social programmes and special services to meet their needs (Acock and Demo, 1994, 231).

The social policy developments which this research identifies as necessary are policies which support women's employment, such as affordable childcare services, combined with the development of workplace flexibility relating to job sharing, sick leave and parental leave. These aspects of family policy would, of course, help to promote qualitatively better family relationships in a changing and insecure economic and social context.

Whilst social policies such as the provision of generous levels of universal child benefits and childcare allowances could alleviate some of the intractable problems faced by lone parents trapped in poverty (see Jordan *et al.*, 1992), the impact that a father's absence has on the disciplinary side of family life remains an issue. This leads to consideration of the relationship between crime and family life.

The criminal underclass family

Dennis is pointing to the actuality that the average child from a one-parent family will, on the whole, do much less well emotionally, educationally and socially than a child from an average two-parent family and, most significantly, will be more inclined towards delinquency and criminality. The qualitative aspect of the family experience is, however, described not in sociological terms, but with reference to social values and social norms which are said to have disappeared from modern social life and which, by their nature, give rise to dispute. Writing in the *Observer*, Oliver James (1993) questions Dennis's interpretation of the data. Specifically he points to the failure of research to isolate the qualitative experience of family conflict which precedes family breakdown. The presence of a father is often considered to be a protection against children slipping into delinquency. However, James observes 'that it is not the father's absence which makes divorce distressing to the child is shown by the repeated finding that children show as much delinquency in the years leading up to the split – while the acrimony is at its height – as in the years afterwards' (James, 1993). James also argues that even when a mother remarries and the child is provided with a stepfather and, presumably, an appropriate male role model and authority figure to follow, the pattern of delinquency which manifested itself in the pre-divorce period continues in the reconstituted family situation. This view is, of course, partly contradicted by Cockett and Tripp (1994); it is the separation per se which seems to be most troubling for some children. The persistence of delinquency in reconstituted families is consistent with this finding. James is correct

to challenge the simplistic structural argument that it is the phenomenon of the lone-parent family which is critical, as if there was
something inherently damaging about the experience of living in
that situation. It is the sense of loss, specifically the loss of whole-
ness of family boundaries, which seems to be the crucial factor. He
directs us towards that research which has been undertaken to isolate the relative importance of *family structure* (which involves variables such as divorce and single parenthood) and *family process*
(which involves the examination of the quality of family interaction).

The essential concern here is parental supervision and discipline
and the conditions under which they are weakened. The emerging
debate about crime and family life is increasingly centred on the
matter of changing patterns of parental authority in general. Whether
it is possible to identify particular patterns of family living which
may be more directly correlated with criminality is a more specific
matter and one which I will address below. A preliminary observation should be made, however, about the general historical trend in
all industrial societies towards more egalitarian and less authoritarian
parent–child relationships.

Jamieson and Toynbee (1990) have addressed the question of
parental authority by way of oral history, contrasting the nature of
parent–child relationships in early twentieth-century Scotland and
New Zealand with the situation since 1950. Including data drawn
from both urban and rural informants, they describe and offer explanations for what many intuitively feel, namely that 'parents in
contemporary Western industrialised societies are less able or willing to control their children's behaviour than in previous generations'. The fundamental shift described by Jamieson and Toynbee
is from a model of 'traditional authority' found in the early decades
of the twentieth-century, characterised as an order considered to be
'natural' and 'immutable' by common custom and practice, to a
model which is essentially pseudo-democratic in nature. As contemporary parents strive to be less distant, more communicative,
and become more concerned about securing the mutual respect and
admiration of their children, they often find it necessary to resort
to the 'power of the hand and the purse' to assert an authority that
is now negotiable rather than accepted unquestioningly by children.
The explanation for these changes is rooted in an analysis of the
changing economic, social and political contexts of family life. Economic and industrial changes in the twentieth century have effected

an altered relationship between the household and the economy, and child labour has lost its significance for the household economy as employment outside the home has risen; this process has been underscored by increasing affluence and the evolution of consumerism in household goods.

> The shift to the 'affluent consumer society' has become associated not only with the multiplication of goods provided for children by parents, but also a reduction in the contributions made by children and young people to their family household. (Jamieson and Toynbee, 1990, 102)

The real problem for many parents in contemporary society is that they are 'under resourced' in relation to the increasing demands of their dependent children. Also, the social and the political context of this issue is characterised by a weakening of both the social and cultural support to parents 'for laying down the law to their children' (p. 103) from an extended family disorganised by rehousing, geographic and social mobility. The rise of new knowledges and forms of advice from social welfare and health professionals, whose responsibility it has been to foster less authoritarian and more caring modes of parenting, has probably contributed to the creation of a more 'child centred' culture, far removed from that of the early twentieth-century Scotland and New Zealand described by Jamieson and Toynbee.

Family relationships have been changing, but the connection between patterns of family living and criminality has been established for a considerable time. The 'moral panic' generated by those on the political right, such as Charles Murray, and the 'ethical left', such as Norman Dennis, which associates the idea of criminality with an 'underclass' family type, mainly fatherless families, has been achieved by claiming novelty for a relationship which is as commonly recognised as its complexities have eluded a full scientific explanation. Joan McCord (1991) reminds us that

> Plato . . . prescribed a regimen for rearing good citizens in the nursery. Aristotle asserted that in order to be virtuous 'we ought to have been brought up in a particular way from our very youth'. And John Locke wrote his letters on the education of children in the belief that errors 'carry their afterwards incorrigible taint with them, through all the parts and stations of life'. (p. 397)

There are two discrete concerns that we must address at this point. First, we need to set out and understand the sociological research which has been conducted into the relationship between family ties and patterns of parental management and delinquency. Second, we need to enquire into social changes and living conditions in contemporary society which may be effecting both a qualitative and quantitative change in the association between family life and criminality. The first type of research reviews attempts to isolate causal variables which lead to delinquency and criminality. The second type of research raises the issue that there may be emerging within many industrialised societies an irregular economy, whose currency is illicit drugs and stolen goods, which is competing with the formal economy for those excluded or marginalised by long-term unemployment. Are there distinct family patterns emerging within the deprived inner-city areas and peripheral housing estates which may, for want of a more precise description, be functional for the episodic dealing and lifestyle found there?

Family life and crime

First, in turning to the empirical research on the relationship between family and criminality we should acknowledge, as do Utting, Bright and Henricson (1993), that 'the statistically significant "predictors" which pepper criminological research, rarely, if ever, approach the realms of certainty' (p. 17). For example, Farrington and West (1990), who have provided one of the most systematic studies of criminality and its causal antecedents in the United Kingdom, identified a number of what Utting, Bright and Henricson call 'false positives': sizeable numbers of adolescents who experienced some of the worst family conditions associated with developing criminality, yet did not subsequently follow a deviant path as the variables might have predicted. Therefore in discussing the empirical research on family and crime a number of methodological problems need to be at least recognised. First, a great deal of this research is based on self-reporting, where the delinquents talk about their own recollections of family life and their delinquent response to the problems that they then experienced. As McCord (1991) observes, studies have shown that 'conscious attention is unnecessary for experiences to be influential, thus adolescents may not notice salient features of their socialisation' (p. 399), and further, that 'reports of family interaction tend to reflect socially desirable perspectives'. With respect to child rearing practices, abused children often perceive their parents to have been less violent and punitive than they actually were, or at least as for as can be assessed by the best objective external measures of these phenomena. Parents in turn also tend to misrepresent their behaviour through feelings of guilt and shame. They employ a vocabulary of motives which will explicitly seek to neutralise the moral censure which they feel to be weighted against them; they will blame social and economic conditions, psychological strain and other factors in mitigation (see Sykes and Matza, 1957). The relationship between delinquency and the attachment, or bonding, between child and parent, which is frequently cited as a crucial variable in either promoting or inhibiting the onset of delinquency, depending on whether it is strong or weak, is very difficult to measure through the use of self-report methods. Weak bonding said to be correlated with increased delinquency could be the product of delinquency just as frequently as preceding it. Caution is therefore required when interpreting data. Nevertheless, there is a clear correlation between delinquency and particular factors of family life which unfortunately has tended to be ignored or overlooked in recent British sociology, if not in American social research. The consequence of this neglect is, of course, that issues of real sociological and policy importance become political footballs, subject to ill-informed comment for the purposes of sensationalism and short-term political advantage in the ideological battle that has emerged over family life in the 1990s.

The pioneering work on family background and criminality undertaken in the 1940s by Sheldon and Eleanor Glueck (1950) showed that variables such as parental discipline, parental supervision, affection and its display towards the child by either the mother or father and family cohesion or the lack of it, were all correlated with delinquency, as either promoters or inhibitors of deviance. That study has acted as a benchmark for subsequent research, including the reanalysis of the original data by Laub and Sampson (1988).

The central theme in much research since the Gluecks' study has been the relative importance to be attached to factors of *family structure* (particularly factors such as divorce, lone parenthood, mothers' employment and parental criminality) and factors of *family process* (which focus attention on social interaction, supervision, modes of discipline and affection displayed). With respect to the concern expressed about 'underclass' family structures in the work of Dennis (1993), Murray (1990) and Segalman and Marsland (1989), recent sociological research on families and delinquency seems to place far more significance on *family process* than on *family structure*, especially with regard to things such as divorce and broken homes; these variables tend to have at best an indirect, and therefore very complex, relationship with delinquency, but more generally tend to have only a weak relationship with patterns of adolescent deviance. Van Voorhis, Cullen, Mathers and Garner (1988) set out to test the importance of variables relating to family structure over measures of family function, as they call it, in influencing delinquency in a sample of 152 boys. The study therefore contrasted data on families where the two biological parents were present with other family forms, such as single-parent households. The general conclusion of their research was that 'bad homes', not 'broken homes', put children at risk of delinquency. The variables which their research identifies as the most significant promoters or inhibitors of delinquency are: the maltreatment of children (this promotes delinquency); affection (which can inhibit delinquency if it is expressed as part of a well balanced child–parent relationship); parental supervision; overall quality of home. The phenomenon of a broken home was correlated only with what the researchers call status offences, such as truancy or running away from home. But the more serious offences involving the use of illicit drugs and property crimes were positively correlated with the variables which relate to *family process*, which directs our attention to the quality of social interaction within the family. Laub and Sampson (1988) arrive at similar conclusions on the basis of their reworking of the Gluecks' 1940s data. *Family process* variables relating to the quality of mothers' supervision, parental styles of discipline and, importantly, feelings of attachment of children to their parents were found to be far more important than structural factors such as broken homes, mothers' employment and even parental criminality. Whilst Gove and Crutchfield (1982) found that the attachment variables relating to parent–child relationships were the best predictor of delinquency, they also highlighted an interesting gender difference in that characteristics of their parents' marriage seem to have a greater effect on boys than on girls. The variables which best predicted delinquency in girls were those relating to parent–child interaction and parental control and supervision. Good family relationships seem to be able to compensate for a range of struc-

tural disadvantages. And, of course, it is precisely this type of research which takes debate beyond surface or superficial associa-
tions, such as the one which links delinquency with certain family
types, to an understanding of the dynamics of the family interactions which make a crucial difference in determining criminality.

Cernkovich and Giordano (1987) have attempted to provide a more
thorough conceptualisation of factors relating to family interaction.
Whilst a number of pieces of research isolate the notion of the child's
'attachment' to its parents as an important inhibitor of delinquency,
the systematic unpacking of this concept has, perhaps, been neglected.
Cernkovich and Giordano's analysis therefore differentiates factors
such as the control and supervision of children by their parents, the
degree of identity support that children receive from their parents
at crucial times in their development, caring and trust, intimate communication, levels of family conflict, parental disapproval of peers,
and instrumental communication between parent and child about
practical and personal problems relating to school and career plans.
Again this research tends to highlight the crucial significance of
the quality of parenting rather than family structure in avoiding juvenile delinquency.

The nature of parental supervision, in particular whether direct or
indirect controls are significant for the prevention of adolescent
delinquency, has also featured in recent research. Wells and Rankin
(1988) and Larzelere and Patterson (1990) stress the neglected significance of modes of direct parental control. The issue which these
pieces of research raise for consideration is whether the parent merely
being 'psychologically present' in the mind of the adolescent is
sufficient to inhibit deviant activity, or whether modes of direct
monitoring and supervision are more significant. In Britain, Harriett
Wilson (1987) has argued that it is the degree of parental supervision and its extensiveness which is important, whereas Riley and
Shaw (1985) are satisfied with the notion that the psychological
presence of the parents is sufficient to inhibit adolescent involvement in delinquency. The analysis by Wells and Rankin (1988) tends
therefore to lend support to Harriett Wilson (1987). Within the concept of 'direct control' they include factors such as the normative
regulation of behaviour and the monitoring of children's where-
abouts so that parents know where and with whom their children
are associating, and also modes of punishment which can be regarded
as an important index of parental control. Hirschi (1969) and others

who have stressed the importance of the notion of the 'attachment' of the child to its parents may be more content with the idea of 'psychological presence'. Both factors are undoubtedly significant, and it is likely that patterns of direct control will be bound up with those indirect controls which influence child behaviour through psychological mechanisms. The difference between control by fear and control through mutual respect is an issue, however, and it should be acknowledged that punitive control of children by parents is often correlated with delinquency, as Van Voorhis *et al.* (1988) have demonstrated.

It is worth reporting research which tends to undermine the view expressed by Dennis and Erdos (1992) and Dennis (1993) that fathers are crucial figures in protecting children, particularly male children, from delinquency, and criminality more generally. McCord (1991) undertook an evaluation of data from a longitudinal study of 232 boys born between 1926 and 1933 in Boston, Massachussetts who were involved in a delinquency prevention scheme. The data includes information, therefore, on well-behaved as well as troublesome boys. The project involved the gathering of data based on monthly visits to the boys' homes and the detailed analysis of official criminal statistics. The general conclusion of McCord's study is that competent mothers insulate children against criminogenic influences by providing leadership, consistent non-punitive discipline and, importantly, affection. Fathers' interactions with their families proved to be comparatively unimportant when contrasted with the central influence and authority of the mother. This was particularly found to be the case for boys during their juvenile years. Fathers only became more influential and significant as the boys matured beyond the adolescent stage. The connection between juvenile delinquency and adult crime was clear. If the protection of a competent mother was absent at the adolescent stage then adult criminality developed out of juvenile deviance. And if this research is discomforting for those who stress the significance of fathers, the conclusion of Riley and Shaw (1985) on lone parents and delinquency is equally discouraging for those who have stressed the particular importance of family structure:

> The notion that one-parent families are . . . 'criminogenic' receives no support from the results of the present survey. Not only were there no differences in the prevalence of delinquency but also largely absent were

differences in factors which might be causally related to delinquency. This suggests it may be unwise to assume that more one-parent families must mean more delinquency or that they are *necessarily* [their emphasis] more lax in their supervision or less able to provide support or affection than two-parent families. (Riley and Shaw, 1985, 45).

They go on to acknowledge that living at the margins of existence, suffering extreme poverty and stress, means that parents are often distracted. Their living conditions 'are unlikely to allow parents the patience, endurance or understanding which they often require in their relations with teenage children' (p. 46). But it is the *quality* of family interactions and relationships which proves to be the most influential factor preventing delinquency. The variables relating to parental stress seemed to be a response to problems in relationships rather than a direct cause of the delinquency.

Finally, Fagan and Wexler (1987) undertook research on the family origins of violent delinquents. Their research confronts the assumption common in the arguments of the political right in the underclass debate that wider social factors outside the family are insignificant influences on criminality. Fagan and Wexler's analysis is based on the self-reporting of delinquent and family experience of 98 violent delinquents and their mothers. The central question they addressed was the one posed by Hirschi's analysis (1969), that weak family bonds lead to delinquency. Fagan and Wexler's study tended to prove that family bonds weakened as delinquency developed; the delinquency preceded the weak bonding. Their analysis classified families into three main types, namely *interactionist families* (with high levels of interaction and bonding), *hierarchical families* (characterised by parental dominance and presence in family interactions), and *anti-social families* (marked by criminality and violence). The influence of peers outside the family, within the immediate community and at school, had a stronger explanatory power when analysing the data than those factors relating purely to social interaction and family bonding. In all probability it is the interaction between family, school and community which is crucial here. Violence, as Fagan and Wexler rightly point out, develops as part of a learning process. And with respect to this more serious category of deviance, it would be quite nonsensical to ignore the influence of factors beyond the family.

The irregular economy and crime

The second major issue that we must recognise is the emergence of
an infrastructure of criminality which appears to be developing within
certain areas of the inner city and peripheral housing estates and
which has served to ground notions of a *criminal underclass family*
form. The image which has surfaced in a number of pieces of American
writing is that of the single female-headed household abandoned by
the males who have fathered her multiple children, and who return
episodically for sexual favours and to supply the family with resources acquired through crime, particularly drug dealing. The debate in America has identified what is called the *violent underclass*
to designate this particular subset (see Jencks and Peterson, 1991).
The factors isolated by criminological research into crime and the
family have, therefore, a particular resonance when discussion turns
to the children's experience of family life in the ghetto underclass
of the large American cities. Debate in British sociology and social
policy is beginning to form around similar issues. The collecting of
anecdotal evidence of growing violence and criminality amongst
children as young as 10 has been continuing for a number of years.
That evidence is now being confirmed as British academic research
into life in peripheral housing estates and the inner cities reveals
the involvement of very young children in the turf wars surrounding
illicit drug supply (see Burrell, 1995).

Recent sociological work based on the method of crime surveys
in relatively deprived areas of London and Merseyside (see Lea and
Young, 1984; Kinsey, Lea and Young, 1986) has revealed that extremely high levels of crime are committed and that these are hidden from public scrutiny because they go unreported. The real victims
of crime in contemporary society are not the affluent residents of
middle-class suburbs but the residents of poor inner-city and peripheral housing estates. Crime tends to be intra rather than inter
class in its predatory nature. An internecine war is being waged at
the heart of many poor areas. The emerging paradigm in the British
sociology of crime is 'new realism' which asserts strongly that both
traditional and left criminology have ignored the 'real' levels of
crime in our society in favour of analyses of the role that the media
plays in structuring public agendas and conceptions of the crime
problem. Without discussing this wider debate, it is sufficient to
say that the 'new realists' have identified an 'underclass' within

these areas who are involved either as victims of crime on a large and repetitive scale or as offenders. The balancing this type of analysis has been the work undertaken on the changing pattern of drug use which recognises the concept of the *irregular economy* as one which has increasing explanatory power (see Auld, Dorn and South, 1984 and 1986). The interesting phenomenon which this work reveals is the use of drugs along with other items of currency to lubricate relationships between those who engage in the illicit buying and selling of cheap, usually stolen, goods. The economic restructuring described above has left many areas of British society with large and increasing populations of never-employed adolescents who find a source of income through their participation in the *irregular economy*. It is described in this way because the trading tends to be episodic, or irregular. Hard drugs are used within this economy in a way described by Auld, Dorn and South (1984) as a 'socially extroverted way'. Gone is the sick role associated with heroin use in the 1970s and 1980s because users and dealers need to be alert and involved in criminal trading; ironically an entrepreneurial culture has grown up whereby dependency is eschewed in favour of the occasional recreational use of drugs. Smoking and snorting heroin, for example, replace injecting because these methods carry fewer health risks for those who control the trading and supply infrastructure. Pharma-ceuticals are also a part of this trade. The interesting question which arises is, if a young male can earn substantial amounts of money through irregular economic activity why should he ever return to conventional employment? And, of course, if successful models of tutelage in drug crime are clearly visible to very young children within a community where drugs are prevalent, then it should not be surprising if they learn to adapt to the ways of life associated with irregular economic activity, which will involve both a rejec-tion of conventional normative frameworks guiding behaviour and the embracing of violent means to obtain economic goals. This phenomenon was described many years ago by Richard Cloward and Lloyd Ohlin in their classic study of juvenile subcultures; the very title of their book directs us to the main issue: *Delinquency and Opportunity* (Cloward and Ohlin, 1960). The emerging image of disorganised family forms in the midst of this innovatory econ-omic activity seduces us into using functionalist vocabulary to de-scribe it. Indeed the idea of a 'colony culture', thriving in Brixton, Handsworth and parts of other large English cities, where inhabitants of those areas straddle the ground between legality and criminality, providing the community with essential goods and services denied by the racism and inequalities of mainstream society, is well documented (see Hall *et al.*, 1978). It is only to be expected that people will be adaptive, and, where legitimate outlets for talent and enterprise are denied, illegitimate opportunities will be grasped, as classical anomie theory has shown (see Taylor, Walton and Young, 1973; Roshier, 1989). Sex codes among the young males involved in this world of episodic wheeling and dealing may lead them to regard the concept of family responsibility as something alien and unnecessarily restrictive for a life living on one's wits: sex becomes another recreational pastime competing with the pleasures of the irregular economy. The role of young females in such relationships is probably under-researched. The image of a helpless and always receptive female partner denies rationality and purposiveness to young women who find themselves alone with children to care for. The rejection of male partners committed more to the deal than to the family may be an act of rationality. It is, of course, as a result of the exercising of this rationality that many young mothers become subject to social work scrutiny and it is to this issue that I now turn. In the final section of this chapter I will discuss the social policy and social work response to family life in the desolate habitats of the inner city and peripheral housing estates.

Social work and social control: the rise of the family centre

The image which emerges from the competing models of the 'underclass family' is one in which family relationships are severely disturbed, either by the workings of an incessantly harsh market economy or by the pathological dysfunctioning brought about by deviant patterns of living. The apparent difference of emphasis between these explanations of marginality can be formulated in a different way: the sociological approach will tend to concentrate on those social and economic forces that give rise to *social disorganisation within the community*, whilst those inclined to social work intervention are increasingly attracted to the model of *the socially disorganised family*. This does not mean, however, that all social workers support those critics of deviant family forms who have been most attracted to the concept of 'underclass'. There is a division within social work between those inclined towards the use of family therapy techniques and clinical models of intervention and those who stress the priority of community work as a way of helping the marginal and socially deviant within society. The former focus their attention on the problems of organisation and *disorganisation* within poor families, whereas the latter concentrate on the development of community institutions and primary relationships to better enhance the community's internal social control and collective problem solving. In Chapter 2 I argued that there are discernible differences in the *classification* and *framing* of knowledge underpinning these different approaches to community and social intervention, with community work tending to adopt a collective and *appreciative* focus, whilst clinical practice tends towards a more individualistic and *correctional* focus. These differences are working themselves out in the development of family centres which are becoming, in policy terms, an important instrument for socially regulating and monitoring problem families. The concept of the problem family has been replaced by that of the 'underclass family'. The concern has been about child protection and the risks to children who may be reared in deviant family situations, which often means in lone-parent families where the mother's partner is not the biological father of the children. Children in this type of family are now considered to be particularly vulnerable to abuse (see N. Parton, 1985; Dale *et al.*, 1987). Whilst debate has raged in politics and social policy analysis about whether an 'underclass' really exists, and about the family factors which are likely promote criminality and violent behaviour, social workers have unselfconsciously continued to deal with the most deviant, the most marginal and the most troublesome members of the community. The focus of those strands of social work inclined towards the methods of family therapy and clinical models of intervention has been on the concepts of the *disorganised family* and the *underorganised* family, characterised by a chaotic family structure, and an absence of conventional gender role models. As Reder (1983) comments with respect to *disorganised families*, 'their principal problem is in consistently defining an executive and caretaking structure to themselves and others' (p. 23). This *disorganisation* leads to an almost daily contact with a range of helping agents such as social workers, health visitors, probation officers, education welfare officers and so on. With respect to the typology of family structures developed by Olson and McCubbin (see Figure 4.1 in Chapter 4) we might expect the debate about the 'underclass family' to centre on the capacity of some family forms to provide the levels of guidance and social support to their members considered appropriate for an active and participatory involvement in community life. Families whose structure of relationships is characterised by the extreme positions on Olson and McCubbin's typology might assist us in conceptualising what might be meant by an 'underclass family'. Social work as an institution has always targeted 'problem families' or 'socially disorganised families' as a central part of its statutory responsibility. The family centre has been seen as an instrument for tackling these multiple problems in a concerted and focused way, particularly in England.

Cannan (1990 and 1992) draws out the distinction which I have alluded to here. Her research describes the different origins and orientations of family centres. Some have grown out of day nurseries, some from children's homes and others have evolved from community centres. They reflect these different origins in their approach to family problems. Centres established within the voluntary sector, such as those managed by the Children's Society, tend to have a community development focus and so they will be open to all potential users within a neighbourhood or community, although they also take families referred to them by the social services. Family centres set up by the statutory services often deal exclusively with families referred to them by social workers concerned about children at risk or about some other issue concerning 'family dysfunction' (see Bourn, 1993). Cannan (1990) maintains that all family centres have as their primary aim the provision of 'preventive services': protecting children at risk of being harmed by their parents and preventing children from entering care (see Bourn, 1993). They are invariably set in areas of multiple deprivation or serve those areas even if the centres themselves are located outside the deprived areas. The link with the idea of an 'underclass' is revealed by Cannan's observation that many of the social workers and volunteers whom she interviewed in her study of family centres subscribed to the 'cycle of deprivation' thesis in some way, if not intellectually, then in terms of their practice. She comments that the cycle of deprivation thesis fashioned in the 1970s by Sir Keith Joseph, which maintained that 'a cycle of poor parenting and maternal deprivation reproduced social problems such as maladjustment, child abuse, delinquency and mental illness', was reflected in family centre planning documents. The aim of the centres was to instil self-reliance and self-discipline into mothers as part of a regime aimed at resocialising them into the parenting role and 'breaking the cycle'.

Two polar types emerge from the research on family centres (see Hasler, 1984; Adamson and Warren, 1983; Cannan, 1992). First, those centres which deal mainly with families referred to them by the statutory services and focus on family therapy tend to offer what Cannan (1990) describes as 'a theoretically grounded, prestigious and medically legitimated technology of intervention' (p. 71). The children's departments of major hospitals such as Maudsley, the Tavistock and Great Ormond Street provide the model here. Family dysfunction is the focus rather than the wider socio-economic environment within which the family lives. Ideas drawn from systems theory prevail, and there tends to be a stress on professionalism and professional distance between the practitioners and their clients. In terms of the framework set out in Chapter 2, this type of family centre works with *strong classification and framing of knowledge*. The distance between the practitioners and clients always remains intact, whilst the *framing* or control over the direction and pace of what happens and what must be known is determined by the professional practitioners who are concerned above all else with accomplishing a *correction* of individual behaviour and family patterns considered to be deviant. Second, those family centres described by Holman (1988) which are run by the Children's Society place an emphasis on providing practical help or a 'resourceful friend' rather than a professionally trained specialist in family problems. These family centres are more obviously located within a project of community participation and development. Cannan (1990 and 1992) suggests that instead of drawing on models of clinical intervention and systems theory, community based centres are influenced by sociological knowledge, which guides them in their dealings with wider political and community issues. There is an emphasis on deprofessionalism in Holman's description of the Children's Society projects. In place of a concern with family functioning there is likely to be an emphasis on social justice. Political bureaucracies are just as likely to be tackled as errant parents. The *classification and framing of knowledge* will tend to be weak, and participation and empowerment of centre users (not clients) will be given greater stress.

The interesting issue concerning family centres irrespective of their orientation is the way that they facilitate social work at the interface between the state and the family. Their primary responsibility seems to be to 'treat' women who are failing to fulfil their culturally prescribed motherhood role. That failure has increasingly been seen as a major cause of maladjustment, criminality and abuse. Family centres have, in some circumstances, therefore, become frontline instruments of social policy intervention in the management of the most marginal problem populations. They are tools for the public management of private dysfunction.

Family centres fit in well with the 1990s emphasis on reducing welfare dependency and increasing the contribution made to social welfare by voluntary agencies. They are likely to grow in importance throughout the decade because of this, but they are also likely to continue to receive official approval because they address the 'moral panic' about deviance in social and family life in a way which appears to be 'clinical'. They focus on the issue of 'dangerousness' in family life and modern society and seek to correct it and control it in an institutional and administratively convenient way. It is to the wider public debate and anxiety about 'dangerousness' in family life that I now turn.

7

Dangerous families, public inquiries and child protection

The 'underclass' debate is one manifestation of public anxiety about family matters and their connection with social deviance. The image of the young never-married woman living in a deprived housing estate may be commonly associated with problems of criminality and incivility, but it is also associated with problems in parenting and, increasingly, child abuse. Concern about 'the underclass' is therefore not solely about welfare dependency and withdrawal from the labour market, as often stressed by the political right, it is also a significant theme in public utterances about child protection (see Hendrick, 1994, 242–57). This is because of attempts in recent years to identify the social and economic characteristics commonly associated with child abuse cases. The profile of the most likely abusing family is one in which the mother lives with a male partner who has a criminal record and is often unemployed; the man is not the biological father of the child or children in his joint care; the family will have financial and accommodation problems; the parents are considered to possess a combination of immature personalities and a tendency to express themselves in aggressive ways. Further, it seems that families associated with child abuse are disproportionately drawn from those at the lower end of the social hierarchy and concern is voiced that child neglect resulting from material deprivation is a phenomenon closely related to the infliction of actual physical harm on a child. The puzzling question for historians of child welfare such as Hendrick (1994) is why there was a gap in public interest between the early years of this century and the 1960s, and further, why there has been an upsurge of concern about child abuse in more recent times. The answer to the first of these questions is basically that for the first sixty years of this century 'in terms of child-protection legislation and the enforcement and interpretation of that legislation by the State through social policy, the *primary* concerns were with the efficient functioning of the family and the maintenance of respectability through socialisation' (Hendrick, 1994, 252). Corporal punishment and firm discipline exercised within the family, irrespective of its form, were accepted as a necessary part of a well ordered society. With respect to more recent interest in child abuse among the general public, Hendrick (1994) has drawn attention to the close association between the so-called 'rediscovery of poverty' in the 1960s and the 'rediscovery of child abuse' in the same period. The public anxiety about child abuse also seems to have been generated by more active movements among professional social workers and doctors to identify and respond to the phenomenon (see N. Parton, 1985, 74–7). The public inquiry into the death of Maria Colwell which was set up in 1973 and reported in September 1974 became a focus for public concern and led to the publicising of cases of child abuse well beyond the confines of their locality.

The molestation of normality: the changing boundaries of deviance

Having located such problem families firmly at the bottom of the social hierarchy, it has to be acknowledged that issues concerning child protection arise in relation to families distributed throughout the social structure. For example, in the United Kingdom the two most significant public controversies surrounding child sexual abuse in recent years in Cleveland and on Orkney attained their heightened notoriety mainly because they involved apparently 'normal' middle-class families. The number of middle-class families associated with child sexual abuse has risen enormously in the past twenty years, leading inevitably to a wider public anxiety about child protection because it no longer seems to be a problem confined to the marginal members of society, or 'the underclass'.

However, a confusion has emerged about the exact nature of the 'crisis' which has supposedly befallen the modern family. Frost (1990) has no doubt about the connection between poverty, deprivation and child abuse, and he has no hesitation in discussing the issue within the context of an emerging 'underclass' in Thatcher's Britain. Those who are the poorest in society are more exposed to life events connected with poverty and social work intervention. They are less able to measure up to the norms of domestic and familial competence in a policy era which stresses family rather than state responsibility for a range of matters relating to family welfare. Pelton (1978) talks about the 'myth of classlessness' in child abuse and neglect cases, and certainly in the United States the evidence points quite clearly to the fact that the frequency and severity of child abuse is related to low socio-economic status. He describes data emerging from a number of social surveys into official child abuse and neglect reporting where the socio-economic status of offenders is known: for example, the American Humane Association survey of child abuse and neglect, reporting in 1975, which revealed that the income levels of 69.2 per cent of offenders was, at that time, below $7,000. He also reports that the survey revealed that very high proportions of offenders were in receipt of Aid to Families with Dependent Children (42 per cent of families in 1976), the main means-tested welfare benefit for American citizens. More small-scale and qualitative survey data reported by Pelton also show that the 'myth of classlessness' in this area of public concern has been exposed: child abuse is, on the whole, correlated with low socio-economic status.

Whilst many people might accept the pattern of public statistics relating to child abuse, they may take issue with Pelton's conclusions. Excessive scrutiny of poor people's lives by welfare professionals might be one explanation for the correlation of low socio-economic status with child abuse and neglect. The socio-economic distribution of child abuse could reflect, therefore, the differential levels of exposure to public inquiry that middle and working class people experience: the relationship between poverty and child abuse is reduced to an anomaly of reporting. The American data does, however, reveal a problem with this line of argument. The research seems to show that child abuse and neglect are correlated with degrees of poverty, that the most severe injuries including the death of a child seem to occur within the poorest families (see Gil, 1970) and, significantly, that 'officially reported incidents are more likely than unreported incidents to involve severe injury, since severity is an important criterion of reporting' (Pelton, 1978, 611). British data also tends to support this general pattern (see Smith, Hanson and Noble, 1975).

[margin handwriting: "most common explanation of Abuse: Child Abuse."]

Despite strong evidence that, overall, child abuse is related to social location, psychopathological explanations remain in the ascendancy, particularly in relation to sexual abuse. Child abuse is popularly regarded as a product either of parental emotional problems (Steele and Pollack, 1968) or of a defect in character structure (Kempe *et al.*, 1962). Psychosomatic illness, self-centredness and a variety of other psychological problems are also advanced as causes (see Gelles, 1973). These diagnoses have served to legitimise psychotherapeutic intervention into family life. Two reasons are offered for the continued popularity of the view that child abuse is a problem distributed throughout the social structure and not generally confined to the poorest families. First, the 'myth' serves the purpose of those who approach social problems and social policy with a singularly clinical eye:

[margin handwriting: "other side of argument" "quote"]

> Maintenance of the myth permits many professionals to view child abuse and neglect as psychodynamic problems in the context of a medical model of 'disease' and 'cure', rather than as predominantly sociological and poverty-related problems. (Pelton, 1978, 613)

The medical model allows those concerned with child abuse to respond to the issue as if it were an epidemic spreading through the social body; it facilitates a perspective which inflates the problem in order to create a space for professional activity. The second reason advanced as to why the 'myth of classlessness' goes on relatively unchallenged is, of course, that it diverts attention away from awkward and searching questions about poverty and social policy which governments in the 1990s associate with increased costs. To enclose the debate about child abuse and neglect within the parameters of a medical discourse means that relatively cheap strategies involving professional intervention and family therapy can be employed, relieving governments of the need to address the fundamental problems of the reward structure in the advanced industrial economies. The advantage of this for policy makers within governmental circles is that the blame for failures in child protection can be contained to the level of negligent professional practice rather than being attributed to insufficient resources and poor social policy direction from the political centre.

Foucault (1978), writing about the apparently obscure topic of the 'dangerous individual' in nineteenth- century legal psychiatry,

illuminates a very contemporary problem: to whom should we del-
egate responsibility for the explanation of violence enacted without
apparent reason? He suggests that by the end of the nineteenth century the problem of who should take on this responsibility of speaking
authoritatively about the 'dangers of the social body' was resolved
as psychiatry established itself in the field of forensic medicine.
The more gratuitous and undetermined violent acts appeared to be,
the more reliance was placed on psychiatry to explain what appeared
to be inexplicable. The necessity for the criminal justice system to
be able to explain an act, either by reference to some instrumental
calculus or motive or by a diagnosis of 'madness', was met by the
ability of psychiatrists to claim to be able to differentiate the 'dangerous' from the merely 'legally responsible'. These same issues
permeate all levels of discussion about child protection today. Indeed the concept of 'dangerousness' has emerged as a key theme in
contemporary professional debates about deviance in social work
(see N. Parton, 1985, 139–44; Parton and Parton, 1989; Dale *et al.*,
1986).

The tendency to reject sociological explanation in the area of child
abuse and the privileging of explanations which centre on *psychopathology* are at the heart of what Charles Krauthammer (1993) has
called the *molestation of normality*. Drawing on an observation by
Daniel Patrick Moynihan (1993), that one way in which modern
American society seems to be responding to the perceived increase
in deviancy, indeed to the perception that crime and deviancy have
reached incomprehensible proportions, is to define it away by lower-
ing the threshold of what we are collectively prepared to call 'normal', Krauthammer suggests that a similar process is occurring upwards
in society. He observes that:

> As part of the vast social project of moral levelling it is not enough for
> the deviant to be normalised. The normal must be found to be deviant.
> Therefore, while for the criminals and crazies deviancy has been de-
> fined down, for the ordinary bourgeois deviancy has been defined up.
> Large areas of ordinary behaviour hitherto considered benign have had
> their threshold radically redefined up, so that once innocent behaviour
> now stands condemned as deviant. Normal middle class life stands ex-
> posed as the true home of violence and abuse and a whole catalogue of
> aberrant acting and thinking. (Krauthammer, 1993)

Krauthammer draws attention to the processes involved in the social construction of public problems. The *molestation of normality* distracts us, therefore, from the pressing problems for which we have no readily available solutions towards problems that are, perhaps, more easily tackled, such as psychopathology and family dysfunction. Possibly the notion 'easily tackled' should be qualified in this context: family dysfunctions divert our gaze inwards to the isolated family and distract us from the wider problems of the social structure which appear to be far too daunting and complex to be confronted. The phenomenon described by Krauthammer as the *molestation of normality* creates a very perplexing environment within which to make sense of such a problematic issue as child abuse and neglect.

The complexities raised by the process of 'moral levelling' are increased by the contribution made by feminist analyses to the issue of child abuse, particularly sexual abuse. The role of men within the family and throughout society is an issue that feminists will not allow to be ignored in the context of discussing violence against women and children. Rather than treating child sexual abuse in isolation, as the act of a socio-pathic individual, many feminists would argue that there is a 'continuum of sexual violence' (C. Parton, 1990) linking everyday male behaviour to acts of severe sexual violence against women and children. However, a conceptual, and indeed political, divide opens up within the feminist perspective with respect to the sociological explanation of abuse: if the problem is patriarchal power, which involves the masculinisation of sexuality and the domination of the gender division of reproductive and productive labour, then the social distribution of child abuse will be found in all social and occupational classes. If this is how child abuse is to be explained, the question which arises is whether aggressive masculinity as a concept exhausts our understanding of the phenomenon. Christine Parton (1990) points out, however, that patriarchal power interacts with other dimensions of cleavage in society such as race, age and social class. The association between material disadvantage and violence may remain. To restate an observation made in Chapter 6 in relation to the underclass debate and the social consequences of lone parenthood, the frequency distribution of child abuse does tend to confirm that whilst it may occur across all social classes, it is more *commonly* encountered where there is poverty, ignorance and subcultural support for aggressive masculinity.

The modern concept of child abuse and neglect is one which is being constructed out of competing public discourses anchored in the conflict between opposing professional interests, and in the midst of wide public anxiety about deviance and 'dangerousness' at the core of society. King and Trowell (1992) make an observation about the distinctive way in which the law courts and therapy clinics deal with issues of child abuse and marital problems. The orientation towards the finding of facts and the engagement with legal reasoning often conflicts with the sympathetic treatment of the frailties of children and their parents in child abuse cases. King and Trowell talk about the distinctive discourses of the court and the clinic in this context. Within the caring professions there is a discernible division between those who subscribe to a medical and therapeutic orientation, seeking family problems in all sections of society, and those who are inclined towards the pursuit of solutions through the development of social policies. This division is further complicated by an almost formalistic and anti-intellectual approach to the issue in Britain compared with the very active multidisciplinary research communities that have grown up in the United States. Diverging approaches to the problem have developed: one theoretical and research oriented, the other grounded in quasi-legal administrative procedures which have been pre-eminently concerned with finding 'managerial' solutions to problems resulting from bad professional practices (see Corby, 1987; Howe, 1992). It might, therefore, be more precise to suggest that four discourses on child abuse have emerged: a clinical discourse rooted in the correction of behaviour deemed to be psychopathological; a quasi-legal discourse rooted in the management of professional practice; a sociological discourse anchored in the social policy analysis of poverty; and a feminist discourse focused on the continuum between male behaviour and sexual violence. The latter two 'ways of seeing' issues have been marginalised, especially within the formal institutions of policy formation and decision-making. I will return to this issue below.

At the heart of this issue is the public's anxiety to know the scale of the problem and how best to protect children. The attempt to inform the public about these disturbing issues is mediated by popular journalism which reports on child abuse cases, offering facile remedies and analyses of what are undoubtedly complex cases. But the central mechanism whereby issues of professional malpractice in the field of child protection have emerged into the public sphere is through the instrument of the public inquiry into infamous cases of child protection failure. The social and political forces which are actively constructing a public agenda and influencing perceptions of the child abuse issue, in Britain certainly, are consolidating their views in the report recommendations of official inquiries with the expectation that professional practice may be influenced. Public understanding of the child abuse phenomenon is being shaped by this process.

The public sphere and public inquiries

Since the 1970s there have been almost forty major public inquiries into child abuse and neglect cases, many of them involving the public examination of the issues and practices surrounding the death of a child in circumstances suggesting professional negligence on the part of social workers and social service and social work departments. These public inquiries are seen as watershed events in which particular insights into the process of managing child protection are publicly identified and used thereafter as policy yardsticks. In fact we have a situation where child protection policy in Britain is driven less by scientific and social research than by quasi-legal administrative processes that signal procedural shortcomings. What is said at public inquiries is obviously of paramount importance to social workers and policy makers, but how proceedings are organised and issues made problematic is also important: there is a tendency to look past the public inquiry process to gain access to information and data without questioning the manner in which problems are identified and solutions proffered. Having already suggested that four prominent discourses have emerged around the child protection issue, it is interesting to observe how public inquiries privilege legal and administrative discourses at the expense of feminist or sociological discourses.

By drawing on the works of Habermas and Bernstein which were discussed in Chapters 1 and 2, and complementing their insights with those of systems theorist Niklas Luhmann (1982 and 1989), a useful perspective on the public inquiry *system* can be acquired. It is important that we understand how public conceptions of problems are shaped and how professional practice is scrutinised. Ultimately we need to know how concepts like 'dangerousness' are reinforced by the public debate about controversial incidents, and how conceptions, or models, of family relationships informing social work practice and intervention into family life are defended and criticised. The way that these themes are discussed in public and the system that is used to select what qualifies as valid and invalid evidence at public inquiries are of vital significance.

The central dynamic of a public inquiry is to shape and delimit the scope of its business by the use of a well defined remit, often given to the inquiry by the statute or governmental body setting up the public hearing. The objective of *establishing the facts* is the prime discipline through which the inquiry ensures that it has a particular focus. All legal and quasi-legal procedures are concerned with fundamental causal relationships as far as these can reasonably be determined. However, the selection of information considered relevant to an issue and the interpretation of what constitutes a fact in public inquiry hearings often lead to controversy and disquiet among those who feel that their point of view has been excluded or assigned a low priority in the hearings' business. King and Trowell (1992) observe that it seems unavoidable that the legal process will seek to 'reduce complex issues to simple choices to be made on the basis of 'the facts' presented on a particular day or days – a snap-shot approach' (p. 52). They contrast this process with that of the family therapy clinic which attempts 'over what may be a lengthy period to unravel a mass of complex information obtained from various external sources and from tests and interviews that their staff con-duct' (p. 52). Whilst King and Trowell may be contrasting the law courts, sitting to determine whether an offence has been committed against a child, with a therapeutic encounter designed to provide healing and care, the same problem of *complexity reduction* applies to the public inquiry sitting to discover 'the facts' relating to a child protection failure. The quasi-legal dimension of public inquiries, involving, indeed dominated by, lawyers, ensures that a legal dis-course narrowly focused on factual events and relationships very often prevails at the expense of what might be described as a *dis-cursive approach* to the evidence, seeking to explore complex issues and indirect relationships. The distinction between what is legally important and what might be considered to be in the interests of *natural justice* is rarely understood by lay participants at public hearings.

I have argued elsewhere that the theoretical debate between sys-tems theorist Niklas Luhmann and critical theorist Jurgen Habermas about the political and democratic implications of modern administrative mechanisms describes different but complementary dimensions of public administrative systems (see Rodger, 1980, 1985a, 1985b). It is a debate between someone sensing a threat to democratic values and institutions from detached functionaries and unaccountable forms of administrative power (Habermas) and a political 'realist' who acknowledges that the ideas of the *Enlightenment* about truth, justice and the public's participation in the processes which govern and control social life are incompatible with modern complex social systems (Luhmann). Habermas originally developed his political position and theoretical perspective in his earliest published work *The Structural Transformation of the Public Sphere* (1989) which was an enquiry into the emergence of what he calls the *bourgeois public sphere* in the late eighteenth century. What was significant about this development was that for a brief historical period, roughly between 1750 and 1880, the propertied middle classes created public spaces of a cultural and political nature where they engaged in open criticism and discussion about matters of public concern at the time. The bourgeoisie were able to establish and institutionalise legal rights and political principles which were used to criticise state action. Jean Cohen (1979) argues that the three key principles of modern civil society – legality, plurality and publicity – were institutionalised in this brief period. All modern western states remain constrained by these principles. Two things, therefore, emerged from this historical development creating the institutional space which we can identify as *the public sphere*: a public space was created in the literary salons, cafe societies and daily and periodic press which established the right to subject public political action and decision-making to the court of public opinion, and this right was secured in law and political institutions guaranteeing free speech. Public inquiries are perhaps one of the best institutional remnants of this 'democratic moment' in western political development. They seek to debate and discover 'facts' about matters of wide controversy in public whilst encouraging the public's participation in their business (see Wraith and Lamb, 1971).

Luhmann takes a quite different look at administrative processes. He views modern societies as too complex to be fettered by the fragments of the *Enlightenment*. The pace of change is so fast and the need to make efficient decisions about complex matters so urgent that subjecting decision-making to open, public participation only complicates procedures whilst tending to 'make a principle out of frustration'. People require only to know that efficient decision-making is proceeding. They do not need to know about the mechanisms by which these decisions are made. Luhmann does not adopt a position which is hostile to democratic values as such; his opposition to Habermas's democratic values is not based on principle but rather on a 'realist' appraisal of how things actually are. He is a sophisticated systems theorist who develops what amounts to a functional-structural approach to systems analysis. The structural limits or boundaries of systems are, therefore, manipulated, or managed, or simply functionally adjust (the emphasis will depend upon the degree of political intention one wishes to incorporate within the perspective) to control the intrusion of complicating matter into the system. Legal systems and public administrative systems operate to *reduce complexity* by excluding complicating data which they are unable to reconcile with efficient decision-making. *Meaning* for Habermas should be realised through the process of open discussion in order that a democratic consensus can be established about 'the facts', whereas Luhmann's system perspective converts the issue of *meaning* to that of the survival and ongoing efficiency of the *system* itself. The concept of the *system* in Luhmann's work literally constructs *meaning* by the exclusion of other *meanings*, displacing competing *meanings* struggling to enter and influence the work of the *system* which might complicate decision-making (see Sixel, 1977). For example, legal reasoning dominates the law courts and public inquiries because it excludes extra-legal discourse. Psychology, psychiatry, sociology and social work theory are permitted limited access to courts and public inquiries dealing with child protection issues, and only in so far as they conform to the dominant reasoning established by the judge or inquiry Reporter/Inspector.

In reality public inquiries, like law courts, are often a tussle between those forms of knowledge validated and permitted entry to the proceedings by the presiding authority, and those ideas and views straining to be heard which lack official recognition. The clash between 'expert' knowledge and lay person's common sense is one area of conflict. Conflict between alternative professional discourses, one of which retains greater social recognition than the other, such as the pre-eminence of medicine over social work, is another area of friction. In other words, we can conceive of public inquiries as simultaneously trying to facilitate what Habermas has called the *ideal*

speech situation (see Habermas, 1970; Mueller, 1973), where discussion can move to ever deeper levels in pursuit of the 'truth', and
what Luhmann describes as *complexity reduction*, where information is systematically excluded and the public's participation is limited to that which is necessary in order to arrive at administratively
efficient and legally legitimised decisions (see Luhmann, 1982;
Mueller, 1973).

Hallett (1989) identifies a number of dimensions around which
inquiries have varied in child abuse cases. For example, inquiries
may vary with respect to the procedural mechanisms adopted to
acquire knowledge of a problem or issue. The adoption of an
adversarial process may be preferred in some cases to that of an
inquisitorial process in which a committee of the 'great and the
good' sit to hear invited evidence and evaluate 'expert' opinion.
Most inquiries tend to follow the inquisitorial model except where
the degree of public anxiety and the sense of controversy surrounding a case lead to a more contentious set of issues. The decision on
whether to hold an inquiry in public or largely in private, though
allowing for the views and submissions of members of the public,
represents a further choice available to those setting up an inquiry.
Public proceedings organised around the adversarial model, which
closely mimics legal proceedings, have been the preferred option
for those inquiries which have dealt with the most infamous controversies in recent years including the cases of Maria Colwell, Jasmine Beckford, Tyra Henry, Kimberly Carlile and also the Cleveland
and Orkney inquiries.

The *classification* and *framing* of knowledge provides the battle-
ground for adversarial processes. The authority to control the inquiry remit, and therefore the power to determine *what is to be
known*, steers the proceedings of any public hearing towards a partial understanding of what are very often complex matters. The
potential of individual social workers, or parents who feel that their
children were removed from the family home and placed in care
without justification, to follow an agenda which is different from
that authorised by the public inquiry is limited. The analytical framework which was set out in Chapter 2 can help us understand this
issue. By way of a reminder, I argued that Bernstein's concept of
framing is useful because it directs our attention towards the relative power of competing interests to initiate consideration of a subject. Where *framing* is strong, the inquiry procedure will be controlled

by the authority presiding over the hearing. The strength or weakness of *framing* will be determined largely by the authority at the political centre which determines the parameters of the inquiry remit. Weak *framing* will be associated with informality and openness in procedure. The adversarial procedure, in some circumstances, can mean that the *framing* of debate will be weak, permitting non-expert knowledge and information to penetrate the proceedings as lawyers draw selectively from the pool of witnesses who best support their case. Weak *framing* is merely a tendency because many adversarial hearings dominated by lawyers incline towards strong *framing* by virtue of the pre-eminence accorded to legal forms of reasoning and argumentation. Strong *framing* will tend to produce feelings of exclusion for some interests and, as with public inquiries more generally, feelings that *natural justice* has been violated.

The Orkney public inquiry into the removal of children from their homes in February 1991 provides a useful example of this issue. Under the Scottish Children's Panel system, the initial examination of the issues surrounding the removal of the children from their homes and their transfer into care on the Scottish mainland was welfare rather than legally oriented. Within the scope of the Children's Panel the primary concern is with the well-being of the children, not the legal finding of guilt or innocence of possible offenders. In order to pursue the legal issue of determining whether an offence has been committed against children, the matter needs to be referred by the Panel Reporter to the Sheriff's court where a legal decision can be taken as to whether there is a case to answer. This procedure inevitably follows if the parents refuse to accept the grounds for referral to the Children's Panel, which was the case on Orkney. The parents of the children and the local Church of Scotland Minister were identified as possible offenders against the children but their opportunity to establish their innocence at the Proof Hearing before Sheriff David Kelbie, and at subsequent legal proceedings, was denied when Sheriff Kelbie concluded that the procedures of the Children's Panel had departed from accepted practice and were therefore incompetent because the children had not been present at the Panel to be advised of the grounds for referral. Because of his unease about the evidence of abuse, Kelbie decided to ignore the legal precedent supporting the decision to exclude the children from the Panel. The higher court in Edinburgh criticised Sheriff Kelbie's legal judgment but the Deputy Reporter on Orkney decided against pursuing the case. In the subsequent public inquiry before Lord Clyde, Church of Scotland Minister Morris MacKenzie and some of the parents were frustrated when they realised that the inquiry remit did not provide an opportunity for them to establish their innocence of the charges. The inquiry remit forced Lord Clyde to consider only the narrower issues surrounding professional practice. Whilst the issues of 'justice', 'truth' and innocence were of the utmost importance to the parents, they were not matters which Lord Clyde's inquiry could consider. The *classification* and *framing* of the inquiry process was, therefore, strong, allowing only material relating to the operation of the Orkney social work department to be considered.

The distinction between an adversarial and an inquisitorial model for public inquiries does not exhaust the possibilities available. It is worth emphasising that the format of public inquiries is seldom a matter of legal rigidity. How an inquiry hearing is to be organised and what procedures are to be followed are often left to the discretion of the authority presiding over the hearing. If a *discursive* approach to the submissions and evidence is considered desirable, then a more open-ended process could, technically, be instituted. In practice the dominance of legal thinking and the preference of public administrators for discipline in public hearings funded by the taxpayer rarely permit such a radical exploration of issues to be undertaken. The cost of public inquiries (the Orkney inquiry cost £6 million) and the expense to lay participants who may be supporting expensive legal representation, militates against an *ideal speech situation*.

Public inquiries as instruments for policy formation

Given that public inquiries lean towards the reduction of complex issues and the restriction of evidence and discussion to 'factual' matters, there tends to be little exploration of the wider issues surrounding child protection and abuse. This, despite criticism from many who participate in public inquiries, makes them ideal instruments for defusing public anxieties; the semblance of activity and policy reappraisal is a substitute for fundamental change, or so it seems. The objective of the hearings is to identify procedural shortcomings in social work practice and to generate an agenda for action in social work bureaucracies. As tools of policy formation, they have become fairly repetitive (see Dingwall, 1986). Whilst most of the well known and controversial public inquiries into child abuse in recent years have considered only the particular circumstances of one case, the final reports emerging from their investigations have offered comments and observations about the childcare and protection system more generally and it has to be acknowledged that the major public inquiries have succeeded in creating a policy agenda by virtue of the public nature of the proceedings. In particular, they have identified procedural problems in professional activity which, by their nature, have a very low visibility for the general public. Further, the process of translating research findings into practical changes in the way that social workers conduct themselves is, by comparison with a major public inquiry event, a longwinded and imprecise route by which to effect change. This is inevitably so because research communities seldom agree about methods and perspectives, and often pursue different goals by different routes, unhindered by the need to deal with pressing and immediate policy problems. Indeed it could be argued that one of the main areas of concern in social work and family therapy in recent years has been the proliferation of theories and therapeutic techniques which have neither attained widespread consensus about their efficacy nor been subjected to the court of public and professional scrutiny. It is only when the mass media have exposed and publicised the more absurd outcomes of bad professional practice, and subsequently created a political climate in which the setting up of a public inquiry hearing has led to some degree of examination of the underlying theoretical and practical assumptions informing child protection work, that professional thinking has been exposed to the scrutiny of a wider and often more cynical audience.

A brief examination of the issues involved in the two most recent public controversies involving child abuse in Britain, at Cleveland and on Orkney, can be used to assess critically the extent to which public inquiries serve a useful purpose in identifying and generating a policy agenda. A distinction ought to be made, however, between the effectiveness of public inquiries for generating a social policy agenda, and the agenda that is generated by the public inquiry. Whilst applauding the use of the public inquiry instrument to examine social work procedures and practices, many critics have pointed to the narrow legalistic approach to child protection work that has resulted from the series of major public hearings in recent years (see Parton and Martin, 1989; Howe, 1992). The first issue to be addressed is the adequacy of the public inquiry system as a mechanism for identifying all relevant issues and subjecting them to public scrutiny.

Cleveland

The detail of the inquiry's findings need not be discussed here (see Lyon and de Cruz, 1988, for a full discussion of the inquiry report). The central controversy of Cleveland centred on the fact that a particular medical examination (specifically, the reflex anal dilatation test) was being over-used, resulting in exceptionally large numbers of children being taken into protective care. As medical practices remain impenetrable to most lay people, the likelihood of that test being named and its shortcomings being identified in public would have been small had the Butler-Sloss inquiry not focused attention on it and on its appropriate use. In fact, once the issue had become part of a widespread public controversy due to both media and political activity, there was no mechanism other than the Butler-Sloss inquiry whereby medical and scientific evidence could be discussed openly and in an accessible way, allowing the medical issues to be placed in a broader social context. For example, as Lyon and de Cruz (1988) point out, in only 18 out of a possible 121 or 125 cases (the inquiry report itself seems to be confused about numbers) was the reflex anal dilatation test relied upon as the sole sign of sexual abuse. This was not the impression given by the more extreme media reports. An accurate recording of events and issues, albeit those delimited by the public inquiry remit, was ensured by the public hearing. The important point to be stressed is that the public nature of the inquiry hearing brought into sharp focus the fact that there should not be reliance on physical signs without also placing those physical signs in a wider social and psychological context. The medical evidence pointed up the complexities of the way the anal muscle works, and indeed that 'physical abnormalities may have an innocent explanation' and sexual abuse of children may occur 'without anogenital contact' (*The Lancet*, 10 October 1987). The absence of an agreed vocabulary for describing physical signs associated with child sexual abuse was also identified, along with a failure to ensure the full medical investigation of symptoms and their meaning. At a procedural level it became clear through the public evidence that forensic medical examinations of children to obtain evidence of abuse had been carried on repeatedly with little consideration being given to the impact of the process on the child's well-being. And there appeared to be a precipitate use of care orders with little regard given to the appropriateness of removing children from their family home irrespective of circumstances. These issues would not have been identified or have entered the public domain in a clear and focused way, necessitating a policy response, without a public inquiry. The dissemination of research findings through academic publications and conferences, whilst an important element in shaping best practice and increasing the knowledge base of professional practitioners, lacks the immediacy of a major public inquiry controversy. The demand that issues and professional practices be subjected to a process of discursive rationalisation within the public sphere is partly met by the public inquiry system.

The way that the inquiry report responded to these identified failures of the child protection network raises different issues. Whether those involved in the Cleveland inquiry, and those charged with amending social work practices in its aftermath, understood the implications of the issues for field social workers and other practitioners working in the field is a matter of debate. I will return to this issue below.

Orkney

The Orkney inquiry revealed something of the limits of the public hearing system with respect to controversial child protection and family issues. What became clear from the proceedings of the public inquiry, and the subsequent report by Lord Clyde, was that well-publicised issues and guidelines resulting from the Cleveland inquiry had not been read and understood. It is one thing to generate a public agenda to amend professional practice, it is quite another to ensure that those practice issues are acted upon. The processes leading up to the removal of the nine children from their homes and their subsequent questioning and treatment were found to be ill-thought-out and badly executed. The Clyde report was sweeping in its criticism of social workers, the Royal Scottish Society for the Prevention of Cruelty to Children (RSSPCC) and the police, but it was also silent about a number of important issues.

The report says nothing, for example, about the adequacy of the judicial supervision of social workers' decisions. The application to the Sheriff for Place of Safety Orders on the nine children contained little of detail about the cases and failed to justify the granting of the orders or indeed to indicate under which statutory powers the orders were being sought. Lord Clyde severely criticised the competence of the social workers for placing such an application before the Sheriff, but he is silent about the competence of the Sheriff who signed the orders permitting the removal of the children to go ahead. This omission directs attention towards the relationship between the judiciary and social work, and the proper checks and balances that are required to ensure the supervision of powers to invade the private sphere of the family. In some respects these issues are pivotal for an understanding of the Orkney controversy. The shaping down of discussion and its containment to 'factual' matters relating only to the events leading up to and immediately after the removal of the children in February 1991 took precedence over an exploration of those wider issues. Whereas the Cleveland inquiry had focused attention on the adequacy of existing social work and medical knowledge relating to child abuse, the Orkney inquiry focused on practice procedures. Whilst the issue of how best to approach and interview children suspected of being abused was discussed, especially in relation to the shortcomings of 'disclosure therapy' as practiced by the RSSPCC, the wider origins and theoretical justifications of the Orkney social workers' understanding of the child abuse field remained uninvestigated.

The limits of the public inquiry instrument in the public sphere compared with other sources of information and critical enquiry can be briefly highlighted by examining the issue of 'satanism' which lay at the heart of the child abuse allegations, but which remained unexamined by Lord Clyde's inquiry. As a theme, 'satanism' has more appeal for the tabloid press who are interested in sensationalising the affair than for policy makers and lawyers charged with the responsibility of shaping childcare law and social work practice. However, academics researching contemporary legend, or the social and psychological mechanisms whereby rumours and fables enter the consciousness of people in modern complex societies (see Cornwell and Hobbs, 1992; G. Fine, 1992), have collected and chronicled the growth in public and professional interest in 'satanic ritual abuse' in Britain through the newsletter of the International Society for Contemporary Legend Research, *Foaftale News* (Issues 22–24, 1991). The research network has compiled a checklist of newspaper reports found in local newspapers, tabloids and quality press, and has been able to identify incidents connecting child abuse with satanism from 1988 onwards, citing a conference in Reading attended by a number of social workers during September 1989 as particularly influential (Ellis, Bennett and Hobbs, 1993). It was this conference, it would appear, that provided the catalyst linking social work theory with more impressionistic accounts of child sexual abuse rife in North America. The extent to which unresearched ideas and badly thought-out theory have infiltrated social work practice, and so influenced the execution of statutory powers, is an issue which has so far not been explored adequately by any public inquiry hearing, although the La Fontaine report (1994) has criticised the prevalence of what she calls 'unproven specialists' working in the field of child protection and has called for a greater degree of professional scepticism in this area. It is very often this issue of overly abstract and sometimes apparently 'cranky' thinking about social relationships, seemingly detached from common sense, however, which is uppermost in the minds of lay people when discussion of child protection failure enters the public sphere. The main outcome of over two decades of public inquiries has been a return to what many critical commentators of the public inquiry process have called 'legalism' (see N. Parton and Martin, 1989; N. Parton, 1991; Howe, 1992), rather than an examination of the central research agendas, theoretical assumptions and received wisdom circulating within the professional worlds of health and welfare practitioners. It is this aspect of public inquiries which represents both their failure as an instrument of open and democratic public debate and their success as a mechanism facilitating policy formation. By focusing on legalities and procedural issues relating to professional practice, the public inquiry limits the extent to which public pressures and anxieties can influence administrative procedures. But, as with all public administrative processes, the lay observer can be left with a sense that 'natural justice' has not been met, and it is that, in a perverse way, which marks the success of the public inquiry as an instrument of policy formation.

The aftermath of the inquiries: dangerousness, legalism and the public sphere

Two main issues have become apparent since the reports of the major public inquiries have begun to be dissected. The first is the impact of the inquiries' findings on the routine practices of welfare bureaucracies, and the second is the broader political question of how failures in the child protection *system* might best be investigated. Both are, in a sense, questions relating to the organisation and political protection of welfare work. The first issue draws our attention to the ways in which welfare work involving child protection has also become involved in protecting welfare workers (social workers, health visitors and educationalists) from public vilification for apparent professional failure. The second issue draws us towards the larger question of the relationship between the state, the family and what Donzelot (1980) has called the social sphere of welfare intervention. However, the concern is not about the state regulation of private family conduct, but rather about the degree of public openness that can or should be tolerated when the child protection *system* is being investigated. Our interest lies, therefore, in what Habermas (1989) has referred to as the *public sphere* in a liberal state.

Dangerousness and legalism

The Scottish Office response to the Orkney controversy was to publish *Scotland's Children: Proposals for Child Care Policy and Law* (Scottish Office, 1993). The document states:

> Any intervention in the life of a child or family should be on formally stated grounds, properly justified, in close consultation with all the relevant parties. (para. 2.15, p. 7)

It goes on to say:

> The separation of children under 16 from their parents against the wishes of any of them should take place only when a competent authority determines that such a step is necessary and where action is subject to *clear legal procedures open to legal challenge.* [my emphasis] (para. 2.16, p. 7)

The move to a more formal and legally supervised system of child protection and childcare seems to be signalled: the Children (Scotland) Act 1995 will consolidate this development.

Nigel Parton and Norma Martin (1989) have suggested that the role of the social worker operating the childcare system is increasingly being regulated and constrained by what they call *legalism*. Referring to Shklar (1964), they define *legalism* in terms of 'the

superimposition of legal duties and rights upon
responsibilities, essentially for the protection of
conduct is deemed to be something that is best ac
following' and moral relationships considered to be a ma
and duties determined by rules. Now this aspect of the pro
role of the social worker is not new. The delicate balance bet
care and control, between statutory powers to intervene into the privat
sphere of the family on behalf of the state and the preservation of
the sanctity of the family, has required careful negotiation since the
inception of welfare work in the nineteenth century (see Donzelot,
1980; Dingwall, Eekelaar and Murray, 1983). The grounding of that
negotiation in legal rules which specify the conditions and limits of
welfare intervention has been acknowledged by professional social
workers for many years. The succession of major public inquiries
into child protection failure, including cases where social work intervention was deemed to have been precipitate and over-zealous,
seems to have refocused concern on the statutory frameworks guiding and controlling social work practice, which may have acquired
a 'taken for granted' status until public debate focused attention on
the competence of some social work interventions into family life.
The outcome of those inquiries is that legal scrutiny of professional
practice has taken precedence over other objectives in social work.

Dale *et al.* (1986) and Dingwall, Eekelaar and Murray (1983)
have pointed to the loss of professional self-confidence in social
work resulting from recent childcare controversies and the movement towards professional protection. That defensive shift has manifested itself in a concern with how potential public criticism can
best be avoided. The view surfacing from the many public inquiries
is that the underlying problem in childcare cases has been due either
to a lack of understanding on the part of social workers about their
statutory powers, or to their failure to use the legal powers invested
in them. The dominant opinion emerging is that social work can
only be defined in terms of its statutory duties and powers: social
workers must work with and through the statutory powers given to
them by the state to ensure that the public regulation of private
conduct is not only effective but also circumscribed by the presence
of a well understood framework of law which can act to protect the
public (the family) from excessive and unwarranted intrusion. The
domination of the public inquiries by lawyers has ensured that the
problems of child protection are defined in a legalistic manner. Parton

and child prot
therapeutic and s
e clients'. Mo
ieved by 'rule
er of rights
ssional
een

changes in an interesting way
gal codes as indices of changing
that the rediscovery of *legalism*
ial work navigate itself out of the
ion failure signals both a fragmenting
British society which typified welfare
-war period and the decline of optimism
welfare work. The mass recognition that
mily, whether it is aimed at children, women
ttered the consensual view of the family as a
world' that may have existed, and generated
con   ing confidence in the ability of the social work
profession to respond effectively to these complex problems.

The concept of the 'dangerous' family, or individual, has replaced that of the vulnerable and troubled family. The emphasis is now on attempts to identify potential problem cases in order that they may be better investigated and monitored and thus professional reputations defended, rather than on engaging with what many within the field of welfare work consider to be the primary duty of social work, that of working to rehabilitate problem populations and reintegrate them within the family and community. Howe (1992) discusses this development in terms of the 'bureaucratisation of social work'. Gone is the language of 'treatment' and 'rehabilitation' focused on the problem of returning families to 'normal' functioning, and in its place is the language of surveillance and investigation concerned pre-eminently with the protection of children from violence. The concern expressed in a number of public inquiries about the failure of agencies working in the field of childcare to co-ordinate their actions and to keep proper forensic records of their practices has been met by resorting to bureaucratic forms of organisation. The key question arising from the child abuse controversies is how can we stop parents killing their children? For Howe, this tendentious question serves to move the fulcrum balancing the care and control functions of social work clearly towards the control end of the spectrum and so tilts the focus of social work practice in the field of childcare towards a *correctional* and away from an *appreciative* code. *Correctionalism* is framed within an administrative and judicial design which accentuates the necessity to monitor and investigate potentially 'dangerous' families who conform to an established profile. The single-female-headed family, where the male partner in the household is not the biological father of the children, is one particularly common profile considered to be potentially 'dangerous'. Other criteria such as unemployment, debt, or an adult or adults living in the household with a criminal record, particularly for any offence involving violence, are also singled out as potentially troubling problems requiring surveillance and possible investigation. Howe (1992) suggests therefore that social work managers have become 'designers of surveillance systems' rather than 'casework consultants'. The bureaucratisation of social work is enshrined in routine practices in the field. In addition to the setting up of specialist teams and case conferences to monitor the handling of all child protection cases, there has been a move to limit the area of discretion in field practice. Professional practice is prescribed: the requirement in childcare cases is to train practitioners who will follow procedures rather than workers who will involve themselves in an empathetic way with problem families. The task which has been set for social workers is now becoming clear. They need to collect and collate sufficient information about problem families to enable a prediction to be made regarding their potential 'dangerousness'. Welfare managers in the field of childcare, as with community care, become the 'obligatory passage point' where all knowledge and data regarding childcare cases are stored and classified. The organisation of this system of knowledge and data is geared towards the production of forensically sound evidence of child abuse which can be used effectively in legal proceedings. The system also, incidentally, affords protection for social workers against the vagaries of childcare work by affirming the collective responsibility of the *system* for the maintenance of child protection rather than the liability of individual field workers.

An inconvenient aspect of this development is that it is fraught with difficulties because there are no reliable predictors of 'dangerousness' in individuals or families. It risks diverting the gaze of social workers away from concerns about community, environment and social structure to focus on the particular deficiencies of an individual or family isolated from those social forces which construct their everyday problems and dilemmas. Whatever else child protection procedures are doing, they are singling out children at the greatest risk of harm in a very imperfect way. Reporting on recent comparative research on child protection, Rikford (1994) suggests that 'child protection workers are spending most of their time policing the parenting habits of extremely disadvantaged people who need practical support more than surveillance'. In fact fewer than a quarter of those children taken into state care have been physically or sexually abused. The vast majority are in care because they are considered to be at risk or neglected. The suspicion is that 'standardised norms' of parenting are being imposed on problem families, instead of effective child protection work being accomplished. The danger is that in the absence of firm evidence of abuse, moral judgementalism is being reintroduced into social work practice under the guise of hard monitoring. A gap seems to be emerging between *family support* work which traditionally has been concerned with keeping families together, and *family investigation* work which is ostensibly about protecting children by anticipating where and when they are likely to be harmed. The latter trend is very much a product of the child protection failures of recent years and has been encouraged by the findings of the major child protection public inquiries which have set the policy agenda in this area since the 1980s. In reality both types of work have been undertaken by the statutory authorities. The question which needs to be posed is, will the *family support* work be allowed to flourish in an unfettered way now that discretionary power in social work has been limited by *legalism*? The important insight of post-structuralist analyses of social work is that very often the work of surveillance and investigation is continued most effectively under the guise of *family support*. The family centre is an ideal setting in which to monitor parenting behaviour whilst offering assistance and tuition on how to be an effective mother or parent. The blurring of the boundary between care and control in social work is developing more rapidly as a result of these changing emphases in childcare.

The public sphere, the child protection system and the liberal state

There are a number of confused issues surrounding the matter of investigating failures in the child protection *system* and, to a large extent, they can be reduced to the tension already alluded to within a public inquiry process which is geared towards *complexity reduction* but also towards attempting to provide an *idealised speech situation*. Beyond the bureaucratic interest in reducing pressures that are complicating the public administrative and political decision-making machinery, there is another interest which favours *complexity reduction*: that of the welfare managers of the child protection *system*. This interest is articulated well by Dingwall (1986). His concern is with the very accessible nature of the public inquiry system combined with its adversarial procedure. He considers that it simplifies the complexities of welfare work in the child protection field, because in part it fulfils a symbolic rather than practical purpose. By seeking to appease public anxieties through the production of 'symbolic victims', the public inquiry system serves badly as an instrument for the improvement of professional practice. He also insists that the public inquiry system, so far, seems to have failed in its attempts to provide clear guidelines and an agenda for child protection work because it has failed to confront the paradoxes inherent in the *social sphere*. Dingwall rightly points to the dilemma facing liberal-democratic societies today: either we accept that there will be more intervention to save children from violent adults, which means devolving more legal and social authority to welfare workers (especially health visitors and social workers), allowing them more access to the private sphere of the family, and risk threatening the basic principles of a liberal society, or we acquiesce to the protection of the private sphere of the family by strictly limiting the extent to which welfare workers can intervene in family life, perhaps at the cost of more children suffering. The public inquiries have contributed to the widespread disillusionment with welfare workers, and encouraged the view that 'someone must be to blame' among the professionals within the child protection *system*, by repeatedly interpreting this difficult choice as a simple matter of professional failure on the part of individual practitioners who were either over-zealous or incompetent. There is a sense in which posing the issues in this way inevitably leads to a rather undemocratic position; by involving the public (which undoubtedly includes the mass media) in the process of investigating child abuse cases 'moral panic' rather than an informed agenda for action in welfare bureaucracies results. Public participation in child protection investigations should therefore be curtailed. Dingwall (1986) suggests that the 'privacy of the family is central to mainstream conceptions of what a free society is' and that any attempt to 'increase the effectiveness of child protection agencies imposes a cost in forgone liberties (p. 503). He then suggests,

> If we accept that some deaths are inevitable, then what is needed is a much more sophisticated approach which investigates every death of a child in care to determine whether it was at all avoidable and general professional lessons could be learned. One possibility might be a multidisciplinary equivalent of the Confidential Inquiry into Maternal Deaths . . . This would entail the formation of standing regional panels of assessors nominated by the principal agencies involved in this work and linked to the Social Work Inspectorate. (Dingwall, 1986, p. 504)

The investigations referred to here would be conducted by panel members from outside of the area where a case arises. An alternative measure would be to use an inquisitorial system where a specialist investigator gathers the 'facts' surrounding a case. The central theme behind these alternative models to the adversarial type of public inquiry is that they would be both more efficient and less likely to cause public anxiety than the large adversarial hearings. The emphasis is on using 'confidential investigations' to assure the public that efficient decision-making is taking place and that professional practice is being amended in the light of the best information and analyses available. This is very much in line with Luhmann's view of efficient public administration, but it raises a number of issues.

First, the replacement of a public process of discovery of 'facts' and debate with a standing committee of expertise unnecessarily places professional and scientific knowledge in opposition to lay common sense. In the area of childcare this would be particularly difficult because there is no clear authoritative voice to claim a privileged right to assess matters relating to child protection. We have a situation where at least three discourses would claim to speak with authority: medicine would tend to reduce cases to issues of clinical diagnoses; the law would seek to impose a legal determination of liability and culpability; while social work, lacking a clear practice paradigm, would tend to offer a contradictory discourse, sometimes favouring a clinical view and at other times stressing social causality. And meanwhile the input of the lay voice would be reduced to the status of the impressionistic, tolerated in order that proceedings should not appear to be too remote from the concerns of ordinary people, but more likely excluded altogether.

Second, by diminishing the role of the public inquiry hearing to that of public symbolism rather than a practical instrument of policy formation, Dingwall prematurely dismisses the importance of publicity as a lever of change. Luhmann (1982) views all publicity as a potential source of 'complicating noise' disturbing the efficient working of political administrative systems. Similarly, the rejection of the public inquiry hearing in favour of a mechanism which involves a standing committee of experts in child protection would exclude an important disciplining influence on the process of investigation, that of an interested public seeking and, in some circumstances, demanding information about matters of wide social concern.

Third, an important issue is raised relating to the public's right to know, and professional practitioners' right to protection from unwarranted criticism of their work in the field of child protection. A number of commentators on these matters have observed that there is a distinction to be made between errors caused by imperfect knowledge of a situation and errors caused by lack of foresight and judgement. Dingwall has observed that it is wrong in principle to criticise professional practitioners' actions when their judgement was based on the best available knowledge at the time, even if, with hindsight, that knowledge is found to be flawed. The assumption, based on a number of the major child abuse inquiries, has been that the very public and adversarial nature of the hearings has led to an eradication of the distinction in order that someone might be found to blame. Such a confusion is a failing of intellect and is not an intrinsic feature of public inquiries. Only if it can be demonstrated that the proceedings get in the way of making fair assessments which can be discursively rationalised can it be said that proceedings should not be open and public.

Fourth, an issue arises relating to the state of knowledge about child protection issues. Medical, psychological, therapeutic and social knowledge should be tested in public for its soundness. It is quite unacceptable that any public administrative *system* should allow a professional discourse to be exempt from making its fundamental principles of knowledge, its epistemology, accessible to those who may be subjected to its influence. To state this principle is, in a sense, to reformulate the second point: the court of public opinion remains an effective regulator of professional practice, as it is with many other activities.

Fifth, and fundamentally, there is a danger that by removing proceedings about matters of public concern from the public sphere and reducing them to acts of routine public administration of a confidential nature, a sense of contempt for lay opinion is expressed. Dingwall (1986) might be right to question whether there is a 'logic to the continuing crucifixion of the child protection system by re-peated public inquiries' (p.504) and to suggest that there may only be a justification for a 'once-in-a-generation shock of a highly sym-bolic inquiry', but we also need to examine the implications of such an opinion. Too often the experts are in possession of rational knowl-edge and this is set against the 'false consciousness' and the 'moral panic' of the non-expert who merely confuses the issues. The main problem here is that whilst Dingwall (1986) rightly raises the ques-tion of which of the available administrative models of inquiry is the most effective mechanism for influencing professional practice and stimulating social policy agendas, I am suggesting that the public political process of open decision-making about matters of professional competence and childcare is as important a defining principle of the liberal state as the protection of the private sphere of the family. Social workers need to be able to justify intervention into the family not only on legal grounds, but also on public political grounds. *Legalism* is not the only factor which is delimiting the discretion-ary power of the welfare worker, *publicity* and *plurality*, those two other principles of civil society in the liberal state, are increasingly encroaching upon the conditions under which welfare work is exe-cuted. *Publicity* ensures as wide a knowledge of facts and events as possible, and *plurality* ensures that the maximum numbers of inter-ests and voices have a right to be heard and be influential in for-mulating policy and justifying conclusions.

Concluding remarks

As with all institutional mechanisms designed to be democratic and administratively efficient, the public inquiry is a very imperfect in-strument with respect to fulfilling its democratic mandate. The domi-nant position achieved by legal discourse within public administration is partly explained by the increasing involvement of lawyers in public inquiries, but also because *legalism,* as a form of reasoning which focuses on 'facts', causal relationships, and the relatively clear issues surrounding culpability, fits in well with the demands of a public hearing system where time and money are in scarce supply. How-ever, we have not so far devised an alternative mechanism whereby the competing claims of democracy and efficient public administra-tion can be reconciled. Certainly Dingwall's suggestions may be intellectually sound but they are politically contentious at a time when the clamour for more and more openness in administration and government is growing. There is a sense in which the political project identified by Luhmann (1982), whereby modern societies trade participatory involvement in politics for a guaranteed assurance that there will be efficiency in decision-making, remains illusory; there will always be a continuous flow of 'complicating noise' from the general public whenever matters of public controversy are to be investigated, especially when the methods of investigation remain incapable of delivering public assurance.

I have identified two established discourses in the field of family studies and child protection which have not been particularly influential in shaping the way in which social work bureaucracies approach family life and child abuse, namely what I have called a sociological discourse, rooted in the social policy analysis of poverty, and feminist discourse, focused on the continuum between male behaviour and sexual violence. The characteristic which both these perspectives on family life share is their radicalism, in the traditional sense that they point to the roots of problems. The problem of poverty is, for example, inextricably bound up with the reward structure in society, but it is difficult to win public attention for a discourse which repeatedly questions the necessity for social hierarchy when inequality appears to many people to be an inevitable feature of modern social systems. Similarly, the entrenched cultural taboos about how males and females are expected to behave, especially towards each other, also draw attention to a set of issues which are difficult for feminism to present, when the pressure in social policy and public administration is to accomplish something which is often of immediate and 'practical' value rather than set a new agenda for living. The public inquiry hearing dealing with the apparent breakdown of the child protection system, and based on an adversarial process dominated by legal reasoning, is not, therefore, the place where sociological and feminist knowledge will be allowed to be influential, even when they have something positive to contribute to our understanding of these issues. The problem is that sociology and feminism will enter the public administrative process as forms of 'expertise' vying for influence with medicine and the law, both of which are better adjusted to offer practical solutions of an immediate kind. The best hope for sociology and feminism to gain influence is to modify the way medical and legal thinking are structured through effectual research rather than by attacking forensic medicine and *legalism* from outside in public where the credibility of the social scientist is much weaker than the doctor or lawyer. *Plurality*, therefore, is not supported by the mechanism of public inquiries, especially when matters relating to family life are concerned. Poverty and male violence remain issues of background 'noise' in most of the major public inquiries; they are often mentioned but their effects are never properly analysed, and rarely are they themes which are given prominence in final reports.

To return to a concept I identified at the start of this chapter, namely the *molestation of normality*, the failure of the many public investigations into child abuse, both physical and sexual, to admit that the phenomenon has a social causation has perpetuated the idea that there is no social patterning to the phenomenon of child abuse, only an increasing incidence of dangerousness among certain kinds of people. The notion of the *social* as a causal influence is in fact converted into a strange abstract force which in a quite *ad hoc* way affects 'certain kinds of people' who suffer from another abstract thing called sociopathology. The problem is very similar to the one raised by Thomas Szasz in his critique of psychiatry (Szasz, 1961). Instead of seeing people with psychiatric disorders as manifesting a struggle to cope with the stresses and strains of modern life, what Szasz calls 'problems in living', as a society we seem to be intent on drawing on the concept of mental illness as an abstract essence which some unfortunate people have and which supposedly causes these difficulties in coping, despite the fact that there is little evidence that there is an organic cause for many of the symptoms which we readily call mental illness. Without admitting the sociological and feminist voice into the business of the large public inquiries to challenge the narrow focus of the public debate, the broader impact of social structures on human behaviour is barely acknowledged. Weak people, feckless people and amoral people are always somehow in our society but not of it. When this way of thinking becomes established the 'social project of moral levelling' which Krauthammer (1993) talks about becomes a reality. Public anxiety turns to the question of why people in modern society are more 'deviant' than they were several decades ago.

The reason offered by an increasing number of social commentators for this troubling problem in contemporary society seems to be that family structures are no longer patriarchal and families no longer take responsibility for their members as they did in the past. The explanation for this can take two main forms: either it is behaviourist and people are choosing to take the amoral path, or it is structural and some attention needs to be given to the social and economic constraints and distractions which make family life a difficult experience for growing numbers in contemporary society. This returns us to the concerns of the previous chapter, debating the emergence of the phenomenon of the 'underclass', a debate which deserves a wide *public* airing.

8

Concluding observations

There have been a number of core themes running through the chapters of this book; sometimes they have been conspicuous, less so at other points in the discussion. It might be helpful to pull out those themes and examine them in the context of debate and analysis about the possible future of family life. The central theme has been that family life is a focus for welfare intervention and public political debate in a number of key areas which Chapters 3 to 7 have identified and examined. In order to explore that theme we have discussed prominent and influential theoretical perspectives, paying particular attention to the most influential theoretical paradigms informing the work of professional practitioners and social analysts of family life in Chapters 1 and 2, and used those theoretical ideas to guide us to a sociological understanding of a range of issues such as divorce, the moral politics of caring, family policy, family deviance and marginality, and child abuse which have stimulated public political debate and innovation in social policy in recent years.

The theoretical orientation of my analysis is eclectic in that it acknowledges the distinctive but partial contributions made to the sociological analysis of the family by post-structuralism, feminism and systems theory. The necessity of adopting an eclectic perspective arises because none of the theoretical positions and their supporting academic literature can provide a complete understanding of family life on their own. However, when the insights of all three are combined they point towards a fruitful and challenging space for social research. Post-structuralism has stimulated an interest in the constitution of knowledges and, especially, directed social analysis towards the inextricable relationship between power and knowledge. Unfortunately this has led to an over-emphasis on the concept of social control in social policy analysis and perhaps on occasion has encouraged sociological analysis to neglect the question of resistance and agency in power relationships. The last section of Chapter 1 reviewed some sociological and historical research which has manifested this shortcoming. Systems theory is valuable because it is thoroughly social in its focus; its main interest lies in the configurations formed through social interaction. The ways in which patterns of social interaction combine to form structural influences on an individual's behaviour and thinking provides an important insight. However, systems theory, too, tends to neglect the question of agency and can become so focused on the matter of social cohesion that it neglects the content of social life; the fact that men invariably have more power than women, and that ideas and beliefs, in short ideologies, can shape and distort the way people interact with each other has to be recognised and made part of the social analysis. Feminism has focused sharply on the patriarchal nature of family life and social thinking, and has been valuable because it has been instrumental in revealing the underlying conflict, power and violence in family life. But feminism is most interesting when it is absorbing concepts from post-structuralism and systems theory and at its weakest when it dogmatically adopts an insular and inward gaze (see Raymond, 1986). The distinctions between the three spheres of social and political activity discussed in Chapter 2, and referred to at various points in my analysis, are an attempt to prepare the foundation for a critical theory of intervention in the family, drawing insights from the three perspectives. The concept of the public sphere developed in the critical theory of Habermas has been fruitfully juxtaposed to the notion of the social sphere developed particularly by Donzelot, writing within the confines of post-structuralism. Increasingly the activities of social welfare workers are exposed to the glare of publicity and subjected to processes of what Habermas might call discursive justification and rationalisation of their activities in public forums, including the mass media and institutions such as public inquiries and commissions of inquiry. The adoption of the theoretical language developed by Basil Bernstein outlined in Chapter 2 has enabled the analysis to move between discussion of practitioner – client relationships contained within the *social sphere* and wider debates and controversies about family life in the *public sphere*. It has enabled me to condense some of the most useful insights of the three perspectives into a single theoretical structure. The *classification* and *framing* of knowledge directs

[handwritten margin note: Conclusion, whether there was a family or not it is deteriorating.]

us to the very important consideration of power relations in discourse analysis, and the idea of *codes* as crystallised forms of orientation to meanings and social relationships directs us to the idea of structure and system in social interaction. The idea of *framing* in discourse analysis points to the differentials of power which are always present in social and communicative interaction. This is, of course, an important aspect of the feminist analysis of family life.

One of the most pronounced arguments in the current debate about family life has been that 'the family' is deteriorating and not simply changing. This view is not universally accepted and a number of sociologists would dispute this interpretation of change in family life (see Fletcher, 1966; Bernardes, 1985, 1986; Acock and Demo, 1994). This disagreement between competing interpretations of social change has been an implicit theme in each chapter, although the debate is addressed more directly in Chapter 6. In Chapter 3, which dealt with the issue of marriage conciliation and divorce, the issue of social change in family life emerges less in terms of the impact of marriage and family on society than in their consequences for individuals and their sense of self-identity. The rise in marriage counselling and conciliation services has coincided with a rise in the divorce rate and a concern for the integrity of marriage as a foundational social institution. There is an anxiety in society and contemporary politics that traditional responsibilities for providing care for children and the elderly are being eroded because the structure of families is less secure. A sense of the family deteriorating has always been an issue for those who would take a punitive or *correctional* view of matrimonial law and marriage counselling. In Chapter 4, which dealt with the issue of who should do the caring in an era when the notion of community care has become the main innovation in personal social services, it was argued that family structures vary enormously in their capacity to care for their members. However, the relentless pursuit of social policies which fundamentally ignore the underlying changes in the normative framework which people use to construct their sense of family has led and will continue to lead to social problems. Elder abuse, in particular, was examined at the conclusion of Chapter 4. The moral politics of caring is altering fundamentally in modern society because of a range of demographic and ideological changes. Whether these changes are bringing about a 'deterioration' in family life will continue to excite debate. Chapter 6 focused our attention on the issue of 'the underclass family', an object of study in which the *deterioration* school of thought has set the pace. The family behaviour of the poor and marginal members of society has always caused alarm throughout history (see MacNicol, 1987). That concern seems to have manifested itself in yet another 'moral panic' in the 1980s which is continuing into the 1990s. The ultimate sign of a society where family life is deteriorating is, perhaps, the fact that its children are mistreated. Child abuse and neglect appears to be a burgeoning problem in modern societies, and what makes it so alarming is the growing presentation of the problem as a cancer spreading throughout the social body; the social structural antecedents of the phenomenon tend to be submerged by a focus on behaviour and sociopathology. In Chapter 7 we examined the official and public reflection on the issue of child abuse and family life by lawyers, administrators and professional practitioners. The public inquiry system has tended to exacerbate a tendency in contemporary society to see problems as being 'in our society but not of it'; *dangerousness* in certain kinds of families seems to be the problem whose solution lies in social workers' involvement in the monitoring of 'deviant family forms' with a readiness to use the power of the law and the state to prevent the occurrence of child abuse.

A slightly different way of looking at the changes in family life is to think about the relationship or interplay between what can be described as 'real movements' which we can see, count and record, such as the number of divorces, lone-parent families, illegitimate births and demographic changes in populations, and 'ideological movements' which we cannot see or count, but which mould the way we think about 'real movements'. I made an observation in Chapter 3 in relation to the change in attitudes to divorce which might help to illuminate this issue. I suggested that the shift in the attitude towards divorce in modern societies of the west was from a *correctional* to an *appreciative* perspective, that marriage was guided by individual emotion and personal choice, and that matrimonial law has been changing in line with 'real movements' affecting economic and social relationships. However, despite the 'real movement' towards no-fault divorces, the 'ideological movement' has been inclined towards a *correctional* rhetoric. The assumption built into my analysis is that the 'real movement' in matrimonial law is directed inexorably towards even greater liberalism to reflect the likely increase in the impermanence of human relationships, and that this will occur despite the potential of 'ideological movements' to interrupt that shift and, conceivably, temporarily reverse it. Marriage as a 'pure relationship' has been formed by fundamental changes in modern social life which I discussed by reference to Giddens's (1991) analysis of modernity and self-identity. Once such changes in human behaviour and thinking have taken place, it is difficult to see how they will be reversed without doing damage to the underlying political, legal and cultural freedoms which sustain those changes. Our attention should always be drawn to the important distinction between what we do and experience and what we talk about in the abstract. Most of what passes for informed debate about family life today is detached and abstract in the sense that it connects with what ordinary people experience in a very imperfect way. The talk is of more *correctionalism,* but the 'real movement' is towards greater *appreciation* of the plurality of family life. In any case, if post-structuralism has taught us anything, it is that discourses work in a subtle way: their power operates through a process of normalisation in which people come to internalise discipline as self-control. This insight, combined with Gramsci's very useful concept of *contradictory consciousness*, which points up the distinction between what we experience as a material reality and the ideas which circulate to assist us in making sense of that material reality, underlines the importance of anchoring 'social control talk' in the material realities of social and family life. People often live with deep-rooted contradictions in their lives. Intellectually they may subscribe to a view of family life which is conventional and laden with the imagery of parental duty and responsibility, but practically, and often emotionally, they pursue a quite different life course involving multiple partners, divorce and an apparent abrogation of responsibility for their children and others.

The implication of this way of thinking about changes in family life is that 'real movements' cannot be affected by rhetoric or ideological currents aimed at changing people's behaviour. The only way that family life can be influenced is by changing its conditions of existence. This raises yet another distinction which has become more evident in the welfare state in recent years between *family policy* and *moral regulation*. The former is concerned with social policy, especially the benefits system, childcare provision and subsidies, maintenance regulations and, most importantly, employment law and policy. The latter is concerned with what Donzelot (1980) has called 'the policing of families' undertaken by social workers, health visitors and a range of other workers in the health and welfare fields operating in places such as family centres. We might include those involved in the pastoral side of education. The relationship between these two branches of the welfare state has been cogently summarised by Davies (1983) in his discussion of the *essential social worker*: 'the social worker has to persuade the poor, the feckless and the deviant to accept the terms currently offered to them by the state' (p. 155). Jordan (1987) underlines this view when he describes the defining aspect of the social work role as being that of 'mixing it with people in their natural settings', and what he calls the *final distribution of welfare*; the social worker is assigned the responsibility of ensuring fairness in welfare in those circumstances where people fail to meet their responsibilities for each other. The social worker is fundamentally defined here by the task of monitoring and regulating family life. What is clear is that only by governments and policy makers attending to the impact of social policies on family life can the conditions of existence of families be affected. Health visitors and social workers are really involved in the same task that they were assigned a century ago, namely, ensuring as far as is possible that a basic level of moral, health and social hygiene is maintained within family situations where there is identified deprivation. The real task remains, of course, that of tackling the conditions which structure that deprivation and can partially alleviate it. Only a comprehensive package of social policies, therefore, tailored specifically to support family life in all its aspects will make a difference. Opinions differ, of course, about how this is to be achieved, as I discussed in Chapter 6.

In Chapter 5 it was pointed up that *family policy* as a concept has been embraced with different degrees of enthusiasm by western countries with developed welfare states. Hantrais (1994a), for example, identifies distinctive policy approaches or styles relating to family matters in her comparison of Britain, France and Germany. In the case of France, considered by many to have the most explicit and most developed notion of *family policy* in the EC, Hantrais remarks:

Social policy in France has always been characterised by its familist orientation. The family is referred to in the Constitution, and government ministries and departments have responsibility for family affairs . . .

The link between demographic trends and family policy is explicit, and pro-natalist policies are actively promoted to encourage population growth . . . The redistribution of social welfare resources has been horizontal rather than vertical, but as a result of the importance attributed to the family, the status of women as mothers has been fully recognised. (Hantrais, 1994a, 154)

Lewis (1992) makes a similarly positive analysis of social policy in France in her comparison of Britain, Eire, Sweden and France. Despite its dual-breadwinner model of welfare, and its reputation as the world's leading welfare state, the Swedish welfare system comes out badly in Lewis's comparison. The French have adopted a parental rather than male-breadwinner model of the welfare state, which means that more generous support is provided for mothers at home, whereas the Swedish dual-breadwinner model presupposes that women will be as active in the labour market as men, but takes no account of the continuing domestic burden carried by working women. The strong emphasis on family life in French social policy therefore marks it out. When the case of Britain is examined, Hantrais makes the following observations.

The view that the United Kingdom lacks an explicit family policy is supported by the fact that the family is not given 'official' recognition, but, unlike France and Germany, the United Kingdom does not have a written constitution. It could be hypothesised that it is the efforts to avoid intervention which are most characteristic of British governments: while they are conducting policies which are likely to have an impact on family life and, ultimately, even the structure of the family, they are reluctant to admit to doing so and do not describe them as family policies. (Hantrais, 1994a, 155)

Again Lewis (1992) points to the traditional view of the family rooted in Beveridge's vision of the welfare state. A male-breadwinner model prevails.

What results from these historical developments in welfare policy is that Britain especially has created social policies without any coherent focus on the idea of family. Yet the contemporary discussion is about modifying the behaviour of family members without a coherent set of policy instruments in place regarding social security benefits, childcare provision and employment which might create the conditions to bring about that modification. The emphasis in social policy in relation to the family has been on responding to problems thought to be caused by internal family structure and pathology. We are left with attempts to set out the rights of children in the Children Act 1989 for England and Wales without corresponding attention being given to the underlying social and economic structures which help to generate child abuse and marital breakdown. The document published by the Scottish Office (1993) presaging the principles informing the new legislation on child care due to be enacted in Scotland during 1996 similarly accentuates the need for governments and professional practitioners to acknowledge parental and children's rights without any corresponding declaration of state responsibility for improving the conditions of existence of family life.

In short, *family policy* as a concept risks being eclipsed by a governmental focus on *moral regulation*. The idea of an *integrated family policy*, combining all strands of social policy which have a bearing on family life, may be required and, perhaps, the 'real movement' within the EC is towards such an idea. However, what seems to be more likely in Britain in the late 1990s is bifurcation, unless European social and political integration can fundamentally change the instincts which have shaped British social and public policy since 1945.

Bibliography

Abbott, P. and Sapsford, R. (1990) 'Health visiting: policing the family?' in P. Abbott and C. Wallace (eds) *The Sociology of the Caring Professions* (Basingstoke: Falmer).

Acock, A. and Demo, D. (1994) *Family Diversity and Well-Being* (London: Sage).

Adamson, J. and Warren, C. (1983) *Welcome to St Gabriel's Family Centre!* (London: The Children's Society).

Agger, B. (1991) *A Critical Theory of Public Life*, London, Falmer

Alcaly, R. and Mermelstein, D. (1977) *The Fiscal Crisis of American Cities* (New York: Vintage).

Anderson, D. (1991) *The Unmentionable Face of Poverty in the 1990s* (London: Social Affairs Unit).

Anderson, E. (1989) 'Sex codes and family life among poor inner-city youths', *Annals of the American Academy of Political and Social Science*, 501: 59–78.

Arendt, H. (1958) *The Human Condition*, 9th edn (Chicago: University of Chicago Press).

Auld, J., Dorn, N. and South, N. (1984) 'Heroin now. Bringing it all back home', *Youth and Policy*, 9: 1–7.

Auld, J., Dorn, N. and South, N. (1986) 'Irregular work, irregular pleasures: heroin in the 1980s' in R. Matthews and J. Young (eds) *Confronting Crime* (London: Sage).

Baistow, K. (1995) 'Liberation and regulation? Some paradoxes of empowerment', *Critical Social Policy*, no. 42.

Baker, J. (1979) 'Social conscience and social policy', *Journal of Social Policy*, 8 (2).

Barclay, P. (1982) *Report of Working Party on Social Workers: Their Role and Tasks* (London: Bedford Square Press).

Barclay, Sir P. (1995) *Joseph Rowntree Foundation Inquiry into Income and Wealth*, vol. 1 (York: Joseph Rowntree Foundation).

Barker, D. (1978) 'The regulation of marriage: repressive benevolence' in G. Littlejohn, B. Smart, J. Wakeford and N. Yuval-Davis (eds) *Power and the State* (London: Croom Helm).

Bean, P. and Mounser, P. (1993) *Discharged from Mental Hospitals* (London: Macmillan).

Bean, P. and Mounser, P. (1994) 'The community treatment order: proposals and prospects', *Journal of Social Policy*, 23 (1): 71–80.

Becker, H. (1963) *Outsiders: Studies in the Sociology of Deviance* (New York: Free Press).

Bell, C. (1968) *Middle Class Families* (London: Routledge).

Berger, B. and Berger, P. (1983) *The War Over the Family* (London: Hutchinson).

Bernardes, J. (1985) 'Do we really know what the "family" is?' in P. Close and R. Collins (eds) *Family and Economy* (London: Macmillan).

Bernardes, J. (1986) 'Multidimensional developmental pathways: a proposal to facilitate the conceptualisation of "family diversity"', *Sociological Review*, 34 (3): 590–610.

Bernstein, B. (1964) 'Social class, speech systems and psycho-therapy', *British Journal of Sociology*, 15: 54–64.

Bernstein, B. (1973) *Class, Codes and Control Volume 1: Theoretical Studies Towards a Sociology of Language* (St Albans: Paladin).

Bernstein, B. (1977) *Class, Codes and Control Volume 3: Towards a Theory of Educational Transmission* (London: Routledge).

Bernstein, B. (1981) 'Codes, modalities and the process of cultural reproduction: a model', *Language in Society*, 10 (3): 327–63.

Black, R. (1993) *Orkney: A Place of Safety?* (Edinburgh: Canongate).

Bookin, D. and Dunkle, R. (1985) 'Assessment problems in cases of elder abuse' in R. Filinson and S. Ingman (eds) *Elder Abuse: Practice and Policy* (New York: Human Sciences Press).

Bott, E. (1957) *Family and Social Network* (London: Tavistock).

Bourn, D. (1993) 'Over-chastisement, child non-compliance and parenting skills: a behavioural intervention by a family centre social worker', *British Journal of Social Work*, 23: 481–99.

Bowlby, J. (1952) *Maternal Care and Mental Health* (Geneva: World Health Organisation).

Bowlby, J. (1965) *Child Care and the Growth of Love* (Harmondsworth: Penguin).

Brannen, J. and Moss, P. (1991) *Managing Mothers* (London: Unwin Hyman).

Broderick, C. (1975) 'Power in the governance of families' in R. Cromwell and D. Olson (eds) *Power in Families* (New York: Sage).

Brophy, J. and Smart, C. (1981) 'From disregard to disrepute: the position of women in family Law', *Feminist Review*, no. 9.

Buck, N. (1992) 'Labour market activity and polarisation: a household perspective on the idea of an underclass' in D. Smith (ed) *Understanding the Underclass* (London: Policy Studies Institute).

Bulmer, M. (1987) *The Social Bases of Community Care* (London: Allen and Unwin).

Burghes, L. (1993) *One-parent Families: Policy Options for the 1990s* (York: Joseph Rowntree Foundation).

Burkitt, B. and Baimbridge, M. (1995) 'The Maastricht Treaty's impact on the welfare state', *Critical Social Policy*, no. 42.

Burns, T. (1992) *Erving Goffman* (London: Routledge).

Burr, W., Herrin, D., Day, R., Beutler, I. and Leigh, G. (1988) 'Epistemologies that lead to primary explanations in family science', *Family Science Review*, 1 (3): 185–210.

208   *Bibliography*

Burrell. I. (1995) 'The "savage generation" hits Britain', *Sunday Times*, 5 February.

Candib, L. and Glenn, M. (1983) 'Family medicine and family therapy: comparative development, methods, and roles', *Journal of Family Practice*, 16 (4): 773–9.

Cannan, C. (1990) 'Supporting the family? An assessment of family centres' in N. Manning and C. Ungerson (eds) *Social Policy Review 1989–90* (London: Longman).

Cannan, C. (1992) *Changing Families Changing Welfare: Family Centres and the Welfare State* (London: Harvester Wheatsheaf).

Castells, M. (1977) *The Urban Question* (London: Edward Arnold).

Castles, F. and McKinlay, R. (1979) 'Public welfare provision, Scandinavia and the sheer futility of the sociological approach to politics', *British Journal of Political Science*, 9 (2): 157–71.

Cernkovich, S. and Giordano, P. (1987) 'Family relationships and delinquency', *Criminology*, 25 (2): 295–321.

Challis, D. and Davies, B. (1980) 'A new approach to community care for the elderly', *British Journal of Social Work*, 10: 1–18.

Challis, D., Barton, R., Johnson, L., Storie, M., Traske, K. and Wall, B. (1989) *Supporting Frail Elderly People at Home* (Canterbury: Personal Social Services Research Unit).

Challis, D., Chessum, R., Chesterman, J., Luckett, R. and Traske, K. (1990) *Case Management in Social and Health Care* (Canterbury: Personal Social Services Research Unit).

Cheal, D. (1991) *Family and the State of Theory* (London: Harvester Wheatsheaf).

Chester, R. (1985) 'Shaping the future: from marriage movement to service agency', *Marriage Guidance*, Autumn: 5–15.

Clark, D. and Haldane, D. (1990) *Wedlocked?* (Cambridge: Polity).

Clark, D. (1991) 'Guidance, counselling, therapy: responses to marital problems', *Sociological Review*, 39 (4): 765–98.

Cloke, C. (1983) *Old Age Abuse in the Domestic Setting: A Review* (Portsmouth: Age Concern).

Cloward, R. and Ohlin, L. (1960) *Delinquency and Opportunity: A Theory of Delinquent Gangs* (London: Routledge).

Cockett, M. and Tripp, J. (1994) *The Exeter Family Study: Family Breakdown and its Impact on Children* (Exeter: University of Exeter Press).

Cohen, J. (1979) 'Why more political theory', *Telos*, no. 40.

Cohen, S. (1985) *Visions of Social Control* (Cambridge: Polity).

Colwill, J. (1994) 'Beveridge, women and the welfare state', *Critical Social Policy*, no. 41: 53–78.

Commons Social Security Committee (1992) *Low Income Statistics: Low Income Families 1979–1989*, Second Report (London: HMSO).

Corby, B. (1987) *Working With Child Abuse* (Milton Keynes: Open University Press).

Corden, J. and Preston-Shoot, M. (1987) *Contracts in Social Work* (Aldershot: Gower).

Cornwell, D. and Hobbs, S. (1992) 'Rumour and legend: irregular interactions between social psychology and folkloristics', *Canadian Psychology*, 33: 609–13.

Corrigan, P. and Leonard, P. (1978) *Social Work Practice Under Capitalism* (London: Macmillan).

Cox, R. (1990) 'Alternative patterns of welfare state development: the case of public assistance in the Netherlands', *West European Politics*, 13, (4): 85–102.

Crellin, E., Kellmer-Pringle, M. and West, P. (1971) *Born Illegitimate: Social and Educational Implications* (Windsor: National Foundation for Educational Research in England and Wales).

Cromwell, R. and Olson, D. (eds) (1975) *Power in Families* (New York: Sage).

Dahrendorf, R. (1985) *Law and Order* (Boulder: Westview Press).

Dahrendorf, R. (1987) 'The erosion of citizenship and its consequences for us all', *New Statesman*, 12 June, pp. 12–15.

Dale, P., Davies, M., Morrison, T. and Waters, J. (1986) *Dangerous Families: Assessment and Treatment of Child Abuse* (London: Routledge).

Dallos, R. (1991) *Family Belief Systems, Therapy and Change* (Milton Keynes: Open University Press).

Dandekar, C. (1990) *Surveillance, Power and Modernity: Bureaucracy and Discipline from 1700 to the Present Day* (Cambridge: Polity).

Davies, J., Berger, B. and Carlson, A. (1993) *The Family: Is It Just Another Lifestyle Choice?* (London: Institute of Economic Affairs).

Davies, M. (1983) *The Essential Social Worker* (Aldershot: Gower).

De Swaan, A. (1990) *The Management of Normality* (London: Routledge).

Dean, H. (1991) 'In search of the underclass' in P. Brown and R. Scase (Eds) *Poor Work* (Milton Keynes: Open University Press).

Decalmer, P. and Glendenning, F. (1993) *The Mistreatment of Elderly People* (London: Sage).

Delphy, C. (1977) *The Main Enemy* (London: Women's Research and Resources Centre). (Originally published in *Partisan*, 1970.)

Delphy, C. (1980) 'A materialist feminism is possible', *Feminist Review*, no. 4.

Delphy, C. (1984) *Close to Home: A Materialist Analysis of Women's Oppression* (London: Hutchinson).

Delphy, C. and Leonard, D. (1992) *Familiar Exploitation* (Oxford: Polity).

Dennis, N. (1993) *Rising Crime and the Dismembered Family* (London: Institute of Economic Affairs).

Dennis, N. and Erdos, G. (1992) *Families Without Fatherhood* (London: Institute of Economic Affairs).

Dingwall, R. (1986) 'The Jasmine Beckford Affair', *Modern Law Review*, 49 (4): 489–507.

Dingwall, R., Eekelaar, J. and Murray, T. (1983) *The Protection of Children: State Intervention and Family Life* (Oxford: Blackwell).

Dingwall, R. and Eekelaar, J. (1988) 'Families and the state: an historical perspective on the public regulation of private conduct', *Law and Policy*, 10 (4): 341–61.

Donzelot, J. (1980) *The Policing of Families* (London: Hutchinson).

210 Bibliography

Eastman, M. (1984) *Old Age Abuse* (Portsmouth: Age Concern).

Ellis, B., Bennett, G. and Hobbs, S. (1993) *The Orkney Islands SRA Case*, ISCLR Occasional Paper no. 1.

European Commission Childcare Network (1990) *Childcare in the European Community 1985–1990*, Brussels: Women of Europe Supplement, no. 31.

Fagan, J. and Wexler, S. (1987) 'Family origins of violent delinquents', *Criminology*, 25 (3): 643–69.

Family Policy Studies Centre (1991) *An Ageing Population: Factsheet 2*.

Farrington, D. and West, D. (1990) 'The Cambridge study in delinquent development: a follow-up of 411 London males', in G. Kaiser and H. Kerner (eds) *Criminality: Personality, Behaviour, Life History* (Berlin: Springer-Verlag).

Fetherstone, B. and Fawcett, B. (1995) 'Feminism and child abuse: opening up some possibilities', *Critical Social Policy*, no. 42.

Field, F. (1989) *Losing Out: The Emergence of Britain's Underclass* (Oxford: Blackwell).

Finch, J. (1987) 'The vignette technique in survey research', *Sociology*, 21 (1): 105–14.

Finch, J. (1989) *Family Obligations and Social Change* (Cambridge: Polity).

Finch, J. (1990a) 'The politics of community care in Britain' in C. Ungerson (ed.) *Gender and Caring* (London: Harvester Wheatsheaf).

Finch, J. (1990b) 'Social policy, social engineering and the family in the 1990s' in M. Bulmer, J. Lewis and D. Piachaud (eds) *The Goals of Social Policy* (London: Unwin Hyman).

Finch, J. and Groves, D. (1980) 'Community care and the family: a case for equal opportunities?' *Journal of Social Policy*, 9 (4): 487–514.

Finch, J. and Summerfield, P. (1991) 'Social reconstruction and the emergence of companionate marriage, 1945–59' in D. Clark (ed.) *Marriage, Domestic Life and Social Change* (London: Routledge).

Fine, G. (1992) *Manufacturing Tales: Sex and Money in Contemporary Legends* (Knoxville: University of Tennessee Press).

Fine, M. (1981) 'An injustice by any other name', *Victimology*, 6 (1): 48–58.

Firth, R., Hubert, J. and Forge, A. (1970) *Families and their Relatives* (London: Routledge).

Fletcher, R. (1966) *The Family and Marriage in Britain* (Harmondsworth: Penguin).

Ford, J. (1988) 'Negotiations (counselling and advocacy): a response to Bill Jordan', *British Journal of Social Work*, 18: 57–62.

Foucault, M. (1967) *Madness and Civilisation* (London: Tavistock).

Foucault, M. (1974) *The Order of Things* (London: Tavistock).

Foucault, M. (1973) *The Birth of the Clinic* (London: Tavistock).

Foucault, M. (1977) *Discipline and Punish: The Birth of the Prison* (London: Tavistock).

Foucault, M. (1978) 'About the concept of the "dangerous individual" in 19th century legal psychiatry', *International Journal of Law and Psychiatry*, 1: 1–18.

Foucault, M. (1980) *Power/Knowledge*, ed. C. Gibson (Brighton: Harvester).

Franklin, A. (1983) 'The family as the patient' in A. Franklin (ed.) *Family Matters* (Oxford: Pergamon).

Fraser, N. (1989) *Unruly Practices: Power, Discourse and Gender in Contemporary Social Theory* (Cambridge: Polity).

Frost, N. (1990) 'Official intervention and child protection: the relationship between the state and family in contemporary Britain' in Violence Against Children Study Group (eds) *Taking Child Abuse Seriously*, (London: Routledge).

Gallie, D. (1988) 'Employment, unemployment and social stratification' in D. Gallie (ed.) *Employment in Britain* (Oxford: Blackwell).

Gallie, D. (1991) 'Patterns of skill change: upskilling, deskilling or the polarisation of skills?', *Work, Employment and Society*, 5 (3): 319–351.

Garfinkel, H. (1984) *Studies in Ethnomethodology* (Cambridge: Polity).

Garland, D. (1985) *Punishment and Welfare* (Aldershot: Gower).

Gelles, R. (1973) 'Child abuse as psychopathology: a sociological critique and reformulation', *American Journal of Orthopsychiatry*, 43 (4): 611–21.

Giddens, A. (1991) *Modernity and Self-Identity* (Cambridge: Polity).

Gil, D. (1970) *Violence Against Children* (Cambridge, MA: Harvard University Press).

Gittins D. (1993) *The Family in Question* (London: Macmillan).

Glendinning, C. and Miller, J. (eds) (1993) *Women and Poverty in Britain in the 1990s*, 2nd edn (London: Harvester Wheatsheaf).

Glueck, S. and Glueck, E. (1950) *Unravelling Juvenile Delinquency* (Cambridge: MA: Harvard University Press).

Goldner, V. (1985) 'Feminism and family therapy', *Family Process*, 24: 31–47.

Goodwin, S. (1990) *Community Care and the Future of Mental Health Provision* (Aldershot: Avebury).

Gough, I. (1975) *The Political Economy of the Welfare State* (London: Macmillan).

Gould, A. (1993) *Capitalist Welfare Systems* (London: Longman).

Gove, W. and Crutchfield, R. (1982) 'The family and juvenile delinquency', *The Sociological Quarterly*, 23: 301–19.

Griffin, L., Devine, J. and Wallace, M. (1983) 'On the economic and political determinants of welfare spending in the post-World War II era', *Politics and Society*, 12 (3): 331–72.

Griffith, R. (1988) *Community Care: Agenda for Action* (London: HMSO).

Grimshaw A. (1976) 'Polity, Class, School, and Talk: The Sociology of Basil Bernstein', *Theory and Society*, 3: 529–552.

Grusky, O. and Pollner, M. (eds) (1981) *The Sociology of Mental Illness* (London: Holt, Rinehart and Winston).

Gubrium, J. (1992) *Out of Control: Family Therapy and Domestic Disorder* (London: Sage).

Gubrium, J. and Holstein, J. (1990) *What Is Family?* (London: Mayfield).

Habermas, J. (1970) 'Towards a theory of communicative competence' in H. Dreitzel (ed.) *Recent Sociology no. 2* (London: Collier-Macmillan).

Habermas, J. (1977) 'Hannah Arendt's communication concept of power', *Social Research*, 44 (1): 3–24.

Habermas, J. (1989) *The Structural Transformation of the Public Sphere* (Cambridge: Polity).

Hadley, R. and Hatch, S. (1981) *Social Welfare and the Failure of the State* (London: Allen and Unwin).

Hall, S., Critcher. C., Jefferson, T., Clarke, J. and Roberts, B. (1978) *Policing the Crisis: Mugging, the State, and Law and Order* (London: Macmillan).

Hallett, C. (1989) 'Child abuse inquiries and public policy', in O. Stevenson (ed.) *Child Abuse: Professional Practice and Public Policy* (Hemel Hempstead: Harvester Wheatsheaf).

Halliday, M. (1978) *Language as Social Semiotic* (London: Edward Arnold).

Hanratty, M. and Blank, R. (1992) 'Down and out in North America: recent trends in poverty rates in the United States and Canada', *Quarterly Journal of Economics*, February (1): 233–54.

Hantrais, L. (1994a) 'Comparing family policy in Britain, France and Germany', *Journal of Social Policy*, 23 (2): 135–60.

Hantrais, L. (1994b) 'Family policy in Europe', in R. Page and J. Baldock (eds) *Social Policy Review*, 6 (Canterbury: Social Policy Association).

Hardey, M. and Crow, G. (eds) (1990) *Lone Parenthood: Coping with Constraints and Making Opportunities* (London: Harvester Wheatsheaf).

Hare-Mustin, R. (1978) 'A feminist approach to family therapy', *Family Process*, 17: 181–94.

Hasler, J. (1984) *Family Centres: Different Expressions, Same Principles* (London: Children's Society).

Hawks, D. (1975) 'Community care: an analysis of assumptions', *British Journal of Psychiatry*, no. 127.

Hearn, J. (1987) *Gender and Oppression: Men, Masculinity and the Critique of Marxism* (Brighton: Wheatsheaf).

Hearn, J., and Morgan, D. (1990) *Men, Masculinities, and Social Theory* (London: Unwin Hyman).

Heisler, B. (1991) 'A comparative perspective on the underclass: questions of urban poverty, race and citizenship', *Theory and Society*, 20: 455–83.

Helmholz, R. (1975) *Marriage Litigation in Medieval England* (Cambridge: Cambridge University Press).

Hendrick, H. (1994) *Child Welfare: England 1872–1989* (London: Routledge).

Hewlett, S. (1993) *Child Neglect in Rich Nations* (New York: United Nations Children's Fund).

Higgins, J. (1980) 'Social control theories of social policy', *Journal of Social Policy*, 9 (1): 1–23.

Higgins, J. (1989) 'Defining community care: realities and myths', *Social Policy and Administration*, 23 (1): 3–16.

Hill, D. (1992) 'The American philosophy of welfare: citizenship and the "politics of conduct"', *Social Policy and Administration*, 26 (2): 117–28.

Hill, R. (1971) 'Modern systems theory and the family: a confrontation', *Social Science Information*, 10 (5): 7–26.

Hills, J. (1993) *The Future of Welfare: A Guide to the Debate* (York: Joseph Rowntree Foundation).

Hills, J. (1995) *Joseph Rowntree Foundation Inquiry into Income and Wealth*, vol. 2 (York: Joseph Rowntree Foundation).

Hirschi, T. (1969) *Causes of Delinquency* (Berkeley: University of California Press).

Hirst, P. (1976) 'Althusser and the theory of ideology', *Economy and Society*, 5 (4): 385–412.

Holman, B. (1988) *Putting Families First* (London: Macmillan).

Homer, A. and Gilleard, C. (1990) 'Abuse of elderly people by their carers', *British Medical Journal*, 301: 1359–62.

Howe, D. (1992) 'Child abuse and the bureaucratisation of social work' *Sociological Review*, 40 (3): 491–508.

Huygen, F. (1978) *Family Medicine: The Medical Life Histories of Families* (Nijmegen, The Netherlands: Dekker and Van de Vegt).

Ignatieff, M. (1983) 'State, civil society and total institutions: a critique of recent social histories of punishment' in S. Cohen and A. Scull (eds) *Social Control and the State* (Oxford: Blackwell).

James, O. (1993) 'Vicious outcome of the poverty trap', *Observer*, 23 May.

Jamieson, L. and Toynbee, C. (1990) 'Shifting patterns of parental authority 1900–1980' in H. Corr and L. Jamieson (eds) *The Politics of Everyday Life* (London: Macmillan).

Jencks, C. and Peterson, P. (1991) *The Urban Underclass* (Washington. DC: Brookings Institution).

Jewson, N. (1976) 'The disappearance of the sick man from medical cosmology 1770–1870', *Sociology*, 10: 225–44.

Jordan, B. (1987) 'Counselling, advocacy, negotiation', *British Journal of Social Work*, 17: 135–46.

Jordan, B. (1989) *Rethinking Welfare* (Oxford: Blackwell).

Jordan, B., James, S., Kay, H. and Redley, M. (1992) *Trapped in Poverty: Labour Market Decisions in Low-Income Households* (London: Routledge).

Jordan, B. and Redley, M. (1994) 'Polarisation, underclass and the welfare state', *Work, Employment and Society*, 8 (2): 153–76.

Kangas, O. (1991) 'The bigger the better', *Acta Sociologica*, 34: 33–61.

Kellerhals, J., Coenen-Huther, J. and Modak, M. (1988) 'Justice norms and group dynamics: the case of the family', *International Sociology*, 3 (2): 111–27.

Kempe, C., Silverman, F., Steele, B., Droegmueller, W. and Silver, H. (1962) 'The battered child syndrome', *Journal of the American Medical Association*, 181: 17–22.

Kiernan, K. and Wicks, M. (1990) *Family Change and Future Policy* (London: Joseph Rowntree/Family Policy Studies Centre).

King, M. and Trowell, J. (1992) *Children's Welfare and the Law: The Limits of Legal Intervention* (London: Sage).

Kinsey, R., Lea, J. and Young, J. (1986) *Losing the Fight against Crime* (Oxford: Blackwell).

Klecker, J. (1978) 'Wife beaters and beaten wives: co-conspirators', *Crimes of Violence*, 15 (1): 54–6.

Kohlberg, L. (1964) 'Development of moral character and moral ideology' in M. Hoffman and L. Hoffman (eds) *Review of Child Development Research* Vol. 1 (New York: Sage).

Kolvin, I., Miller, F., Scott, D. and Gatzanis, S. (1990) *Continuities in Deprivation: The Newcastle 1000 Family Study* (Aldershot: Avebury).

Korpi, W. (1991) 'Political and economic explanations for unemployment: a cross-national and long-term analysis', *British Journal of Political Science*, 21 (3): 315–48.

Krauthammer, C. (1993) 'The molestation of normality', *The Guardian*, 18 November.

La Fontaine, J. (1994) *The Extent and Nature of Organised and Ritual Abuse*, (London: HMSO).

Langley, W. (1995) 'A break and make time', *Sunday Times*, 5 February.

Larzelere, R. and Patterson, G. (1990) 'Parental management: mediation of the effect of socioeconomic status on early delinquency', *Criminology*, 28 (2): 301–23.

Lasch, C. (1977) *Haven in a Heartless World* (New York: Basic Books).

Laub, J. and Sampson, R. (1988) 'Unravelling families and delinquency: a re-analysis of the Gleucks' data', *Criminology*, 26 (3): 355–79.

Lea, J. and Young, J. (1984) *What Is To Be Done About Law and Order* (London: Penguin).

Lenoir, R. (1991) 'Family Policy in France since 1938' in J. Ambler (ed.) *The French Welfare State* (London: New York University Press).

Leonard, D. (1978) 'The regulation of marriage: repressive benevolence', in G. Littlejohn *et al.* (eds), *Power and the State* (London: Croom Helm).

Lewis, J. (1992) 'Gender and the development of welfare regimes', *Journal of European Social Policy*, 2 (3): 159–73.

Lewis, J., Clark, D. and Morgan, D. (1992) *Whom God Hath Joined Together: The Work of Marriage Guidance* (London: Routledge).

Lewis, J. and Meredith, B. (1988) *Daughters Who Care* (London: Routledge).

Lockhart, C. (1984) 'Explaining social policy differences among advanced industrial societies', *Comparative Politics*, 16: 335–50.

Luhmann, N. (1982) *The Differentiation of Society* (New York: Columbia University Press).

Luhmann, N. (1989) 'Law as a social system', *Northwestern University Law Review*, 83 (1&2): 136–50.

Lyon, C., and de Cruz, S. (1988) 'Child sexual abuse and the Cleveland report', *Family Law*, 18: 370–8.

McCord, J. (1991) 'Family relationships, juvenile delinquency and adult criminality', *Criminology*, 29 (3): 397–417.

MacNicol, J. (1987) 'In pursuit of the underclass', *Journal of Social Policy*, 16 (3): 293–318.

McNay, L. (1992) *Foucault and Feminism: Power, Gender and the Self* (Cambridge: Polity).

Maluccio, A. and Marlow, W. (1974) 'The case for the contract', *Social Work* (USA), 13: 28–36.

Mann, K. (1991) *The Making of an English 'Underclass'?* (Milton Keynes: Open University Press).

Marklund, S. (1990) 'Structures of modern poverty', *Acta Sociologica*, 33 (2): 125–40.

Marshall, T.H. (1965) *Class, Citizenship and Social Development* (New York: Anchor Books).

Martin, F. (1984) *Between the Acts: Community Mental Health Services 1959–83* (London: Nuffield Provincial Trust).

Martin, J. and Roberts, C. (1984) *Women and Employment* (London: HMSO).

Matthews, R. and Young, J. (eds) (1992) *Issues in Realist Criminology* (London: Sage).

Matza, D. (1969) *Becoming Deviant* (Englewood Cliffs, NJ: Prentice-Hall).

Mayo, M. (1994) *Communities and Caring: The Mixed Economy of Welfare* (London: Macmillan).

Melossi, D. and Pavarini, P. (1981) *The Prison and the Factory* (London: Macmillan).

Meltzer, J. (1978) 'A semiotic approach to suitability for psychotherapy', *Psychiatry*, 41: 360–76.

Miller, W. (1958) 'Lower class culture as a generating milieu of gang delinquency', *Journal of Social Issues*, 14 (5): 5–19.

Morgan, D. (1985) *The Family, Politics and Social Theory* (London: Routledge).

Morgan, P. (1995) *Farewell to the Family?: Public Policy and Family Breakdown in Britain and the USA* (London: Institute of Economic Affairs).

Morris, L. (1994) *Dangerous Classes: The Underclass and Social Citizenship* (London: Routledge).

Morris, S., Gibson, S. and Platts, A. (1993) *Untying the Knot: Characteristics of Divorce in Scotland* (Edinburgh: Scottish Office Central Research Unit).

Moynihan, D. (1993) 'Defining deviance down', *American Scholar*, Winter.

Moynihan, D. (1965) *The Negro Family: The Case For National Action* (Washington: United States Department of Labor).

Mueller, C. (1973) *The Politics of Communication* (London: Oxford University Press).

Murray, C. (1990) *The Making of the British Underclass* (London: Institute of Economic Affairs).

Murray, C. (1994) *Underclass: The Crisis Deepens* (London: Institute of Economic Affairs).

Nietzsche, F. (1974) *The Gay Science* (New York: Vintage).

Norris, P. (1984) 'Women in poverty: Britain and the USA', *Social Policy*, 14 (4): 41–3.

Oakley, A. (1974) *The Sociology of Housework* (London: Martin Robertson).

Oakley, A. (1991) 'Eugenics, social medicine and the career of Richard Titmuss in Britain 1935–50', *British Journal of Sociology*, 42 (2): 165–94.

O'Connor, J. (1973) *The Fiscal Crisis of the State* (London: St James Press).

Offe, C. (1984) *Contradictions of the Welfare State* (London: Hutchinson).

Oliveri, M. and Reiss, D. (1981) 'The structure of families' ties to their kin: the shaping of role constructions', *Journal of Marriage and the Family*, May: 391–407.

Olson, D. and McCubbin, H. (1983) *Families: What Makes them Work* (London: Sage).

Osborne, K. (1983) 'Women in families: feminist therapy and family systems' *Journal of Family Therapy*, 5:1–10.

Pahl, R. (1984) *Divisions of Labour* (Oxford: Blackwell).

Pahl, R. (1988) 'Some remarks on informal work, social polarisation and the social structure', *International Journal of Urban and Regional Research*, 12 (2): 247–67.

Pampel, F. and Williamson, J. (1988) 'Welfare spending in advanced industrial democracies 1950–1980', *American Journal of Sociology*, 93 (6): 1424–56.

Parsons, T. (1951) *The Social System* (London: Routledge).

Parton C., (1990) 'Women, gender oppression and child abuse' in Violence Against Children Study Group (eds) *Taking Child Abuse Seriously* (London: Routledge).

Parton, C. and Parton, N. (1989) 'Child protection: the law and dangerousness', in O. Stevenson (ed.) *Child Abuse: Professional Practice and Public Policy* (Hemel Hempstead: Harvester Wheatsheaf).

Parton, N. (1985) *The Politics of Child Abuse* (London: Macmillan).

Parton, N. (1991) *Governing the Family: Child Care, Child Protection and the State* (London: Macmillan).

Parton, N. and Martin, N. (1989) 'Public inquiries, legalism and child care in England and Wales', *International Journal of Law and the Family*, 3: 21–39.

Payne, J. and Payne, C. (1994) 'Recession, restructuring and the fate of the unemployed: evidence in the underclass debate', *Sociology*, 28 (1): 1–19.

Pelton, L. (1978) 'Child abuse and neglect: the myth of classlessness', *American Journal of Orthopsychiatry*, 48 (4): 608–17.

Penhale, B. (1993) 'The abuse of elderly people: considerations for practice', *British Journal of Social Work*, 23: 95–112.

Perelberg, R. and Miller, A. (eds) (1990) *Gender and Power in Families* (London: Routledge).

Persaud, R. (1993) 'Talking your way out of trouble', *Sunday Times*, 26 September.

Philips, D. (1977) *Crime and Authority in Victorian England* (London: Croom Helm).

Pierson, C. (1991) *Beyond the Welfare State?* (Cambridge: Polity).

Pincus, A. and Minahan, A. (1973) *Social Work Practice: Model and Method* (Itasco, IL: F.E. Peacock).

Pinker, R. (1983) 'Social welfare and the education of social workers' in P. Bean and S. MacPherson (Eds) *Approaches to Welfare* (London: Routledge).

Piven, F. and Cloward, R. (1972) *Regulating the Poor* (London: Tavistock).

Platt, A. (1977) *The Child Savers* (Chicago: University of Chicago Press).
Policy Studies Institute (1991) *Britain in 2010* (London: Policy Studies Institute).
PP. (1947) Cmd.7024 *Final Report of the Committee on Procedure in Matrimonial Causes*.
PP. (1948) Cmd.7566 *Report of the Departmental Committee on Grants for the Development of Marriage Guidance*.
Pratt, J. (1985) 'Juvenile justice, social work and social control: the need for positive thinking', *British Journal of Social Work*, 15: 1–24.
Qureshi, H. (1990) 'Boundaries between formal and informal care-giving work' in C. Ungerson (ed.) *Gender and Caring* (London: Harvester Wheatsheaf).
Qureshi, H. and Walker, A. (1989) *The Caring Relationship: Elderly People and their Families* (London: Macmillan).
Raymond, J. (1986) 'I am the world', *New Statesman*, 30 May.
Reder, P. (1983) 'Disorganised families and the helping professions: who's in charge?', *Journal of Family Therapy*, 5: 23–36.
Reiss, D. (1981) *The Family's Construction of Reality* (London: Harvard University Press).
Relate (1993) *Family Policy Briefing*, January, Rugby.
Rickford, F. (1994) 'The lottery of life', *The Guardian*, 30 March.
Rieff, P. (1966) *The Triumph of the Therapeutic* (Harmondsworth: Penguin).
Riley, D. and Shaw, M. (1985) *Parental Supervision and Juvenile Delinquency*, Home Office Research Study no. 83 (London: HMSO).
Robinson, M. (1991) *Family Transformation Through Divorce and Remarriage* (London: Routledge).
Rodger, J. (1980) 'Inauthentic politics and the public inquiry system' in R. Parsler and D. Shapiro (eds) *The Social Impact of Oil in Scotland: A Contribution to the Sociology of Oil* (Farnborough: Gower).
Rodger, J. (1985a) 'On the degeneration of the public sphere', *Political Studies*, 33 (2): 203–17.
Rodger, J. (1985b) 'Natural justice and the big public inquiry: a sociological perspective', *Sociological Review*, 33 (3): 409–29.
Rodger, J. (1992) 'The welfare state and social closure: social division and the "underclass"', *Critical Social Policy*, no. 35: 45–63.
Rojek, C., Peacock, G. and Collins, S. (1988) *Social Work and Received Ideas* (London: Routledge).
Roll, J. (1991) *What is a Family? Benefit Models and Social Realities* Family Policy Studies Centre, Occasional Paper no. 13, London.
Room, G., Lawson, R. and Laczko, F. (1989) '"New Poverty" in the European Community', *Policy and Politics*, 17 (2): 165–76.
Roshier, B. (1989) *Controlling Crime: The Classical Perspective in Criminology* (Milton Keynes: Open University Press).
Rosser, C. and Harris, C. (1965) *The Family and Social Change* (London: Routledge).
Rothman, D. (1971) *The Discovery of the Asylum* (Boston: Little, Brown).
Rowe, D. (1994) *The Limits of Family Influence: Genes, Experience and Behaviour* (London: Guildford Press).

Saville, J. (1957) 'The welfare state: an historical approach', *New Reasoner*, no. 3.
Scanzoni, J. (1979) 'Social processes and power in families' in W. Burr, R. Hill, I. Nye and I. Reiss (eds) *Contemporary Theories About the Family* (Glencoe: Free Press).
Scharpf, F. (1984) 'Economic and institutional constraints of full employment strategies: Sweden, Austria and West Germany' in J. Goldthorpe (ed.) *Order and Conflict in Contemporary Capitalism* (Oxford: Oxford University Press).
Scheiwe, K. (1994) 'Labour market, welfare state and family institutions: the links to mothers' poverty', *Journal of European Social Policy*, 4 (3): 201–24.
Schmidt, D. (1983) 'When is it helpful to convene the family?' *Journal of Family Practice*, 16 (5): 967–73.
Schneider, C. (1990) 'The struggle towards a feminist practice in family therapy: practice' in R. Perelberg and A. Miller (eds) *Gender and Power in Families* (London: Tavistock/Routledge).
Scottish Office (1993) *Scotland's Children: Proposals for Child Care Policy and Law*, Cm 2286 (Edinburgh: HMSO).
Scull, A. (1979) *Museums of Madness* (London: Allen Lane).
Seebohm, F. (1968) *Report of the Committee on Local Authority and Allied Personal Social Services*, Cmnd. 3793 (London: HMSO).
Segalman, R. and Marsland, D. (1989) *Cradle to the Grave: Comparative Perspectives on the State of Welfare* (London: Macmillan and Social Affairs Unit).
Sennett, R. (1974) *The Fall of Public Man* (Cambridge: Cambridge University Press).
Shilling, C. (1991) 'Educating the body: physical capital and the production of social inequalities', *Sociology*, 25 (4): 653–72 .
Shilling, C. (1993) *The Body and Social Theory* (London: Sage).
Shklar, J. (1964) *Legalism* (Cambridge MA: Harvard University Press).
Sinfield, A. (1986) 'Poverty, privilege and welfare' in P. Bean and D. Whynes (eds) *Barbara Wooton: Essays in Her Honour* (London: Tavistock).
Sixel, F. (1977) 'The problem of sense: Habermas versus Luhmann' in J. O'Neill (ed.) *On Critical Theory* (London: Heinemann).
Smart, C. (1982) 'Regulating families or legitimating patriarchy' *International Journal of the Sociology of Law*, 10: 129–47.
Smart, C. (1984) *The Ties That Bind* (London: Routledge).
Smart, C. (1989) *Feminism and the Power of Law* (London: Routledge).
Smart, C. (1992) 'Disruptive bodies and unruly sex: the regulation of reproduction and sexuality in the nineteenth century' in C. Smart (ed.) *Regulating Womanhood: Historical Essays on Marriage, Motherhood and Sexuality* (London: Routledge).
Smith, D. (1976) 'Codes, paradigms and folk norms', *Sociology*, 10: 1–20.
Smith, S., Hanson, R. and Noble, S. (1975) 'Parents of battered children: a controlled study' in A. Franklin (ed.) *Concerning Child Abuse* (Edinburgh: Churchill Livingstone).

Social Security Department (1993) *The Government's Expenditure Plans 1993/94 to 1995/96* (London: HMSO).

Squires, P. (1990) *Anti-Social Policy* (London: Harvester Wheatsheaf).

Stedman Jones, G. (1971) *Outcast London* (Oxford: Clarendon Press).

Steele, B. and Pollack, C. (1968) 'A psychiatric study of parents who abuse infants and small children' in R. Helfer and C. Kempe (Eds) *The Battered Child* (Chicago: University of Chicago Press).

Stoesz, D. and Karger, H. (1992) 'The decline of the American welfare state', *Social Policy and Administration*, 26 (1): 3–17.

Sykes, G. and Matza, D. (1957) 'Techniques of neutralisation: a theory of delinquency', *American Sociological Review*, 22: 122–4.

Symonds, A. (1991) 'Angels and interfering busybodies: the social construction of two occupations', *Sociology of Health and Illness*, 13 (2): 249–64.

Szasz, T. (1961) *The Myth of Mental Illness* (New York: Hoeber-Harper).

Taylor, I., Walton, P., Young, J. (1973) *The New Criminology* (London: Routledge).

Thane, P. (1982) *The Foundations of the Welfare State* (London: Longman).

Therborn, G. (1986) *Why Are Some Peoples More Unemployed Than Others: The Strange Paradox of Growth and Unemployment* (London: Verso).

Théry, I. (1989) 'The interest of the child and the Regulation of the post-divorce family' in C. Smart (ed.) *Child Custody and the Politics of Gender* (London: Routledge).

Tholfesen, T. (1976) *Working Class Radicalism in Mid-Victorian England* (London: Croom Helm).

Titmuss, R. (1958) *Essays on the Welfare State* (London: Allen and Unwin).

Titmuss, R. (1987) *The Philosophy of Welfare: Selected Writings of Richard Titmuss*, ed. B. Abel Smith and K. Titmuss (London: Allen and Unwin).

Turner, B. (1987) *Medical Power and Social Knowledge* (London: Sage).

Ungerson, C. (1987) *Policy is Personal: Sex, Gender and Informal Care* (London: Tavistock).

Urry A. (1990) 'The struggle towards a feminist practice in family therapy: premisses' in R. Perelberg and A. Miller (eds) *Gender and Power in Families* (London: Tavistock/Routledge).

Utting, D. (1995) *Family and Parenthood: Supporting Families, Preventing Breakdown* (York: Joseph Rowntree Foundation).

Utting, D., Bright, J. and Henricson, C. (1993) *Crime and the Family: Improving Child Rearing and Preventing Delinquency*, Occasional Paper 16 (London: Family Policy Studies Centre).

Uusitalo, H. (1984) 'Comparative research on the determinants of the welfare state: the state of the art', *European Journal of Political Research*, 12: 403–22.

Van Every, J. (1992) 'Who is the family? The assumptions of British social policy', *Critical Social Policy*, no. 33.

Van Kersbergen, K. and Becker, U. (1988) 'The Netherlands: a passive Social Democratic welfare state in a Christian Democratic ruled society', *Journal of Social Policy*, 17 (4): 477–99.

Van Krieken, R. (1986) 'Social theory and child welfare: beyond social control', *Theory and Society*, 15: 401–29.

220   *Bibliography*

Van Krieken, R. (1991) *Children and the State: Social Control and the Formation of Australian Child Welfare* (Sydney: Allen and Unwin).

Van Voorhis, P., Cullen, F., Mathers, R. and Garner, C. (1988) 'The impact of family structure on delinquency: a comparative assessment of structural and functional factors', *Criminology*, 26 (2): 235–61.

Van Wel, F. (1992) 'A Century of Families under Supervision', *British Journal of Social Work*, 22: 147–166.

Wallerstein, J. and Blakeslee, S. (1989) *Second Chances* (London: Bantam).

Wasoff, F., Dobash, R. and Harcus, D. (1990) *The Impact of the Family Law (Scotland) Act 1985 on Solicitors Divorce Practice* (Edinburgh: Scottish Office Central Research Unit).

Webber, D. (1983) 'Combatting and acquiescing in unemployment: crisis management in Sweden and West Germany', *West European Politics*, 6 (1): 23–43.

Wells, L.E. and Rankin, J. (1988) 'Direct parental controls and delinquency', *Criminology*, 26 (2): 263–85.

Wennemo, I. (1992) 'The development of family policy: a comparison of family benefits and tax reductions in 18 OECD Countries', *Acta Sociologica*, 35: 201–17.

Whitehead, B. (1993) 'Dan Quayle was right', *Atlantic Monthly*, April: 47–84.

Wicks, M. (1987) 'Family matters and public policy' in M. Loney (ed.) *The State or the Market* (London: Sage).

Willmott, P. and Young, M. (1960) *Family and Class in a London Suburb* (London: Routledge).

Wilson, H. (1987) 'Parental supervision re-examined', *British Journal of Criminology*, 27 (3): 275–301.

Wilson, W. (1985) 'Cycles of deprivation and the underclass debate', *Social Service Review*, 59 (4): 541–59.

Wilson, W. (1987) *The Truly Disadvantaged: The Inner City, the Underclass and Public Policy* (Chicago: University of Chicago Press).

Wilson, W. (1989) 'The underclass: issues, perspectives and public policy', *Annals of the American Academy of Political and Social Science*, 501: 182–92.

Wolfe, A (1989) 'Market, state and society as codes of moral obligation', *Acta Sociologica*, 32 (3): 221–36.

Worrall, A. (1990) *Offending Women: Female Law Breakers and the Criminal Justice System* (London: Routledge).

Wraith, R. and Lamb, G. (1971) *Public Inquiries as an Instrument of Government* (London: Allen and Unwin).

Young, J. and Matthews, R. (eds) (1992) *Rethinking Criminology: The Realist Debate* (London: Sage).

Young, M. and Willmott, P. (1957) *Family and Kinship in East London* (London: Routledge).

Zimmerman, S. (1988) *Understanding Family Policy* (London: Sage).

Zinn, M. and Eitzen, D. (1990) *Diversity in Families*, 2nd edn (New York: Harper & Row).

Index